LEARNING THEORY AND LEARNING OUTCOMES

The Connection

Pauline Grippin
Sean Peters
The College of Saint Rose
Albany, New York

UNIVERSITY PRESS OF AMERICA

LANHAM • NEW YORK • LONDON

University Press of America,[™] Inc.

4720 Boston Way
Lanham, MD 20706

3 Henrietta Street
London WC2E 8LU England

Printed in the United States of America

ISBN (Perfect): 0-8191-3795-2
ISBN (Cloth): 0-8191-3794-4

TABLE OF CONTENTS

Preface

This text was written out of desperation. We searched and searched for a theories of learning text that met our student's needs. Every text we reviewed was either a serial listing of theories by chapter, or a promotion of the author's own theory of learning. Neither kind of text offers an appropriate theoretical basis for decision-making in the day-to-day life of the teacher or social worker or psychometrician. We felt we needed a text that said to readers "if you can identify the learning outcomes you want to accomplish, then here are the theoretical foundations for your instructional planning. They are eclectic in nature, but integrated by the outcome you desire."

The rationale and approach of the text are unique. The student is led to analyze a learning event according to the expected outcomes and then to apply the theory or theories which appropriately apply to that learning outcome. Using the Gagne domains of learning outcomes as a framework, we discuss the major theories and research pertinent to each identified learning outcome: motor skills, intellectual skills, verbal information, attitude, cognitive strategies. This approach allows us to help the student make sense of the myriad, often contradictory, theoretical explanations of learning. Classical conditioning, for example, is useful in understanding attitude formation, but not very useful for understanding how we acquire intellectual skills. Other texts either offer a unitary theory of learning ("all learning can be explained by my theory."); or they describe a different theoretical approach in each chapter. In either case, the student is poorly served. Little wonder that students find theory of little value in their day-to-day experience.

By concentrating throughout the text on the *outcomes* of learning (e.g., attitudes, motor skills) and exploring the extant theory and research which speak to each domain, the authors hope to help the student be able, in his/her own professional setting, to:

1. Analyze desired student outcomes in terms of

type of learned capability

2. Recall appropriate theory and research for that domain

3. Demonstrate comprehension of recalled theory and research by developing an appropriate application

4. Have a positive attitude about the practicality of theory in the everyday world

5. Continue to educate yourself by intelligent consumption of theory and research on learning.

The book is intended for master's level or upper division students in Educational Psychology, education, curriculum, or psychology. It would be especially useful in programs which train persons for the helping professions, e.g. teaching, social work.

Pauline Grippin
Sean Peters

September 1983

This first chapter reminds the reader of the benefits of having a good theory from which to work, looks at the characteristics of a good theory and gives some examples of such theories. The final portion of the chapter is devoted to a few basic definitions of terms.

1. What are the characteristics of any good theory?

2. What "good" is theory?

3. In what ways does someone who follows the cognitive tradition differ from one who holds a behaviorist position?

CHAPTER ONE

THEORY

INTRODUCTION

Learning theory and learning outcomes, is there a connection? The psychologist claims, "There is nothing so practical as a good theory." The third grade teacher replies, "Don't give me any of those theories; tell me what to do on Monday mornings."

The objective of this book is to help you find the connection between theories of learning and learning outcomes. The authors adhere to the old adage: "Give them a fish and you feed them for a day; teach them to fish and they feed themselves." Learning to fish in this instance is learning how to use theory as your most practical and valuable tool.

Two People. Let us begin with a comparison. In the morning Ms. Jones gets up and turns on the all-news station in her city. She takes ages to dress in a three-piece grey suit with a white high-necked blouse, sort of dragging herself around the house in an effort to "get started." She sits quietly in the kitchen while she downs a cup of coffee. Later she goes to the office where she walks right past the secretary who has a new hairdo. Ms. Jones doesn't even say hello. At about ten Ms. Jones steps out of her office to ask the secretary for the two reports she had asked her to type the day before. She takes the reports with no comment. At lunch time she instructs the secretary to send out for a ham and cheese sandwich which she eats in her office.

Ms. Smith on the other hand gets up and immediately turns on the local pop-music station with the talkative DJ. She hustles through her morning preparations and, as she sits down for a quick cup of coffee, telephones her friend who had a date with a new man last night. The conversation finished, she's off to the office in a chic new bright green dress, she greets her secretary with a compliment on her lovely new blouse. About ten Ms. Smith steps from the office to ask the secretary if she has had time to prepare the reports that she had requested yesterday. After complimenting the secretary on her efficiency Ms. Smith returns to her office reminding the secretary to call her for her 12:30 luncheon date with the friend she had called at breakfast.

Obviously your experience of Ms. Smith and Ms. Jones is very limited, but imagine that you have known the two of them for about three months. They have been interacting in ways similar to those outlined above. What would you say to describe Ms. Jones in a word or two? And what word or two would describe Ms. Smith? I might describe Ms. Jones as shy and retiring and Ms. Smith as outgoing or extroverted.

A Theory. My ability to describe the two women in this way is not based on "only the facts" but on the way in which I connect the facts together. I have an underlying hypothesis about how people who are shy and retiring act. When I first interact with Ms. Jones I begin to form an opinion of her to gather data about what kind of person she is. From my first information, I might think that she is tired but other evidence suggests that this is not the best description. I may try other hypothesis but "shy and retiring" is the one that accounts for or "fits" most of the data. It systematizes or puts the facts together in a way that helps me to see the connections between them.

Further, such a theory helps me to decide what to do. Once I label Ms. Jones as "shy and retiring" and Ms. Smith as "outgoing" I treat them differently. I may be more reserved when interacting with Ms. Jones and more exuberant with Ms. Smith. Or I may decide that the best way to get my ideas across to Ms. Jones is to state them very precisely on a formal memo, while Ms. Smith would be more likely to listen over lunch in an "in" restaurant.

Theories, then, are the answer to the issue posed in the first paragraph, that is, just tell me what to do on Monday morning. Theories coordinate the facts and they give a basis of action. Without a "theory" each encounter with Ms. Smith is a new experience. With a theory I know how to plan interactions with her for the greatest comfort of both of us. For the teacher theory "Tells me what to try Monday morning."

Implicit Theory. We create theories all the time. Based on prior experience, prior data gathering, we build up sets of expectations about how our world works. For example, I may have certain expectations about how friends treat one another. I expect that a friend will seek me out and try to include me in her activities. I expect my friend to tell me of the joys and sorrows of her life. If someone whom I consider my friend snubs me at a party I decide that she did not see me, or was distracted, or was tired or upset, or...

I also probably have a theory of "stranger." I have different expectations of this person. If a "stranger" snubs me at the party (fails to pay attention to me) I take this as a part of the behavior that I would expect from a person who has no particular relationship to me. The explanation of the behavior is "this stranger has no need or responsibility to notice me." These kinds of theories by which we make sense out of our every day world are called Implicit Theories. We build them from our experience but we rarely test them. We assume that they are true. For example, once I have decided that the reason for the "snub" is that my friend is fatigued, I make further decisions based on that theory. Rarely do I test that "theory" to see if it can account for the data. It may not be until the person snubs me two more times that I begin to investigate the possibility that our relationship has seriously changed or is temporarily interrupted.

The assumption of validity in implicit theories can get us into some serious problems. Consider the number of sticky communication situations you have been involved in that could have been avoided or quickly remedied by the clarification of the underlying assumptions. John, who is sincerely busy at college, writes home to Jane, his high school beaux, to say he cannot keep their planned date next weekend. Jane, with an implicit theory that high school romances never last if one member goes on to college, assumes John is trying to let her down gently. Jane now begins to let the relationship cool from her end. John feels the coolness and assumes Jane has become interested in someone new at her job. So he begins to look elsewhere too. They go their separate ways not because of any clear decision but because Jane assumed her theory was true. She never checked or tested her facts. She acted on her assumed data. This is a rather "classic" example but most readers will be able to think of several similar but "closer to home" examples.

Humans are theory builders combining and recombining facts to make sense out of their interactions. These theories are full of inaccurate assumptions that are assumed correct and acted upon; sometimes with a sad end; sometimes with comic results; sometimes with great success.

Formal Theories. Formal theories are built up in a similar fashion to implicit theories; that is, they are initiated to attempt to account for the behavior of certain phenomena using the data from prior experience of that phenomenon. (In psychology, the phenomenon studied is the behavior of persons and animals.) Formal theories differ from implicit theories in one major way: they are tested. Formal theories are not assumed to account for data. This ability to appropriately connect the data must be demonstrated. The hypothesized relationships of a formal theory must be supported by the collected facts. Formal theories must have certain characteristics to be treated seriously by researchers.

CHARACTERISTICS OF A GOOD THEORY

1. Theories help to organize or systematize the facts. Theories should help us to put the facts together in a useful way. The facts are like a list of ingredients for a pie. A theory is the recipe that tells us how to put the ingredients together to make a cherry pie. A theory puts the facts into a useful form like the directions for putting together a tool. Without directions we still have all the pieces but we cannot make

use of the tool until we put the pieces together in a certain way...We may have a list of all the major cities in the world (facts) but we need an atlas (theory) to decide the best way to travel to one of the cities. Theories connect facts in ways that make them meaningful and useful. We may have a number of interactions with Ms. Jones and Ms. Smith but until we put the results of these interactions together into a system (theory) we do not know how to treat the two women differently.

Theories also tell us what facts to pay attention to. In any situation there is much more data than we can reasonably use. If my theory about Ms. Jones' and Ms. Smith's behavior at work is based on their basic attitude toward life, then I am going to look for data that tells something about that basic attitude, hence I look at the interaction with the radio in the morning, the activities surrounding the coffee drinking, the color of the clothes and the interaction with the secretary. I disregard other available evidence such as the colors of their office walls, the type of furniture they have in their office, and the names of their secretaries. If my theory about their behavior were based on the work environment, however, I might well attend to the office appointments and disregard the activities surrounding the coffee drinking.

Theories are useful, then, if they help us to tie the facts together into a meaningful whole and help us select the facts we will attend to during future interactions with the phenomenon under examination.

2. Theories provide explanations. Snelbecker (1974) states, "An event is said to be explained when it is shown to be an example of a familiar principle or set of principles (p. 30)." Theories provide a set of principles which can be related to the events experienced in the data collection. Theories give a sort of superstructure to which new data can be attached. In my theory of "shy and retiring" I have a principle which says "Shy people avoid crowded public places." This helps me "explain" why Ms. Jones decides to eat lunch at her desk rather than "brave" the crowded city restaurants.

Theories explain in two different ways, descriptive and prescriptive. A descriptive theory attempts to tell what phenomena exist, Piaget's Theory, for example. There is no intent in a descriptive theory to explain why the phenomena exist. Prescriptive theories, on the other hand, attempt to answer the why question and thus suggest potential intervention strategies. Of course, some theories are a combination of descriptive and prescriptive approaches. Herein, the practitioner needs to carefully consider which aspects of the theory tell "what" and which aspects tell "why."

3. Theories have a heuristic value. Good theories not only aid us in organizing our information and using it to explain phenomena, they also help us to ask good questions. Once the scientist establishes a basic theory, she can begin to see two things: where new connections seem likely and where there are loopholes in the information. These factors imply new hypotheses which should be examined and tested. If, based on prior experience, I adopt a theory with a basic tenet, "older children are less anxious than younger children when speaking to adults," I can begin to see possible extensions and refinements of this principle. Does the socio-economic-status of the child make a difference? Does race or cultural background matter? Does familiarity between child and adult increase or decrease anxiety? Does setting of the interaction or topic of the conversation enter in? Without a basic theory these questions are simply several interesting bits of information. With a theory the researcher can build a "set of principles" that interact in specific ways. The scientist can create a sort of checklist and gradually investigate, incorporate, reject and refine the data until the theory either stands tall or falls under the weight of the data. Growth of the theory by intention results when new hypotheses refine the concepts of principles of the theory. Extension occurs when research hypotheses attempt to apply the theory to new situations.

Whether the new hypotheses generated by the basic theory stand up under the examination or are proven false is irrelevant in terms of their value to the theory building. Frequently discovering that a particular hypothesized relationship does not "hold water" is equally, if not more, informative than discovering other relationships do hold true. For example, suppose in testing out the theory above, one assumed that the familiarity between the adult and child would significantly reduce the anxiety of the child while in conversation. If the investigator discovered that familiarity did not reduce anxiety in the child, this is an important piece of data to the entire theory and its implications.

4. Theories make predictions possible. Once I have asked several questions about a set of hypotheses that helped me systematize and explain a set of facts, I should be able to make predictions or "safe guesses" about what will happen in a given situation. For example, I may be a bit pinched for funds. I work with Ms. Jones and Ms. Smith. I hesitate to invite one out to lunch without inviting the other, but I'm not really sure I have enough money for all of us to have an enjoyable lunch. If I invite both to a busy, noisy restaurant I may come out okay because it is a safe bet that Ms. Jones will refuse. I "look good" because I did not leave either out of the invitation but I also manage to stay within a reasonable budget for the day. Without a theory I would not be able to make such predictions. Of course, there is always a possibility that I will get burned and Ms. Jones will accept. This is particularly true with unchecked implicit theories. Formal theories attempt to reduce the unexpected results by careful description of the necessary circumstances for the theory to predict events. For example, the theory of adult/child interaction would have to specify whether it made a difference if the participants were in a formal or informal situation and give descriptions for the characteristics of formal and informal. Another aspect might address the importance of the adult/child ratio in the group and make clear distinctions about what ratios made different results, if any. Vague theories tend to be fairly useless as predictors because practitioners do not have enough information to know whether or not a given situation is an appropriate application of the theory or not.

5. Theories can be tested. Good theories, therefore, can be used to predict. Such theories can also be tested. If the theory is precise enough to predict a certain behavior in a specific, clearly defined situation and the behavior does not reliably occur, the researcher can begin to build a set of data to dispute the theory. (It may be the researcher's own theory, but disputing or disproving it is a healthy, scientific thing to do.) By disproving one theory or modifying it

significantly, the theoretician continues to build up theories which do predict reliably.

Vague theories cannot be disproved. Since a vague theory states no precise definition of the circumstances when the theory holds, it is impossible to decide whether or not a given circumstance is an appropriate test situation. If there is no clear test situation, there can be no clear test. A vague theory cannot be tested, nor constructively modified. Such a theory may continue to be informally used, but it ceases to be seriously considered by the scientific community. A good theory then, can be tested.

6. Theories are parsimonious. One final attribute characterizes a good theory. In addition to organizing, explaining, generating questions, predicting and being testable, a good theory must be the simplest formulation possible that takes into consideration all the data while still maintaining appropriate precision. An implicit theory that hypothesizes that Ms. Jones acts the way she does on Monday because she is tired from the weekend, on Tuesday because her office is pale green, on Wednesday because she had weak coffee for breakfast and on Thursday because she is shy is simply too complicated to be a useful way to explain the world. Besides any one of the hypotheses could be fairly easily tested and either supported or refuted. A theory should be parsimonious.

The professional knows what observations lead to what theory and therefore knows when the theory is appropriately utilized to decide the Monday morning questions. That's the trick--making the right connection between learning outcomes desired and the theoretical principles which predict the greatest probability for success. If you want to know "what to do Monday morning" get yourself a good theory.

A UNITARY THEORY OF LEARNING

With the notable exception of Edward Tolman, until recently psychologists have hunted for and hoped for a single theory of learning that would explain all human learning. The result of all this endeavor is that we have many theories of learning, each of which tells us something about learning, but none of which generalizes very far. Each theory of learning predicts successfully in some area of learning; no theory of learning successfully predicts all learning. This lack of generalization has led some researchers to new lines of questioning and research. The accumulating evidence suggests that Edward Tolman was a man way ahead of his time when he said in 1949: "There is more than one kind of learning."

Although some contemporary psychologists continue to believe the data support a unitary theory of learning (Wolpe, 1978), other researchers have directed their energies to integrating the disparate experimental results into a larger matrix that can accommodate contradictions and contrasts. Educational psychologists began to ask the question: "What are the differences among learning experiences that make it impossible for one theory to successfully predict all learning?"

The answer to this question is still emerging, but much is already known. Two significant contributors are individual differences among learners and different conditions of learning for different learning outcomes. Most people recognize that three-year olds learn differently from thirty-year olds. Psychological research is currently demonstrating important differences in learning styles and strategies within age cohorts. Differences among learning outcomes are also being discriminated. The way we learn to type is not the same process as the way we learn to appreciate poetry. The conditions for learning to "Love our neighbor as ourselves" are different from the conditions necessary for becoming good problem-solvers.

In order, then, to utilize learning theories as prediction formulas in instructional settings, it is necessary to discriminate among learner characteristics and among learning outcomes. Once these essential discriminations are made, the appropriate theory of learning can be selected and used to facilitate learning.

TWO GOOD BASIC THEORIES

Two of the most universally applied learning theories are the Behaviorist and the Cognitive Theories.

Behaviorist. The basic tenet of the Behaviorist tradition is that learning results in a change of behavior in the student. The change may be quite subtle but it must be observable in some way in order to "count" as learning. There is a sort of underlying premise that learning takes place through a process of accretion, that is, one learning attaches to the next and that to the next, much like a mason building a brick wall. The mason keeps adding bricks until the wall is sufficient to the need of the learner. Most Behaviorists also structure their theories around an external reinforcer which stimulates continued change in behavior. Names like Pavlov, Skinner, Hull, Thorndike are usually associated with the Behaviorist tradition.

Cognitive Theory. Cognitive theory grew up in opposition to the ideas of the behaviorists. The cognitive theorist, believing that learning is more than simple accretion, looks not for changes in behavior, but rather for changes in the way in which the learner understands or organizes the elements of the environment. The skills which the learner has may or may not change significantly, but the way in which the learner is now able to use the skills may be totally different from the way she used them before the learning (reorganization) took place. Names typically associated with the Cognitive Tradition are Piaget, Ausubel and the classical Gestalt school.

Behaviorism and Cognitive Theory are Good Theories. These two theories possess the characteristics of a theory discussed in an earlier part of the chapter. You will remember that theories not only help people structure the facts that they have, they also indicate which facts the researcher should attend to. A Cognitive Theorist and a Behaviorist may observe the same learning situation, for example, a child learning to solve a complicated puzzle. The Behaviorist would look at ways in which the learner's behavior changed each time that she interacted with the puzzle. He would look for patterns that are built up over time and are either rewarded by an outside helper or rewarding because they seem to lead the puzzler to a solution to the puzzle. The Cognitive theorist on the other hand would look for evidence that the puzzler was continuously reconstructing the problem in her head and building and testing hypotheses about how the problem might be solved. In fact the identical behaviors of the puzzler might be interpreted and organized quite differently by the two observers. The two theories would also make different suggestions to the practitioner about what "next steps" to take to help the puzzler reach the goal of becoming an efficient puzzler (one who solves puzzles quickly, with low stress and with good success). Both theories have a certain parsimony, suggest helpful, if different questions, allow practitioners to make predictions and can be disproved, that is, shown to be inappropriate in some situations. Therefore, we may consider them "good" theories. After some preliminary discussion of some broad issues relating to all learning theories, we will take up an extended discussion of these two "good" theories and how they might help us plan for instruction in different outcomes of learning.

SOME DEFINITIONS

At this point some distinctions between various terms used in discussion about theory may be helpful. Theory, model and paradigm will be distinguished from one another. The differences between hypothesis, principle, law and construct will also be explored.

Theory. A theory is a set of propositions that are logically related to one another. Although theory may be defined in a variety of ways, almost all definitions include the idea that theories are abstract formulations of the connections between various phenomena. The theory is not the phenomena themselves but the interrelationships. Theories have the characteristics described above.

Model. A model is more concrete than a theory. Models attempt to represent the processes involved in a theory in an analogous or in some cases even physical form. Architects use drawings or scaled down replicas as models. Chemists use a sort of "tinkertoy" arrangement to represent certain molecules. Psychologists may use diagrams or flow charts to manifest their theories. Not all models have direct relationships to a specific theory. Some models are atheoretical or perhaps are "in search of" a theory.

Paradigm. A paradigm is a verbal pattern or a diagram "which serves to describe recurring basic features of the phenomena being studied and which mainly serves to provide rather specific guidelines for conducting research" (Snelbecker, 1977, p. 33). Paradigms are frequently less complex than theories or models. They usually are an attempt to represent a subset of the total theory. A paradigm is a sort of formula describing a set of interactions within the theory.

Hypothesis. An hypothesis is the untested statement of a specific interaction of two phenomena. An hypothesis forms the basis for experimentation. It becomes the focus relationship of a specific piece of research. Theories are built through continued testing of hypotheses. Each hypothesized relationship is either supported or weakened by a good piece of research.

Law. A law is a principle which has virtually universal support of a great variety of data. It holds in all appropriate circumstances. Only by significantly tampering with the circumstances will the law cease to hold, for example, the law of gravity anywhere on earth except where an artificial vacuum is created. Psychological and sociological theory does not admit of many, if any, laws.

Principle. A principle is a tested hypothesis which has received support from the collected data, but is not clearly fundamental or is not sufficiently well-established to be called a law.

Construct. A construct is a phenomenon which cannot be directly observed but which is presumed to exist because of its results or effects. No one can directly observe "personality" but personality is presumed to exist because persons exhibit fairly consistent behavior patterns under some variety of circumstances. Personality, then, would be a construct.

REFERENCES

Snelbecker, G. E. *Learning Theory/Instructional Theory and Psycho-educational Design*. New York: McGraw-Hill, 1974.

Wolpe, J. Cognition and Causation in Human Behavior and Its Therapy. *American Psychologist*. 1978, *33*, 437-445.

Chapter Two introduces the concept of learning outcomes. Gagne's theory is presented in considerable detail followed by the models of Norman, Bloom, Merrill and Reigeluth. Interwoven with these models is an introduction to the concepts of memory, transfer and evaluation.

1. Give examples of each of the following: Intellectual Skills, Attitudes, Verbal Information, Motor Skills, Cognitive Strategies.

2. How does Gagne's theory differ from the other models presented in the chapter?

3. In what ways are the outcomes presented in this chapter related to the general theories of learning overviewed in Chapter One?

CHAPTER TWO

LEARNING OUTCOMES

INTRODUCTION

Chapter One introduced Learning Theory. The other half of the connection is learning outcomes.

Learning Outcomes. Learning outcomes are changes in behavior that cannot be explained by maturation or medication and are persistent over time. Gagne (1977) postulates that there are at least five different kinds of learning outcomes, each of which requires unique "conditions of learning." The discriminations he makes among learning outcomes are derived from the essential attributes for successful learning in each of the described domains. Gagne's answer to the question, "What are the differences precluding a unitary theory of learning?" is that process and product in learning experiences fall into the independent domains of attitudes, motor skills, intellectual skills, verbal information, and cognitive strategies.

Intellectual skills are the learned capabilities which permit symbolic interaction with the environment. Verbal information involves the capability to recall learned facts and generalizations. The way the learner approaches a novel learning experience reflects cognitive strategies; while attitudes are internal states that influence behavior. Motor skills are the capabilities which mediate purposeful motor activity. These domains set the limits of generalizability of research findings concerned with learning. Generalization is possible within a domain across subject matter, but is not possible across domains, even within one subject matter. For example, theory and research on attitude formation has application in learning to enjoy social studies, feeling positive toward one's case worker or developing prejudices. But theory and research on learning the intellectual skill of reading does not generalize to learning to enjoy reading.

GAGNE'S OUTCOMES

Intellectual Skill. Using the printed word (or oral, for that matter) to convey messages, using a recipe to make a pie crust, converting a fraction to a whole number, understanding in what way Lincoln was "Captain" of his nation, all involve interacting with the environment symbolically. The capabilities which enable these interactions are termed by Gagne intellectual skills. They are applied knowledge and lead to rule-governed behavior. The learner may not be able to verbalize the rule being used, but clearly is performing in accordance with such a rule. The three-year-old sorting the silverware into piles of spoons, forks, and knives; or the forty-year-old mason laying a straight line for bricks may not be able to explain to you how to do the task being done, but is demonstrating the capability to interact with the environment using a mediating symbol system.

Gagne (1977) believes that having the prerequisite sub-skills is the key to learning new intellectual skills. The rule reflected in the performance of an intellectual skill can be broken down into sub-categories of intellectual skills. Such an analysis yields a hierarchy of capabilities of decreasing complexity. Understanding a metaphor requires application of a higher-order rule (a rule about the relationships between other rules). The prerequisite intellectual skills are rules (relationships among concepts) which have as prerequisites the understanding of the concepts involved. Understanding of the concepts requires the prerequisites of the appropriate discriminations which permit classifying something as a member of a class of things. And making discriminations is dependent upon the prerequisite learned associations and chains.

New intellectual skills are rapidly learned if the prerequisite skills are known, but they may easily be forgotten, also. The poor retention of unrehearsed intellectual skills is in direct contrast to the long range retention of motor skills. Compare your ease at swimming after a long hiatus with your ease at figuring percentages. This comparison illustrates another aspect of learning outcomes.

Memory. The mechanisms of memory appear to be somewhat different for each domain of learning and the ways to facilitate retention will reflect the learning outcome desired. For intellectual skills, much practice and frequent review is implied by the appropriate theory and research.

Verbal Information. Using a ruler for measuring is an intellectual skill; being able to give a definition of a ruler is verbal information. The critical difference between intellectual skills and verbal information is in the "telling." Defining "ruler" requires the use of intellectual skills (e.g., using symbols to convey messages, etc.), but the purpose in defining the term "ruler" is to convey information.

Answer the following questions. In what year did Columbus discover America? What color is grass? How many quarters in a dollar? What is Ohm's law? What kind of bird delivers babies? Why do we have an American and New York Stock Exchange? Your capability to give a verbal response to these questions is the essence of the domain of verbal information. Contrary to common student belief, this is an important capability. We persons need to know a body of knowledge shared with others, e.g., there are four quarters in a dollar. In addition, verbal information is often a necessary component for further learning, e.g., to become skillful as a stock speculator (an intellectual skill), one probably needs to know the difference between the American and New York Stock Exchange. To be a successful doctor, one probably needs to be able to recall descriptions of symptoms and remedies.

Gagne (1977, p. 99) makes a distinction between

<u>meaningful verbal learning</u> and <u>rote verbal learning</u>. Later chapters will expand on this distinction in more detail. Since most memory research has utilized the retention of nonsense words or unrelated words, the generalizability of this research to recall in general or to verbal information in particular is questionable. Research on meaningful verbal material indicates that the internal cognitive structure of the learner is crucial for retention. When verbal material is presented in an organized, meaningful context, it is easily learned and retention is long-range. A meaningful context is one that ties new verbal information to previously acquired verbal information conceptually rather than in a verbatim fashion. Retention depends upon a network of conceptually related ideas. When the learner doesn't possess a network of ideas to which can be attached a new piece of verbal information, retention may depend upon the artfulness of the mnemonics utilized. Simple repetition may suffice -- 2 + 2 = 4, 2 + 2 = 4, 2 + 2 = 4, but most learners acquire a "bag of tricks" (cognitive strategies) for remembering unrelated bits of information. Did you recite "Columbus sailed the ocean blue" in order to recall in what year Columbus discovered America? Yet another aspect of acquiring and recalling verbal information involves the perception of the context. How did you respond to the question "What color is grass?"? If you are over thirty, you probably said green.

A major proportion of schooling involves acquiring verbal information. As we shall see, theory is divided and contradictory unless we approach the issue from the point of view of learning outcomes: meaningful or verbatim.

<u>Transfer</u>. Memory of verbal information has been highly researched and so has <u>Transfer</u>, another aspect of learning outcomes. Facilitating positive transfer is different for different learning outcomes. Promoting <u>transfer</u> of a positive <u>attitude</u> from one subject to another requires different facilitation than promoting <u>transfer</u> of appropriate motor skills from down hill skiing to water skiing.

<u>Attitudes</u>. Attitudes are "mental states which influence choice of personal actions" (Gagne, 1977, p. 28). They are "learned dispositions" and therefore are amenable to instruction. Do you love classical music, but

despise country-rock? Do you have a favorite color? Have you ever dropped a course because you couldn't tolerate the mannerisms of the professor? Does the thought of a snake throw you into a panic? Are you frigid? Impotent? Attitudes influence the choices we make and the actions we take. Therefore, they are directly tied to the issue of motivation. Identifying desired attitudes in the learning situation is often critical to successful learning. Memory for attitudes is long-term and transfer is highly probable. Gagne finds great explanatory power for the learning of attitudes in Bandura's Social Learning Theory, but other theorists also have interesting things to say. A later chapter will explore theory and research on attitude formation.

Motor Skills. Swimming, writing, playing a musical instrument, walking, flying a space craft, urinating, talking, using a microscope: organized, patterned, smoothly executed motor performances. What are the capabilities that allow us to learn to perform such complicated acts with such precision that they appear deceptively simple? What are the conditions under which such learning takes place?

We know that motor skills continue to improve with practice over long periods of time. We know that retention is superior to the retention of intellectual skills and verbal information. We know that much of the learning of motor skills has to do with the feedback we receive from our own body: proprioceptive cues. We know that part of what is learned is the procedural sequence -- what comes after what in the execution of the movement.

Two major approaches to the study of motor skills are found in the literature. One approach has been to carefully describe the component parts of motor skills and to look for interrelatedness of sub-skills. Most of this work has been done with adult subjects and with correlational techniques. This text refers to this approach as the "psychometric approach" (measurement approach). A second major theoretical thrust has been to study the development of motor skills in children. This approach necessarily takes into account nature as well as nurture. We refer to this as the "developmental approach." Increasingly, the developmental approach is being influenced by the work of ethologists which indicates that teaching animals to perform motor acts that are not species-specific is quite different from teaching them motor acts they would perform in a natural habitat. The implication is that many motor behaviors (perhaps many other types of learning as well) are under partial genetic control. Theorists within the Behavioristic tradition study associations between stimulation and motor response, as well as documenting the effects of reinforcement on shaping performance. Cognitive psychologists, on the other hand, are interested in the information processing required to acquire and integrate motor routines.

Memory and Transfer. Although performance of a motor skill may deteriorate over time, memory for motor skills is very long term. Transfer from one motor skill to another is usually positive, but some special transfer problems do arise.

Evaluation. The fourth component of an adequate study of learning is evaluation. There are (1) initial learning, (2) retention (memory), (3) transfer, and (4) evaluation. A distinct advantage of thinking in terms of learning outcomes is never again teaching one thing and testing another. Do you teach the motor skill of changing a tire and then give a pencil and paper test requiring a listing of the steps involved? Do you teach the dictionary definitions for democracy and republic and later on a test require students to list 3 republics and 3 democracies? Do you tell your child how to swim and then throw her in the lake? Unless evaluation mirrors the learning outcome taught, it lacks validity and reliability. It is also unfair.

Cognitive Strategies. Cognitive strategies are our machinery for thinking. Verbal information may be the content of our thought; intellectual skills may be the application of our thought; attitudes may influence what we think about; motor skills may mediate the expression of our thought; but cognitive strategies make thinking possible. They are the internal mental structures that determine the way in which an individual approaches a learning experience.

Gagne (1977, p. 34 ff) defines cognitive strategies as those capabilities which "manage learning, remembering and thinking" and points to Bruner's "cognitive strategies;" Rothkopf's "mathemagenic activities;" Skinner's "self-management behaviors;" and Greeno and Bjork's "executive control processes" as examples of the domain. Gagne's own work on cognitive strategies has been primarily in the area of problem-solving, which he believes encompasses both intellectual skill learning and cognitive strategy learning. Faced with a novel problem (for the learner), the learner applies previously learned rules in new combinations arriving at a solution which is a new higher-order rule. This involves using intellectual skills to derive a new intellectual skill, but it also involves managing the search for old rules that are applicable, managing the selection of combinations to try, and so on. These management systems Gagne calls cognitive strategies. Managing the approach to one problem results in refined or new cognitive strategies to be used on later problems.

This text will also examine other aspects of the domain of cognitive strategies; the role of the development of cognitive structure from sensori-motor through formal-operational thought, the role of cognitive style and the "meta" process of cognition. As the child develops, changes in the underlying cognitive structure strongly influence the way a novel problem is approached. For example, the ten-year-old is tied to personal life experiences and probably cannot handle more than two or three ideas simultaneously. The twenty-year-old is freed from total reliance on personal experience and can probably handle 7 ± 2 pieces of information at a time.

Cognitive style is a term used to denote a characteristic way of interacting with the environment cognitively. Several cognitive style variables have been identified and researched. Among them are impulsivity, focusing, scanning, reflectivity, conceptual style. This text will mainly emphasize the cognitive style variable field dependence-independence. This construct describes a characteristic way of analyzing environmental stimuli (Witkin, et. al., 1962). Some individuals habitually analyze stimuli into their component parts, while other individuals habitually take a wholistic approach. The interaction of cognitive style and cognitive structure on cognitive strategies is a relatively new theoretical area of great promise (Pascual-Leone, 1972). A major and important implication is that instructional techniques are not necessarily generalizable over age groups. Appropriate conditions for learning verbal information or motor skills by the 4th grader are not necessarily appropriate for the college sophomore because different management systems (cognitive strategies) may be used by the two.

The theories of meta-processes in cognition are also new avenues of research. These processes concern our conscious knowledge about our own capabilities (Flavell, 1979). How many items in a list can we recall? What kinds of problems can we solve? Are we creative, shy, clumsy? Our definition of cognitive strategies is much broader than Gagne's, encompassing (1) executive-management strategies, (2) cognitive developmental level, (3) cognitive style, and (4) meta-processes/knowledge. We denote this difference by using the term "cognitive strategies/cognitive structures," (CS/CS).

Are there other learning outcome theories?

Although this book utilizes Gagne's domains of learning to illustrate the connection between learning outcomes and learning theories, the Gagne model is only one of many approaches to differentiating learning outcomes. As you read the following descriptions of four other models, compare them with the Gagne model in terms of parsimony, clarity and comprehensiveness.

THEORY OF COMPLEX LEARNING: NORMAN

Norman (1978) presents a model of learning outcomes for what he terms complex learning. Complexity is defined by the existence of experts in the topic. Since there are expert cooks, cooking is a complex learning topic. The topics include motor skills, intellectual topics, procedurally-based topics, fact-based topics, and mixtures among topics.

The _outcomes of learning_, however, are not topic-related but rather are _knowledge modules_. Knowledge modules are units of memory within an interconnected and hierarchical structure. Regardless of the specific complex topic being learned, knowledge modules are acquired in the same way, through the stages of _accretion_ learning, _restructuring_ learning, and _tuning_ learning.

Accretion learning consists of acquiring new

verbal information. Prior knowledge modules provide scaffolding for accretion. The learning strategies for accretion suggested by Norman are somewhat vague, "Study, probably using mnemonic systems and good depth of processing" (p. 44). Memory, transfer and evaluation of accretion learning are specified in the model. Accretion learning is hypothesized to be highly susceptible to interference from related topics and to have little transfer capacity. Evaluation of accretion learning would involve recall and recognition tests.

Restructuring learning is a process of reorganizing accretion learning into more meaningful structures. No new accretion learning takes place. Norman likens restructuring learning to the "aha" experience described by Gestalt psychologists. The outcome for the learner is a new insight, a new sense of understanding of previously learned information. The prerequisite for such learning is existent knowledge modules available to be restructured. Experiencing a Socratic dialogue would be most conducive to restructuring learning, according to Norman. Teaching strategies include use of analogy, metaphor and example. Memory for restructured learning should be relatively good; interference from related topics is hypothesized to be moderate. Restructured learning has high transfer value to other topics. Evaluation of restructuring should require inference and/or problem solving.

Tuning learning involves the refinement of knowledge modules previously accretioned and restructured. During tuning the structures are streamlined, made more efficient. Supportive systems may be dropped as the module becomes automated. Tuning does not require any new knowledge or any new restructuring. Tuning is accomplished by practice and is evaluated by performance. Interference is low. The transfer value of tuned knowledge modules depends on the generality of the knowledge topic in question. The more specific the knowledge the less the transferability of that knowledge.

Norman calls for the teaching of learning strategies and developing a focus, but does not include these as separate learning outcomes in his model of complex learning. He suggests that faulty learning strategy and lack of purpose are the result of inadequate or incorrect knowledge. Developing appropriate learning strategies and foci are theoretically, then, learned through accretion, restructuring and tuning.

Norman's theory of complex learning is, therefore, a theory which defines different learning outcomes: Accretion, restructuring, tuning. However, the theory is a unitary theory of learning, applying these recursive phases of learning outcomes to all complex learning topics. Accretion, restructuring and tuning are the outcomes of learning/instruction for fact-based topics or motor skills; procedurally-based topics or intellectual to restructuring to tuning, the inference is that all complex learning is an outgrowth of verbal information learning.

TAXONOMY OF EDUCATIONAL OBJECTIVES: BLOOM

Bloom and associates (1956, 1964, 1971) developed taxonomies of educational objectives in three domains: cognitive, affective, and psychomotor. These taxonomies reflect an intuitive sequencing within each domain. Attempts to empirically validate the hierarchical nature of the taxonomies have not been successful (Miller, 1979; Seddon, 1978). However, the taxonomies have demonstrated heuristic value for test designers since most instructional outcomes can be subsumed under the sub-categories described.

The taxonomy for the cognitive domain covers the broad range of learned capabilities of symbol manipulation. The sub-categories in intuitive hierarchical order are: knowledge, comprehension, application, analysis, synthesis, evaluation. The learned capabilities range from recall of facts to making judgements about the value of facts.

The taxonomy for the affective domain attempts to place into sub-categories different learned states of feeling which motivate behavior. The major categories are receiving, responding, valuing, organization and characteristic life style. The learned affective states range from attending to instruction to emotional adjustment to a particular life style, for example, maintaining good eating habits after a diet.

The psychomotor domain describes a variety of subskills that are reflected in educational objectives ranging from the eye-hand coordination necessary for drawing a simple picture to the creation of new motor patterns such as skillful manipulation of a space craft.

While useful for purposes of test construction, the taxonomies cover wide categories of learning not consistently related to any theoretical or empirical basis. Instructional analysis and prescriptions for learning based on this model therefore lack reliability and validity.

COMPONENT DISPLAY THEORY: MERRILL

Component display theory developed by Merrill and his associates (Merrill, 1979) makes the assumption that _type of content_ and _task level_ define learning outcomes. Type of content may be (A) fact, (B) concept, (C) procedure, or (D) principle. Task level may be (1) Remember instance verbatim (2) Remember instance in an alternate form, (3) Remember generality, verbatim (4) Remember generality in an alternate form (5) Use a generality, or (6) Find a generality.

Task level and type of content form a matrix with 24 cells, each representing a different learning outcome. For example, giving a dictionary definition of "chair" would be "remembering a concept verbatim." Or, figuring out how to mix concrete so that it doesn't crumble when dry would be "finding a principle." Or, dividing fractions would be "using a procedure."

Component display theory further assumes that all cognitive instruction occurs through either _telling_ or _questioning_, using either _generalities_ or examples. Combining this matrix with the learning outcomes matrix provides prescriptions for instruction. The theory offers rules for instructional prescription under which optimum learning should occur. These additional rules are necessary because the nature of the instructional matrix is different for different task levels of the learning outcome matrix. "Telling" an "example" for learning a "remember instance verbatim" would be different from "telling" an "example" for "finding a generality."

In addition to specifying the appropriate instructional components and the optimal combination of instructional presentation forms, the prescription rules include what are called "adequacy rules." These prescription rules address instructional strategies like feedback and attention-focusing. The theory also prescribes specifics for evaluation of learning outcomes.

Component Display theory has been utilized by its developers to design instructional packages for commercial dissemination. Their empirical research suggests considerable success in achieving desired learning outcomes with their packages. The complexity of the theory may limit its utilization to only those intimately involved in developing and testing its hypotheses, however.

ELABORATION THEORY: REIGELUTH

Elaboration theory is an extension of Component Display Theory (Merrill, 1979). The learning outcomes of the task/content matrix of Component Display Theory define only <u>single constructs</u> of facts, concepts, procedures and principles. More complicated learning outcomes involve relationships among constructs. Such relationships result in learning outcomes that are best labelled <u>structures</u>. Structures may take the form of <u>lists</u>, <u>taxonomies</u>, <u>parts hierarchies</u>, <u>procedures</u>, <u>models</u> or other kinds of relationships. The major emphasis of Elaboration theory is that the <u>structural relationships</u> are learning outcomes and should be taught.

To use Elaboration Theory in designing instruction, the facilitator of learning would first determine the structures of the subject matter and the purpose for learning. From this the instructional designer evolves an <u>organizing structure</u> for the instructional unit. If the organizing structure turned out to be a model such as the theory of aerodynamics, the instructor would extract from the basic theory an <u>epitome</u>. This would be the most general and simple statement of the theory that was possible. The epitome would be presented first and later be elaborated with details, refinements, exceptions. Instruction would proceed in a cycle of epitome, elaboration, expanded epitome, elaboration. The epitome would always be a more general and more simple presentation and discussion of paper airplanes, kites, and gliders. The second epitome might be a presentation of air flow over powered airborne surfaces, elaborated by a discussion of bats, birds, and biplanes.

Elaboration theory posits mastery of subject matter structure as the most desired learning outcome and suggests epitome-elaboration as the facilitating instructional medium. The theory does not take learner cognitive structure into account and has had minimal empirical testing. (The epitome device shares common characteristics with Ausubel's concept of the advanced organizer to be discussed in a later chapter.)

Are there other learning outcomes?

The theories and their models discussed above are a fair representation of the state of the art/science. Much has been done, but much remains to be discovered. Are social skills adequately discriminated and defined? Are they a combination of attitudes, intellectual skills and cognitive strategies or are they distinct learning outcomes not covered by the Gagne model or other models? Can you identify other learner outcomes which fit like the Procustean bed?

How can I make the "connection" with so many unknowns?

Current theory has much to offer the practitioner in some areas of learning outcomes, for example, memory of verbal information. In other areas where research and theory is not as advanced, for example, the cognitive strategies involved in attitude formation, the connection between theory and outcome is tentative. A tentative theory, however, is far superior to no theory at all.

The practitioner who hopes to develop effective and predictable instructional techniques, whether for learning algebra or for learning to live with one's neighbors, must keep current with work in the field. However, the task to be aspired for in one course in theories of learning is the building of a foundation for future intelligent decision making and consumerism. Become familiar with the various approaches to studying learning, the inherent strengths and limitations of each approach, the probable type(s) of learning outcome to which research findings can be generalized and, therefore, applied.

REFERENCES

Bloom, B.S. (Ed.) Taxonomy of educational objectives: Handbook I: Cognitive domain. New York: David McKay, 1956.

Bloom, B.S. Hastings, J.T., & G.F. Handbook on formative and summative evaluation of student learning. New York: McGraw-Hill, 1971.

Flavell, J.H. Metacognition and cognitive monitoring: A new area of cognitive-development inquiry. American Psychologist, 1979, 34 (10), 906-911.

Gagne, R.M. The Conditions of Learning 3rd edition. New York: Holt, Rinehart and Winston, 1977.

Gagne, R.M. Educational technology and the learning process. Educational Researcher, 1974, January, 3-8.

Gagne, R.M. Domains of learning. Interchange, 1972, 3, 1-8.

Krathwohle, D.R., Bloom, B.S., & Masin, B.B. Taxonomy of educational objectives: Handbook II: Affective domain. New York: David McKay, 1964.

Pascual-Leone, J. Cognitive development and cognitive style: a general psychological integration. Indianapolis: Heath-Lexington Books, 1972.

Merrill, M.D., Kowalls, T., & Wilson, B.B. Instruction design in transition. Paper presented at the annual meeting of the American Educational Research Association in Boston, 1980.

Miller, W.G., Snowman, J., & O'Hare, T. Application of alternative statistical techniques to examine the hierarchical ordering in Bloom's taxonomy. American Educational Research Journal, Summer, 1979, 16 (3), 241-248.

Norman, D. Notes toward a theory of complex learning. In Lesgold, A.M., J.W. Pellegrino, S.D. Fokkema, & R. Glaser (Eds.), Cognitive Psychology and Instruction. New York: Plenum Press, 1978.

REFERENCES CONTINUED

Seddon, G.M. The properties of Bloom's taxonomy of educational objectives for the cognitive domain. Review of Educational Research. Spring 1978, 48 (2), 303-323.

Witkin, H., Dyk, R., Faterson, H., Goodenough, D., & Karp, S. Psychological differentiations. New York: Wiley, 1962.

The overriding issues presented in Chapter Three include memory, transfer and evaluation. Several theories of memory are discussed, followed by a section on the distinctions between various types of transfer. The final portion introduces the essential questions to be considered in evaluation. This chapter actually consists of three small chapters, each with an introduction and some conclusions, which have been combined into three parts of this one chapter. Chapters six through ten, which delineate the various learning outcome areas, have a final section presenting overriding issues as they relate to each specific outcome.

1. Define memory, transfer, evaluation.

2. Describe several theories of memory.

3. Discuss several different ways to categorize transfer phenomenon.

4. What are the three basic steps in any evaluation process?

CHAPTER THREE

OVERRIDING ISSUES:

MEMORY, TRANSFER, EVALUATION

INTRODUCTION

Connecting learning outcomes with learning theories requires making distinctions among characteristics of different learning products and discerning which of several theories of learning offers a model most likely to facilitate the acquisition of that outcome. Parallel with that effort, the instructional designer should keep in mind the overriding issues of memory, transfer and evaluation. Initial learning must persist in memory, be retrievable and have transfer value to other new learning situations. Adequate and appropriate evaluation is essential throughout the learning process in order to guide the learning process. Part I of this chapter concerns memory. Part II concerns transfer. Part III concerns evaluation.

PART I: MEMORY

Introduction and Definition. "I know I read that, I just can't remember what it said." "I'm so embarrassed! My memory fails me. I can't remember your name." Surely one of the banes of human existence and interaction and a major problem for any student resides in the human memory.

Memory or retention is loosely defined as "the extent to which material originally learned is still retained" (Deese & Hulse, 1967, p. 371). Adams (1967) attempts a more complete definition.

> Memory is the habit state of a subject that gives the capacity for correct occurrences of a criterion response. There is an initial acquisition session in which the subject makes a discriminative response to a stimulus, followed by a period of time called a "retention interval" when the criterion response does not occur. After the interval there is a retention test in which the subject is asked to recall the criterion response to its original form when a stimulus is presented or, in the case of recognition, to indicate with an identification whether he has experienced this stimulus or this criterion response before (p. 9).

Adams' rather lengthy definition of memory elaborates what Deese and Hulse's (1967) contains in brief, that is, memory implies three separate parts, aspects or stages: an acquisition/encoding stage in which the individual makes some decision about how to classify the "information" to be stored; a storage phase in which the "information" is put aside, out of the immediate consciousness; and a retrieval stage in which the individual attempts to return the "information" to the conscious mind for use or further consideration (Hulse, Deese & Egeth, 1975). Forgetting, the opposite of remembering, may result from difficulty at any one of these stages. Memory, then, is a rather complex system.

In the long history of memory research (Ebbinghaus' classic monograph was first published in 1885) theorists have refined and modified earlier theories in an attempt to understand and, perhaps, subdue this unruly human ability. Some theories emphasize the importance of one stage of memory while others suggest that the problem lies at another stage or in some combination of stages.

IMPORTANCE OF THE LEARNING PHASE

Association. Associationists see memory as closely related to the general laws of association, that is, when two facts, events or other such phenomena occur at the same time, they become associated or connected in the human consciousness. If the two items are well learned, that is, clearly associated, memory will endure. According to the associationists humans can reproduce (retrieve) past happenings in three ways. Each illustrated the importance of the learning phase. One can remember voluntarily, through attempts to recollect. If "good" learning has occurred, bringing one item in the association to mind should bring the other also. For example, if a student who has learned the mathematical rules well in solving a problem, he should be able to "remember" the rules associated with that problem almost without any effort. Again, if learning has been thorough, the chance occurrence of one "mental image" will elicit the associated image. Suppose, for example, that a child always drinks a root beer float at her grandmother's house and only there. If she enters a soda fountain and whiffs a root beer odor she will probably think of her grandmother's house. As a third alternative, individuals remember in an unconscious way through the occurrence of processes similar to the original happening. A child plays with his sand pails on the beach. Later his mother asks him to select the correct size plastic bowl to store some dinner leftovers. Although the child does not actually recall the beach-pail experience in his bowl selection, the earlier event unconsciously influences his choice. For the associationists, then, original learning forms the essential base of memory.

Use-Disuse. Learning also relates closely to the popular notion of use-disuse of memory. How often do we hear people say or say ourselves, "I can't remember that because I haven't thought about it in a long time." On the other hand, we have much evidence, that there are hundreds of things that we remember in spite of years of disuse. Think of a motor skill that went untapped for years and then was reinstituted or some piece of a nursery rhyme that you may not have recited since early childhood, yet it is still there in your memory store. It seems then that if something is well "stamped in" as Thorndike (1913) would say, even long periods of disuse will not disturb it.

Interference. Interference theorists such as Melton and Irwin (1940) suggest that it is not mere disuse that causes forgetting, not merely the passage of time, but what happens in the time between learning and memory. They attempt to illustrate how one experience affects another through the use of two paradigms: Retroactive Interference (Fig. 1A) and Proactive Interference (Fig. 1B).

Retroactive Inhibition	Proactive Inhibition
Experimental Group	Experimental Group
Learn Task 1	Learn Task 1
Learn Task 2	Learn Task 2
Test Task 1	Test Task 2
Control Group	Control Group
Learn Task 1	Rest
Rest	Learn Task 2
Test Task 1	Test Task 2
(A)	(B)

Fig. 1. Paradigms for Retroactive (A) and Proactive (B) Inhibition.

One can see that in the retroaction paradigm the experimenter is attempting to see the effect of the second task on the retention of task 1, while in the proaction paradigm the researcher is interested in how task 1 affects the learning of task 2 for the experimental group. These two distinct types of interference can be found in memory.

In a more every day example, imagine that Sally learns Spanish in sophomore year and then switches to French in junior year. If Sally forgets the Spanish she is suffering from retroactive interference, the French has taken the place of the Spanish. If instead, she remembers the Spanish, she has experienced proactive interference. The Spanish has, in a sense, prevented the remembering of the French.

Whether proaction or retroaction occurs depends on a number of circumstances. How well practiced was the Spanish? How important is it that Sally remember the Spanish? Does she plan to spend a year of college in a Spanish speaking country? Does she have a Spanish heritage? Perhaps Sally found the Spanish teacher difficult to work with and therefore did not learn as well as she did from the French teacher. Whether proactive or retroactive interference (inhibition) is the problem, the learning stage is at least in part the bugaboo to memory here.

Information Processing. If one assumes a two-stage learning process as Hebb (1949) does, another support for the importance of good learning comes from the "information processing" literature. Hebb (1949) suggests that when the student attends to something in the environment, a group of nerve cells is activated which recurrently excite one another. Hebb claims that this accounts for memory of short duration (also called primary memory, PM, short-term memory, STM, or short-term storage, STS). If the attended-to event is not rehearsed the electrical activity in the nerves disappears and the activity subsides. If, however, the event is rehearsed, a structural change occurs in the nerve network and permanent or long-term storage (LTS) begins. (Long-term storage is also called secondary memory, SM, long-term memory, LTM.) One need not be aware of the rehearsal for it to take place. Rehearsal, even in some unconscious form, will "cement" the experience into long-term memory. According to information processing theory, items in LTM do not need continual rehearsal. They can be retrieved after they have left the conscious mind for long periods of time.

An interesting hypothesis of Miller's (1956)

impacts on this theory of the importance of short-term memory in the learning phase of memory. Miller suggests that the STM is limited to a very few (7 ± 2) unrelated items. Once past this relatively small limit (whatever its number) further items "bump out" prior items which have not been rehearsed, preventing learning and therefore subsequent storage and retrieval possibilities.

Mental Imagery. Another area that relates to successful learning and memory is mental imagery. Bugelski (1977) supports the belief that virtually all stimuli, even the most abstract, can and do elicit some mental image in the subject. Some learning conditions may inhibit imagery, for example, if presentation rate is too rapid, but Bugelski reports evidence which suggests that encouraging the use of imagery, including "nonsense" imagery, enhances recall. In fact, the more ridiculous or "memorable" the image is to the person trying to remember, the better one can be expected to remember. The imagery is introduced in the learning phase. While it surely influences storage and retrieval, the learning phase receives the emphasis.

Dual Encoding. A further delineation of the idea of the mental imagery idea is found in the dual encoding theory (Paivio, 1974). According to this theory, two separate areas of the brain exist, a verbal area and a non-verbal area. The two systems encode data separately but activity in one area can initiate activity in the other. Although both systems may encode the same external data, one system may work independently on external events and later "create" a corollary in the other system. A person, then may simply take in an impression (image) of an event. Later, after the external phenomenon has ended, the individual produces an accompanying verbal "memory." The reverse may be more typical in the use of mnemonic devices. Initially the memory taps into only the verbal system. In an effort to enhance memory, the individual uses some mental imagery. Paivio (1977) cites much evidence to demonstrate that imagery does indeed lead to success in memory. Certainly this imagery interacts at every stage of memory but its greatest impact reverts to the learning stage.

Behaviorism. One final position which supports the emphasis on the learning phase is the behaviorist viewpoint as stated by Skinner (as cited in Hergenhahn, 1976). For Skinner, memory is intimately related to learning. An individual learns to associate some operant with some reward. When the experimenter removes the reward, she produces extinction.

Extinction (forgetting) is basically unlearning. The original connection between the behavior and the reward is unlearned and the behavior returns to the preexperimental operant level. The learner acts as though no conditioning has ever taken place. If the experimenter has succeeded in arriving at a reinforcement schedule with high production of behavior for very low reward, the behavior is virtually impossible to extinguish. Under the most successful teaching in Skinner's system forgetting does not occur spontaneously. Rather the student learns to forget. Skinner clearly rates learning as the most important aspect in memory. For him memory is learning, the two processes are identical.

The learning phase of memory, then, boasts several supporters from somewhat divergent viewpoints. Although all memory specialists recognize the importance of good learning, some look to other phases for the problem areas in memory.

THE IMPORTANCE OF THE STORAGE PHASE

Those who look to the storage phase for their understanding of memory processes are interested in what happens to the "memory" after the learning has taken place. What processes seem to affect the memory almost spontaneously after the original learning has been accomplished?

Internal Transformation. Some researchers (for example, Koffka, 1935) suggest that a memory trace is formed in original learning and that the trace can be modified both internally through a process of progressive simplification toward the ideal and externally through the influence of similar experiences with which the trace interacts. An example of an internal transformation would be when a figure such as /_\ changes to △ , a more ideal figure perceptually, while in storage. External influences can be seen when someone engages in some repeated action, for example, dining with Grandmother each week. One trace, Grandmother's dinner the first week in June, becomes intertwined with subsequent weeks. The trace of the first week alone is no longer retrievable or even existing as a separate trace. According to Koffka, then, each of these influences may act on a trace individually or both influences may interact in some undetermined manner. Thus, the original trace does not really decay, but neither is it available to the person's conscious memory. Ausubel, whom we will discuss in greater detail later in the text, has a theory that relates closely to this idea of Koffka's.

Interference. Some aspects of interference theory also lend emphasis to the storage phase of memory. For example, Osgood (1935) shows that in well learned experimental lists of words, semantic similarity may cause interference. If the first list requires learning WARM-HOLE and a second list demands WARM-OPENING, interference occurs. One explanation is that in the storage phase HOLE and OPENING become indistinguishable. Interestingly, in short-term memory, acoustic similarity causes interference (Conrad & Hull, 1964). Since there is some evidence that short-term memory storage is acoustic, storage again emerges as the culprit in memory failure.

Reorganization. Others who emphasize the importance of the storage phase (Cofer, 1973; Jenkins, 1974) argue that subjects reorganize data in memory. Jenkins and his associates, for example, asked subjects to listen to several sentences which revealed one, two or three facts about a specific event. After hearing each sentence, the subjects responded to some question which focused their attention on the statement for a moment. When Jenkins later asked the subjects to identify sentences which they had heard before, they successfully discriminated true statements from false statements, but they were unable to distinguish true sentences which they had actually heard before. The subjects apparently had used the various bits of information to construct a complete event. Once the event was established, a true sentence about that event was "recognized" whether or not the subject had ever heard that specific sentence before. The storage system reorganized the specific bits of data into a cohesive whole. The learner remembered not the original experiences but the reorganized event.

THE IMPORTANCE OF THE RETRIEVAL STAGE

Learning and storage, then, are named as the essential focus points for various theorists. The retrieval stage also comes into play. All researchers involved in memory would agree that some event, real or imagined, must "cue" memory. Even our most spontaneous memories are initiated by some subtle prod. If we lose the cue, we lose the ability to pull out the memory.

Penfield (1959), however, demonstrated that the *memory trace* itself probably exists regardless of whether we can consciously recall it or not. In his work in brain surgery he showed that stimulation of the sensory areas of the brain produced verbal reports of experiences. For example, stimulation of the visual area resulted in experiencing lights, colors and so on, but these lacked meaning. Stimulation of the temporal lobes, however, led to detailed reports of meaningful, integrated experiences. It seemed that anything a person ever attended to could be found in this store if the clinician knew the exact spot to stimulate. Certainly this is interesting support for the essential place of adequate retrieval procedures.

Psychoanalysis. Perhaps the reason we do not remember some things is that we do as Barbra Striesand suggests in the song "The Way We Were," "Things too painful to remember, we simply choose to forget."

Freud (1943) would agree that the memories still exist and subconsciously affect behavior, but they are unavailable to the conscious mind. For the psychoanalyst healing happens when circumstances exist in which the client brings back the painful memories and reintegrates them into conscious memory. Retrieval, for the psychoanalyst, is essential, learning and storage are automatic.

Interference. Proponents of the interference concept of forgetting also "pop-up" here, stressing the importance of retrieval. McGeoch (1932) for example, claims that when two responses are learned to the same or very similar response they are both stored, but when the cue to remember them occurs one response is more powerful than the other and therefore occurs first and is taken as *the* memory. To illustrate, if you went to a party and met two beautiful, long-haired women, one named

Annette and the other named Theresa, McGeoch claims that you will store both names. Later, however, when you again meet one of the two women, the name which is more familiar to you will emerge first, and you will "remember" that name.

Most memory theorists conclude that retrieval is essential to memory but some do not see it as a separate phase of memory but rather as intimately related to the learning phase. Particularly in arbitrary learning situations, such as learning a person's name, specific cues or plans for retrieval must be integrated into the learning phase of memory.

CONCLUSIONS ABOUT MEMORY

This section has lightly touched on some beliefs and theories of memory and forgetting. It has totally ignored others, for example, the tentative chemical encoding theory (Babich et al., 1965). Further, it has put aside the questions of different measures (Is memory the same for recall, recognition, and reconstruction?), and a long history of "How to Remember" literature (for example, Loisette, 1899; Luria, 1968). It has concentrated instead on the three phases of memory.

PART II: TRANSFER

Research and theory on memory and forgetting concentrate on storage and retrieval of experience. The mental representation of prior experience is examined and predictions are made concerning the retrieval of that experience. The utilization of stored experience to facilitate new learning is the province of research and theory on _transfer_.

DEFINITIONS

Definitions of transfer vary from simple statements of "the effects of prior learning on subsequent learning" (Houston, 1981, p. 231) to complex qualifying statements such as that given by Royer (1979, p. 53). He defines transfer as "the extent to which the learning of an instructional event contributes to or detracts from the subsequent problem solving or the learning of subsequent instructional events."

Positive Transfer. Both definitions imply that transfer can be either a positive or a negative phenomenon. Positive transfer occurs when a prior learning experience increases the speed or mastery of new learning. Reading skills have positive transfer value in many learning situations; if your reading skills are poor, learning from this text would be extremely difficult. Positive transfer may also involve very specific details of prior learning. Having learned to float in water, I can use that experience to learn the dog paddle. Or, having learned that the prefix "pre-" means "before," I can use that knowledge to deduce the meaning of "precede," "preview," "prepare."

Negative Transfer. Negative transfer occurs when prior learning interferes with or slows down new learning. Proactive interference is a form of negative transfer. Memory of a prior learning experience inhibits new learning. Repeated failure at learning to read creates an attitude toward future reading that inhibits or interferes with later learning. Having learned to float while lying on my back increases the difficulty I have learning the dog paddle. Or, having learned that words starting with "pre" have a meaning related to "before," I may experience difficulty in learning the meanings of "preceptor," "precious," or "preen."

Other Terms. As illustrated above, transfer effects may be very broad or very narrow, may be negative or positive. In the historical search for the parameters of such effects, researchers have identified and labelled other sub-categories of transfer. These subcategories are not mutually exclusive. In fact, there is considerable over-lap among them. Their existence in the literature is the result of different theoretical and empirical approaches to the study of transfer.

Generalization. When a response to a particular stimulus is learned, that response may later be performed to a similar, but not identical, stimulus. Sally learned to shoot a basket through a hoop attached to a pole. Later she learns to shoot a basket through a hoop attached to a plate of tempered glass. The same response is transferred to a new stimulus. John learned to do the two-step to the strains of "Anniversary Waltz." Later he learned to dip. He now delights his dancing partners by two-stepping and dipping to the graceful chords of "Anniversary Waltz," a new response to an old stimulus. Generalizations of either old responses to new stimuli or old stimuli to new responses appear to occur in a predictable pattern that can be represented by a normal curve. Generalization (transfer) is most probable when the greatest similarity exists between the original learning and the new learning. As the similarity decreases, the probability of transfer decreases. Sally would probably not try to shoot a basket through a hoop attached to a flying airplane. John probably would not hop-scotch to "Anniversary Waltz."

Discrimination. Sally and John would not do these last mentioned acts because they would not see a similarity between the situation described and their previously learned stimulus-response patterns. They would discriminate between the situations. The discriminations necessary for Sally and John in these last instances are not difficult discriminations. The attributes of dipping are far removed from those of hop-scotch, as are the attributes of a hoop on tempered glass far-removed from those of a hoop on a flying plane. Transfer from one situation to the other is possible, but not probable.

Where situations are more similar, but transfer is inappropriate, discrimination learning would be necessary to prevent transfer. Sewing machine needles come in different sizes. Although very similar in appearance, differences among them are crucial to excellent tailoring. The good seamstress will not generalize (transfer) the properties of a size 16 needle to a size 9 needle and attempt to use them the same way.

Secondary Generalization. Primary generalization, described above, occurs when the similarity from situation one to situation two is environmentally defined. Generalization from a size 16 needle to a size 9 needle (negative transfer) might occur because both are patterned the same way with a pointed end that contains a thread hole and a blunt end that has one flat side. Secondary generalization occurs when the similarity from situation one to situation two is previously learned semantic similarity. Houston (1981) cites a study in which children were taught to move a lever in one direction on a white-colored cue and the opposite direction on a black-colored cue. They were then divided into two groups. One group was taught to call grey-colored cues "white," the other group was taught to call grey-colored cues "black." Put back in the original learning setting, the children demonstrated secondary generalization (transfer). Presented with a grey cue, the children who were taught to call grey "black" moved the lever in the direction previously learned for black, if taught to call grey "white," they moved the lever in the opposite direction. The similarity creating the conditions for generalization was not in the external environment, but in the internal representation of the learner.

Specific Transfer. Specific transfer is said to have occurred when there is clear similarity between attributes of the old stimulus and attributes of the new stimulus. Sharing the "pre" prefix would be an example of clear similarity between attributes of words already learned and new words to be learned. For transfer to occur, the learner must notice or respond to the similarity.

As a child Oscar lived next door to a very grouchy white-haired lady whom he learned to fear. After 30 years of marriage Oscar's wife became a real estate agent and their life style had to be relearned. At the same time Oscar's wife's hair began to grey. Oscar had great difficulty learning (adjusting to) their new life style. He was anxious and uncomfortable in the new clock hours he and his wife had set aside for shared activities. Neither one had any idea that Oscar's failure to learn was related to his experience as a child.

Nonspecific Transfer. Nonspecific transfer is a term used to describe effects of prior learning on new learning when no apparent similarities exist between old and new stimuli. The characteristics of nonspecific transfer are often described under the concepts "learning to learn" and "warm-up."

Learning to Learn. Experimental research with both humans and infra-human subjects demonstrates that learning efficiency increases over repeated trials. Animals learning to discriminate colors and humans learning lists of paired-associate words learn more quickly with increased experience at similar learning tasks although the specific elements being learned are different. The aspects of transfer appear to be knowing what to attend to, using the same mnemonic strategies, etc. The learner develops a strategy for learning that can be transferred to all similar learning tasks. Learning to learn usually results in positive transfer, but not always. Negative transfer can occur when a learner stays with a learning strategy that is inappropriate. This phenomenon is called functional fixedness. A classic experimental study of Duncker (in Houston, 1981) demonstrates this aspect of negative transfer. Subjects were given a box of tacks, a candle and matches and instructed to attach the candle to the wall in such a way that it would burn properly. Few subjects used the box as a candle holder. Their previous experience with tacks and candles had developed strategies for using tacks and strategies for placing candles in safe positions for burning. However, their prior learning strategy involving tacks included taking tacks out of the box and using them to attach things, not taking tacks out of the box and using the box. Therefore, they experienced negative transfer.

Warm-up. Warm-up has to do with the transitory effects of engaging in a learning experience. Such things as sitting in the right position, preparing to be attentive, cueing the appropriate learning-to-learn strategy and so forth. Learners who have warmed-up have an advantage over learners who have not; therefore, warm-up has positive transfer effects that are nonspecific.

Vertical Transfer. In vertical transfer, prior learning impacts upon new learning that is higher in a hierarchy. Any learning in which prerequisite skills are necessary requires positive vertical transfer. In order to figure percentages, the learner must already know how to divide and multiply. Division and multiplication skills have vertical transfer value for learning to figure percentages.

Lateral Transfer. When prior learning affects new learning at the same level in the hierarchy, it is called lateral transfer. Jennifer at three years of age learned to discriminate between red and blue blocks; at four years she received poster paints and easily learned to discriminate between red and blue paints. Susan learned to roller skate backwards while living in Florida. When she moved to Albany, she discovered the ice rink at the Empire Plaza and decided to learn to ice skate. She now can ice skate backwards. In the process of learning, however, she experienced both negative and positive transfer from her roller skating knowledge. She had to discriminate between those old moves which helped and those old moves that didn't work.

Near Transfer. When new stimulus elements are similar but not identical to old stimulus elements the term near transfer might be used to describe the phenomenon. When Jennifer uses her prior knowledge about the differences between red and blue to learn to discriminate between pink and lavender, we might call it near transfer (we might also call it vertical transfer.). Susan's experience of using roller skating skills to learn ice skating could also be called near transfer.

Far Transfer. Far transfer is used to describe those situations in which the stimuli are quite different from the relevant prior learning. Having learned to discriminate between red and blue blocks probably has positive transfer value for later learning to discriminate between black and navy blue suits. Another example would be learning to figure the amount of wallpaper you need for the living room on the basis of your prior classroom experience in figuring the area of rectangles.

Literal Transfer. Knowing that all my furniture is upholstered in shades of gold-tan-brown, I chose wallpaper for my living room with a light beige background and turquoise highlights. Literal transfer describes using a piece of knowledge or an intact skill directly in a new learning situation. Henry had great difficulty mastering the eye-hand coordination necessary to print his name. However, he didn't have to relearn eye-hand coordination to write cursive. He experienced literal transfer from his printing days. While studying the American Revolution, Dave learned that wars may be caused by desires to control natural resources. When he began to study World War I, he immediately began to look for natural resources control as an explanation.

Figural Transfer. Figural transfer "involves the use of some segments of our world knowledge as a tool for thinking about or learning about, a particular problem or issue" (Royer, 1979, p. 60). Calling Lincoln the captain of his ship is asking the reader to use figural transfer. All the "world knowledge" (prior relevant experience) the reader has about being a ship captain is called into play to enhance the appreciation of Lincoln's role as President. Enjoying and appreciating the Super Bowl is possible for persons with no literal knowledge of the game or the players, if figural transfer from the World Series is possible. Figural transfer is different from other forms of transfer in that it involves a whole complex of prior learning experiences that is brought to bear on a new learning experience. The epitome of figural transfer is the use of metaphor and simile.

Where did all these terms come from? As noted above, the terms used to describe transfer effects are not mutually exclusive. Learning to learn (nonspecific transfer) is probably literal transfer. Near transfer includes, at least both vertical transfer and specific transfer. Are specific transfer and literal transfer the same phenomenon with two names?

The proliferation of terms with definitions ranging from slightly to very different is the result of research and theory building supported by quite different theoretical viewpoints. The distinctions made previously between Behaviorism and Cognitive Psychology should have positive transfer value for you here.

Behaviorists theorize that environmental manipulation explains behavior. They therefore study the environment, manipulate environmental elements, predict changes in behavior based upon that manipulation, and test their hypotheses. Behavioristic research on transfer then has involved describing the stimulus elements in prior and new learning to deduce the transfer effects. The assumption of Behaviorists is that the environment can be manipulated in such a way that the learner will notice the similarities between old and new, therefore facilitating (or inhibiting) learning.

Cognitive Psychology attempts to explain the phenomena internal to the learner. Cognitive psychologists, therefore, study the learner, manipulate variables like processing skills, make predictions about how information/skills are stored and retrieved, and test their hypotheses. The assumption of cognitivists is that what the learner brings to the learning situation will determine the kind and degree of transfer. Retrieval of prior information/skills is the concern of much cognitive research. Bransford and McCarrell (in Royer, 1979) demonstrated the importance of the internal structure of the learner for transfer effects in new learning. The new task is to understand the following sentences. "The trip was not delayed because the bottle broke." "The notes were sour because the seam split." "The haystack was important because the cloth ripped."

What prior knowledge are you using to decipher the meaning of these new pieces of verbal information? Was your first attempt literal or figural? Are you able to make any connections between the concepts connected grammatically in the statements? If you are experiencing difficulty in comprehending the meaning of these statements, can you explain the source of the difficulty?

Cognitive psychologists hypothesize that our memory structure is analogous to a filing cabinet. When appropriately cued, we enter into a search process that leads directly to the right drawer, file, and paper. If the cue misleads us, we don't find the right paper immediately and we start looking in other files or other drawers semantically connected in our memory structure with the cue. We continue this process until we find the right paper or give up. Have you found the right "papers" to gain meaning from the above statements? Ship launch, bagpipe, parachute. Are you now experiencing positive transfer?

A relatively recent development in psychological theory and research is Aptitude Treatment Interaction (ATI). Such theory assumes that learning is the result of the interaction between the characteristics of the learner and the characteristics of the "to-be-learned." This marriage of Behaviorism and Cognitivism is in its infancy and few substantial significant findings exist. Research on transfer effects is a promising area in which this marriage may thrive. The chapter on Cognitive Psychology will describe some current theories on transfer in which ATI is a basic assumption.

PART III: EVALUATION

Evaluation of learning outcomes includes the evaluation of learner change in the desired direction and evaluation of the instructional program designed to achieve the learning outcome. Gronlund (1976) lists the three basic steps in any evaluation process. They are (1) determine the intended learning outcomes, (2) choose (or construct) appropriate measurement instruments, and (3) use the results of measurement to improve both learning and instruction.

SELECT MEASURES

Constructing or selecting a measurement instrument involves matching the intended outcome, assuring the validity of the measurement and assuring its reliability. As noted above, a measuring instrument must be relevant to the learning outcome. Assessing what you claim to be assessing is the issue of validity. If you teach learners how to change an auto tire, and evaluate the learning by giving a paper and pencil test in which learners are asked to list the steps in changing a tire, you violate the principle of validity. A valid test would measure the learner's performance in changing a tire, not the learner's ability to articulate the steps. A learner could rotely memorize the steps, but be totally unable to change a tire. Some of the difficulties of assuring the validity of a measurement tool can be illustrated with an example from the domain of attitudes.

Attitudes are not clearly defined. Valid measurement tools demand clearly and precisely defined constructs. Therefore, researchers find it difficult to attest to the validity of their measures. If we do not know precisely what it is that we wish to test, how will we design an appropriate tool to test it? By analogy, suppose you were asked, for some reason, to evaluate whether or not several surfaces were "fuzzy." You would first have to develop an operational definition of "fuzzy" that would give all the defining characteristics of "fuzzy." Only then could you develop an appropriate rating scale to test for fuzziness. Any other investigator who wanted to call his surfaces "fuzzy" would have to use the same defining characteristics or else use a different term to discuss his construct. At the present level of sophistication of attitudes, researchers do not have this common operational definition. Therefore a test which might be constructed to test attitudes in one situation with considerable validity might not be used with the same assurance in a second situation.

Reliability of evaluation is also essential. Can the learner consistently reproduce the test performance; is the sample of behavior large enough to assess performance over time and circumstance? Can the tire changer always succeed in changing the tire on the demonstration car? Or only seven out of ten times? Can the learner change tires on other makes and models? A difficult to "capture" learning outcome, such as attitudes, can create havoc with reliability.

Attitudes are largely unconscious. Therefore, the way in which we construct our attitudes in one situation might differ markedly from the way in which we construct them at a later time. This will clearly reduce the reliability of measures of attitudes. Further a problem of "fakability" enters into attitude measures. Frequently attitude measures are self-report scales on which even the relatively naive test-taker can ascertain the attitudes that are being scaled. The test-taker also knows what attitudes are "acceptable" in regard to a particular attitude object. For example, a school child "should" like arithmetic. The test-taker may answer with acceptable attitudes not because she believes that these are her attitudes but because she wants to look acceptable to the tester. Also, the attitude measure may ask the individual to recognize rather than generate attitudes. She may tend to "recognize" acceptable attitudes as her own even if her "generated" attitudes were different. The results of such a test, then, may say nothing about the attitudes that really do mediate this individual's behavior. A second scale that took specific behaviors as indicators of attitudes will tell a very different story about the individual resulting in low predictability between the measures.

Matching evaluation instruments to learning outcomes is essential. When tests unintentionally mix assessment of different learning outcomes, the resulting "grade" has little meaning. For example, suppose that an instructor states a learning objective of "The learner will divide three digit numbers by one digit numbers." To assess learning, the instructor gives a test on which the learner is asked to define terms, list the steps in division, and do several problems.

The student who can do only the problem part of the test has achieved the learning outcome, but probably will not pass the test.

Evaluation Methods. The most familiar form of evaluation of learning is the classroom paper and pencil test. Properly selected/constructed to assess the intentional learning outcomes, classroom tests can be very effective tools.

The Standardized test of achievement, or aptitude, or attitude developed by professional psychometricians is another familiar assessment tool. Standardization allows the user to make comparisons among learners that would not always be appropriate using classroom tests. The test creators pilot their test questions on representative individuals and groups. Only questions which produce the desired psychometric properties are retained. Items are carefully chosen to assure the reported validity and reliability. When the test constructors are satisfied that the test is valid and reliable, they then test representative groups. The scores from the representative groups provide "norms," a set of scores that may be regarded as typical for all groups similar to the norming group. Therefore, the user may compare the scores of his or her students with the scores of the norming group to make judgements about the performance of the students. Such comparisons should not be made if the norming group is not similar to the group being tested. For example, if the norming group consisted of only white students, the norms should not be used to judge the performance of Mexican-Americans. Another caveat concerns the content validity of the test. Content validity concerns the degree to which the content on a test is consistent with the learning objectives and instructional procedures. A standardized test can be an excellent test and yet not have content validity for a particular class or school. The test may cover content that is not taught, or it may not cover content that is taught. In terms of learning domains, the test will almost certainly be some combination of different domains. The analysis of the resulting scores will be complicated in the same ways as those resulting from improperly developed classroom tests, as discussed above.

Observation is a frequently used evaluation tool in both formal and informal educational settings. To appropriately use observation techniques, define clearly the learning outcomes being assessed and look for only those outcomes. Objectivity in observation is extremely troublesome. Subjectivity destroys both reliability and validity of observation measures.

Another evaluation method is peer-appraisal. As with observation, objectivity is crucial to meaningful peer-appraisal. The appraisers must have a clear understanding of the learning outcomes being assessed. They also must have working definitions of what behaviors constitute achievement of the specific desired outcomes.

The learner may be able to evaluate his/her own learning achievement. Such evaluation is called self-report. The reliability and validity of self-reports are difficult to determine. Individuals often respond differently at different times -- the reliability question. They also perceive the learning experience in idiosyncratic ways that can influence validity. This is especially true if the learning outcome is socially desirable and can be faked. For example, lack of prejudice toward ethnic groups can be self-reported and yet be totally inaccurate. (Readers interested in more detail are referred to any of the many excellent textbooks on educational and psychological measurement.)

USE THE RESULTS

Evaluation techniques are largely misused if the only result is a set of scores or observations filed somewhere. When evaluation instruments are carefully chosen to assess specific learning outcomes, improvement in future learning and instruction is a real possibility.

A score of 60 on a test of division skills which unintentionally mixed verbal information and intellectual skills would typically be followed by remediation on the entire unit. If the learner does have the division skills, but failed the test because she/he could not "tell" the verbal information, hours more of drill on division will only have negative effects. The learner will be discouraged, confidence and self-concept will suffer. If the verbal information is important for future instructional success, the remediation should center on that outcome. The learner should be told that the division skill is well-learned, but she/he also needs to be able to "tell" some things about division, so that learning other math skills will be easier in the future.

Using evaluation to *improve instruction* also is enhanced by careful coordination between desired outcomes and assessment. When learners learn to divide, but cannot "tell" about division, the instructor knows that the place for *instructional improvement* is on teaching verbal information. If analysis of your learner's performance on your evaluation instrument does *not* suggest ways to improve learning and/or improve instruction, the evaluation instrument is probably inappropriate or being used inappropriately. The results of evaluation should lead to (1) improved learning, (2) improved instruction *and* (3) improved evaluation.

REFERENCES

Adams, J.A. Human Memory, New York: McGraw-Hill, 1969.

Babich, J.R., Jacobson, A.L., Bubash, S., and Jacobson, A. Transfer of a response to naive rats by injection of ribonucleic acid extracted from trained rats. Science, 1965, 144, 656-657.

Bugelski, B.R. Words and things and images. American Psychologist, 1970, 25, 1002-1012.

Cofer, C.N. Constructive processes in memory. American Psychologist, 1973, 61, 537-543.

Conrad, R. and Hull, A.J. Information, acoustic confusion and memory span. British Journal of Psychology, 1964, 55, 429-432.

Deese, J. and Hulse, S.H. The Psychology of Learning (3rd Ed.), New York: McGraw-Hill, 1967.

Ebbinghaus, H. Memory, New York: Teachers College Press, Columbia University, 1913.

Freud, S.A. A General Introduction to Psychoanalysis, New York: Garden City, 1943.

Gronlund, N.E. Measurement and Evaluation in Teaching (3rd Ed.), New York: Macmillan Publishing Co., Inc., 1976.

Hebb, D.O. The Organization of Behavior, New York: Wiley, 1949.

Hergenhahn, B.R. An Introduction to Theories of Learning, New Jersey: Prentice-Hall, Inc., 1976.

Houston, J.P. Fundamentals of Learning and Memory, Second Edition, New York: Academic Press, 1981.

Hulse, S.H., Deese, J., and Egeth, H. The Psychology of Learning, (4th Ed.), New York: McGraw-Hill, 1975.

REFERENCES CONTINUED

Jenkins, J.J. Remember that old theory of memory? Well forget it. American Psychologist, 1974, 29, 785-795.

Koffka, W. Principles of Gestalt Psychology. New York: Harcourt, Brace and World, 1935.

Lesgold, A.M., Pellegrino, J.W., Fokkema, S.D. and Glaser, R. (Eds.) Cognitive Psychology and Instruction, New York: Plenum Press, 1978.

Loisette, A. Professor (Marcus Dwight Larrowe) Assimilative Memory, New York: Funk & Wagnalls, 1899.

Luria, A.R., The Mind of Mnemonist, New York: Harper and Row, 1965.

McGeoch, J.A. Forgetting and the law of disuse. Psychological Review, 1932, 39, 352-370.

Melton, L.N. and Irwin, J.M. The influence of degree of interpolated learning on retroactive inhibition and the overt transfer of specific responses. American Journal of Psychology, 1940, 53, 153-203.

Miller, G.A. The magical number seven, plus or minus two: Some limits on our capacity for processing information. Psychological Review, 1956, 63, 81-97.

Osgood, C.E. Method and Theory in Experimental Psychology, New York: Oxford University Press, 1953.

Paivio, A. Language and knowledge of the world. Educational Researcher, 3, 5112, 1974.

Penfield, W. The Interpretive cortex. Science, 1959, 129, 1719-1725.

Royer, James M. Theories of the Transfer of learning, Educational Psychologist, 1979, 14, 53-69.

Thorndike, E.L. Educational Psychology, New York: Teachers College Press, Columbia University, 1913.

Chapter Four considers the theories of learning related to the Behaviorist tradition. Behaviorists look to external events for both the cause and the demonstration of learning. This chapter presents an overview of the Behaviorist School and then looks more closely at the Classical Conditioning, Operant Conditioning and Neo-Behaviorist positions.

1. What are the major characteristics of all behaviorists?
2. How do theories within this general category differ from one another?
3. What are the main points of the various positions within this school?

CHAPTER FOUR

BEHAVIORISM

INTRODUCTION

Humans can and do learn. This statement surely raises no eyebrows nor causes much disagreement. The difficulty arises when individuals attempt to explain how the learning occurs. In the early days of experimental psychology eager scholars believed that comprehensive theories could explain all human learning. They ambitiously set out to build such theories. This chapter will overview some of these attempts. The behaviorist school of theories will be looked at in some detail.

Characteristics of all Behaviorists. Although there are several different frameworks in which behaviorists encapsulate their theories, all behaviorists have certain fundamental commonalities. All behaviorists look for behavioral change in the learner. Although they do not deny the existence of a "mind," they claim that such a construct is inaccessible to observations of science and is therefore an unworthy subject for scientific research. The behaviorists define learning as a relatively permanent change in behavior which cannot be explained by injury, drugs, fatigue or other such phenomena. That the change occurs in behavior is the important process for the behaviorist, whether or not some internal change took place is not central to their thinking.

Further, all behaviorists concentrate on the importance of the environment in the learning of the individual. It is the environment which controls what the learner will learn, not the individual who decides what to learn. Other people become part of this environment, providing feedback to learners on whether or not they are achieving appropriately. Even perception is externally controlled for the behaviorist. It is not the person or animal that structures the external world, rather it is elements of the environment which structure the organism. The characteristics of the event call the attention of the learner or demand a response. Perception of one item rather than another results from the salience, distinctiveness and evoking power of the item, not from some characteristic or structure within the learner.

For the behaviorist, then, that which is outside the learner creates the learner; the environment is the essential control mechanism. The behaviorist would say, "Construct the appropriate habitat and you can create any individual you wish." One is reminded of Watson who claimed "Give me a child for the first seven years of his life and I will give you back any individual you choose."

Two other issues that are addressed, if not agreed upon, by all behaviorists are: The importance of contiguity and the value of reinforcement in learning. Contiguity concerns how close in time two events must occur in order for an association between them to be learned. Reinforcement denotes the consequences of a response to an event. Different Behavioristic theories emphasize these issues differentially. Some focus more on the relationship between stimuli and study the importance of timing (contiguity). Other theories focus more upon the relationship between behavior (responses) and consequences (change in the environments) and, therefore, study reinforcement contingencies. While the relative emphasis on contiguity and reinforcement varies across theories, all behaviorists must address these aspects of learning in building a comprehensive behaviorist theory.

TERMS

Before beginning to look at individual behaviorist theories, some terms that are common to many, if not all behaviorists, will be introduced and briefly discussed.

Behavior. Any action, internal or external, which is engaged in by the learner is called behavior. This behavior may be overt and easily observable like pushing a button, or it may be detectable only to sophisticated instruments like the change in skin acidity when the individual is anxious.

Contiguity. Contiguity means proximate in some way. Events are said to be contiguous when they occur at the same time and in the same place. Not all behaviorists agree that both events must be physically present to be contiguous. Some allow for memory to bring one of the events to the present situation. For example, a child may be spanked an hour after writing on the living room wall. If, however, the parent reminds the child of the writing and tells him that the writing is the reason for the spanking, the events can be said to be contiguous because the writing is brought to the present situation through memory.

Stimulus. A stimulus is any event which calls forth some behavior in the individual. A ringing phone is a stimulus to answer it. Food in the mouth is a stimulus for the digestive system to begin work. Pounding on a thumb is a stimulus to shout "ouch."

Response. A response is any behavior called forth by a stimulus. The action of answering the phone, the working of the digestive system and the shouting of "ouch" are all examples of responses to stimuli.

Reinforcement. A reinforcement is any event which increases the likelihood that an event will occur again. Reinforcement may be a response of the environment, for example, a pleasant sound when the person blows on a horn; it may be an automatic response of the organism, for example; the slakening of thirst when water is ingested; or it may be something added to the situation by another individual, for example, a pat on the back from a third party when a job is well done. This third type of reinforcement is peculiar to a given individual. For example, what is reinforcing to a "sweet-tooth" may be uninteresting to someone whose snacks revolve around salt.

Punishment. Punishment is any event which suppresses a behavior. Punishment, for most behaviorists, does not lead to learning. Rather, it suppresses one behavior so that another behavior may be initiated and, therefore, learned.

Extinction. Extinction is the process of unlearning or forgetting. Forgetting only occurs when something in the environment causes one to learn a new combination of actions or associations in the presence of the same stimulus. Extinction is a sort of planned (at least planned from outside the learner) forgetting.

Intervening Variable. An intervening variable is some action or event that comes between the stimulus and the response. The behaviorist does not try to modify the intervening variables but rather discusses how the variable impacts upon the probability of a given response to a stimulus. Some behaviorists acknowledge that these variables exist and build them into their theories.

THEORETICAL PERSPECTIVES WITHIN BEHAVIORISM

Behaviorists come in three flavors: Associationists, functionalists, and neo-behaviorists. Each theoretical perspective will be introduced in turn, its basic theory and terminology will be delineated and then a few examples of the theory will be explored.

Association Theory. The basic premise of associationism states that when two experiences occur together, they become associated or learned. As long as the two items continue to occur together in the initial "learning," the association will be strengthened. If the two items cease to occur together or if some other item is substituted for one of the items, then the earlier association will be weakened. The association of the two events is called learning, the weakening of the connection between the two events is called extinction or forgetting. Associationists disagree about the need for reinforcement for learning to occur and the types of situations where the theory applies. Some have a rather narrow idea of where the theory can be used and some have a wider application. The theories which will be considered in the associationist tradition are Pavlov, Guthrie, and Rescorla. First some terms will be introduced which are common in association theories and then three examples of this theoretical perspective will be examined.

Unconditioned Stimulus. An unconditioned stimulus (UCS) is a stimulus that occurs with regularity in the environment of the individual.

Unconditioned Response. An unconditioned response (UCR) is a response to an unconditioned stimulus. In a way the UCR is elicited by the UCS. Given the UCS the organism cannot help but respond with a UCR.

Conditioned Stimulus. The conditioned stimulus (CS) is a stimulus which is paired in some way with the UCS.

Conditioned Response. The conditioned response (CR) is the response elicited by the conditioned stimulus.

Classical Conditioning. Perhaps the most famous of the associationist theories is Ivan Pavlov (1955, as cited in Hergenhahn, 1976). Pavlov did not start out to be a learning theorist. His interest in learning arose out of the physiological experiment he conducted. His theory, Classical Conditioning, concerns the autonomic nervous system (the involuntary nervous system which controls eyeblinks, digestive muscles and other similar responses which are not under the conscious control of the individual). Pavlov's basic paradigm is simple. An unconditioned stimulus elicits some unconditioned response. A second stimulus, the conditioned stimulus, is consistently paired with the UCS. After several pairings the CS alone elicits the CR which is a response very similar to the UCR.

In Pavlov's oft-cited example, meat powder (UCS) was placed on the tongues of experimental dogs. The powder caused the dogs to salivate (UCR). Pavlov then consistently rang a bell (CS) immediately before giving the dogs meat powder. Eventually the dogs salivated at the sound of the bell when no meat powder was presented. This salivation to the sound of the bell is the conditioned response. Its only difference from UCR is a slight difference in amount of salivation. Figure 1 illustrates this event.

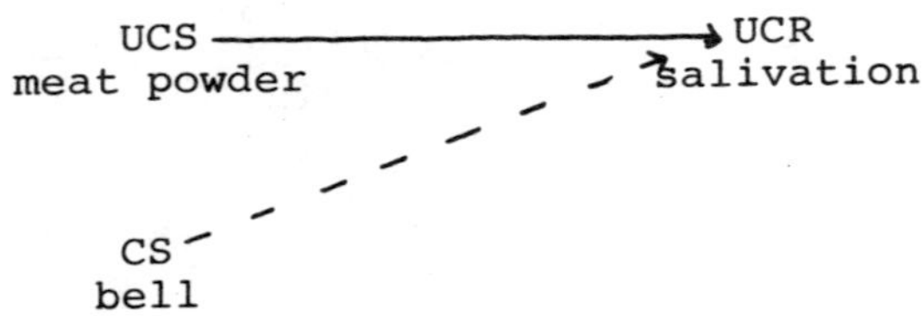

Fig. 1 Pavlov's paradigm

Pavlov's system can be called *stimulus substitution* theory since a new stimulus (CS) is substituted for the original stimulus (UCS) to elicit the same response. No new responses are learned. Rather the same responses are associated to new stimuli.

After initial learning the UCS must occasionally be reintroduced into the paradigm. If the UCS is never again paired with the CS the power of CS to elicit the UCR will fade and eventually disappear or extinguish. In cases where high levels of *overlearning* have taken place, however, it is almost impossible to achieve extinction. That is, when the student continues practice for many trials after initial learning the CS-UCR pairing is difficult to extinguish. In a way this overlearned CS begins to function as a UCS in its own right and new stimuli can be attached to that. A human example of this phenomenon is money. Initially money (CS) is paired with acquisition of material goods (UCS) which elicit the UCR, pleasure (warmth from housing, satiation from food and drink, a sense of security). Eventually, the money becomes so consistently paired with access to the necessities of life that it becomes a UCS. Other stimuli may be paired with it. For example, hard work may be consistently paired with money. Eventually, hard work, in itself, will elicit the same feelings of pleasure and security as the money did before. However if money is *never* repaired with hard work -- hard work will slack off.

Pavlov's work was seen as a breakthrough by some psychologists. Among his greatest contributions to the field is the careful experimental habits that he built into all his research and the complete codification of the effects of different time sequences in the pairing of UCS anc CS.

One Trial Learning. Another example, and perhaps the ultimate example, of the associationist position is Edwin R. Guthrie (1952). He claims only one law of learning: Whatever you do in the presence of a stimulus, you do again when that stimulus is re-presented. For any of us who have found ourselves making the same typing mistake again, and again, Guthrie's theory has some intuitive appeal.

Guthrie admits no need for reinforcement, no intervening variable, only a combination of stimuli accompanied by a movement. Learning occurs in one trial; that is, the full associative strength between the stimulus and the movement occurs in one pairing of the two events. When challenged by those who demonstrated that practice does affect learning, Guthrie pointed out that all movement within the organism is not observable. Between the environmental stimuli and the observable response, several minute stimulus and response associations are built up. These mini S-R combinations are fully associated in one trial. Practice appears to have an effect, claims Guthrie, only because more of these stimulus-action pairs are built up until the observable response appears as "learned" to an outside observer. This observable response, of course, is made up of multiple unseen S-R sets. To explain the demonstrated effect of reinforcement on learning, Guthrie suggested that reinforcement marks the end of an event so that no further stimuli are associated with a particular movement. In itself reinforcement adds nothing to the strength of mere contiguity.*

Among Guthrie's most practical suggestions for learning are his rules for forgetting or extinction.

---

* Guthrie's theory provides an excellent example of a poor theory because it is not testable. The variables that Guthrie includes in his theoretical paradigm, the sort of mini S-R's, cannot be subjected to empirical testing. Guthrie's theory has some intuitive appeal and so it "hangs

If there is one-trial learning, there is also one-trial forgetting. The teacher simply has to create a situation where the student makes a new response to the same set of stimuli. Having made this new response, the student will replace the old response with the new. An individual does again what he/she last did in the presence of that set of stimuli. Punishment enters here in his rules for forgetting. Like most behaviorists, Guthrie saw little value to punishment unless it caused the substitution of some desirable response in the presence of the stimuli formerly associated with the undesirable response.

Guthrie, then, developed a theory based on pure contiguity. Although there are _some_ _few_ applications of the theory, its explanatory power is fairly limited.

Differential Contingency. As discussed above, Pavlovian conditioning depends upon the contiguity between the stimulus and the response. The two events, according to Pavlov, must occur at the same time in the same place in order for the individual to learn to associate the two. In the late 1960's _Robert_ _Rescorla_ began to question whether or not mere contingency were enough (Schwartz, 1978). Contiguity is necessary, he agreed, but is it sufficient? He demonstrated instances where the CS and the UCS were both present in the situation, but the CS in no way indicated that the UCS would follow in any regular pattern. One can think, for example, of an ineffective and inconsistent parent who frequently and randomly deprives her child of love and affection. Threats and loss of love are both present here but threats come in what appears to be a random sequence and love or lack of it is just as capricious. This situation provides no clear predictability for the child that this particular threat will lead to loss of love and affection. Rescorla, then, suggests that the key factor in conditioning is not the presence of the two stimuli in the same situation, but rather the _differential_ _contingency_ between CS and UCS.

---

on" in spite of its obvious flaws. Estes attempted to correct Guthrie's shortcomings by carefully quantifying Guthrie's system. Since such mathematical systems remain at a relatively primitive level, they have not made a serious impact on the study of learning.

The question that Rescorla claims is essential is, "Does the CS predict the presence or absence of the UCS with a fairly high level of probability?" If this high level of probability exists, then conditioning will take place. If the probability is low (random or chance) then no conditioning takes place.

This finding sounds very similar to Pavlov's contiguity conditioning. What Rescorla demonstrated through his experiments, however, is that specifically unpaired CS-UCS combinations lead to conditioning if the subject has built up an expectation or probability calculation that a particular CS will lead to a particular UCS. For example, in one of Rescorla's experiments he trained dogs to avoid a shock (UCS) when they heard a tone (CS) administered immediately before the shock. He then divided the dogs into four groups. Group A received the traditional CS-UCS pairings. Group B experienced a situation where tone (CS) and shock (UCS) were never paired; Group C had totally random pairings, sometimes UCS followed CS and sometimes it did not; Group D received a semi-random pairing, that is the shock (UCS) never immediately preceded the tone (CS). Pavlovian or contiguity conditioning would predict that fear would be developed at the sound to the tone in Group A and no conditioning would occur in Groups B, C, and D. Rescorla, however, showed that in Group B the dogs learned that the tone meant that the shock would not come immediately, and Group D learned fear because the tone was sometimes followed by the shock. In both these cases the contingency theory of Rescorla would suggest that there was information to be gained from the stimulus situation. Only in the totally random situation is there no information about the connection between the CS and the UCS. Contingency between the two stimuli, then, and not mere contiguity, is the variable of interest.

Rescorla and his associates went further to demonstrate this "information" hypothesis. They showed that animals seem to build up expectations from their prior experience. For example, certain animals were conditioned to expect a shock after a noise, later these same animals had several trials in which a complex CS included both light and noise before shock. When the animals were then tested on the effects of light alone on their behavior, no conditioning had occurred. The noise was the important predictor, the light was redundant information, and thus ignored in the complex stimuli learning. If, however, the complex stimulus of light and noise was never followed by a shock, the conditioning occurred to the light. Light in this situation gave new information to the animal: Noise alone means shock is coming; noise plus light means no shock is coming. The two stimuli are differential predictors of the outcome. Rescorla and his co-workers have since attempted to discover the mechanism that allows for the building up of sets of predictions or contingencies. They hypothesize, as usual, that certain stimuli are automatically more salient to certain organisms. In addition, they hypothesize an automatic mechanism which processes the accumulated data of experience making predictions possible much the way that predicting the arc the fork must take from the plate to the mouth is virtually automatic.

In sum, the importance of Rescorla's theory is to show the possibility of a much broader application of the classical conditioning paradigm through the processes of probability calculations and information evaluation. Far more complex behaviors can be explained by Rescorla than could be explained by the Pavlovian classical conditioning paradigm.

Functionalism. A second theoretical perspective in the Behaviorist tradition is represented by the functionalists.

Basic Premise. The basic premise of the functionalists is that learning helps the individual to adapt to the environment. Adapt, for the functionalist, means how the individual gets the most out of the environmental conditions. Therefore, reinforcement is an important ingredient in the theory. Functionalists theorize that individuals arrange their behavior to maximize the reinforcement available in the environment. The functionalists that will be examined here are Edward L. Thorndike and B. F. Skinner.

Connectionism. Edward L. Thorndike, surely one of the most prolific psychological writers, exemplifies the functionalist position. Thorndike's theory, Connectionism, focused on the bond or connection between the sensory impression or stimulus (S) and the behavior or response (R) which followed.

In the earliest formulation of his theory, Thorndike delineated three distinct laws as the backbone of his ambitious effort. His first law, the Law of Readiness, though somewhat obscurely stated, implies that when someone is ready to do something, doing it is satisfying; not doing it is annoying. The reverse also holds, that is, when someone is not ready to do something, being forced to do it is annoying.

The Law of Exercise formalizes a practice phenomenon. When the individual uses the connection between a stimulus and response, the connection becomes stronger. Conversely, an unused connection weakens.

Thorndike's third major law, the Law of Effect, postulates a relationship between the connection and the consequences of the connection. If the connection leads to a "satisfying state of affairs" (reward), the connection is strengthened; if an "annoying state of affairs" (punishment) results, the connection becomes weaker.

Having developed these three major laws and several minor concepts to support them, Thorndike set out on an experimental program to demonstrate them. By 1929, the evidence demanded restructuring of the theory.* Thorndike, (at the International Congress of Psychology, 1929) boldly admitting his error, drastically reduced the import of both the Law of Exercise and the Law of Readiness. Further, he truncated the Law of Effect, stating that while reward strengthened a connection, punishment had minimal or no effect on the bond between stimulus and response.

Operant Conditioning. From this final theory of Thorndike, it is a short step to the ideas of B. F. Skinner, (1953) probably the best-known Behaviorist. Skinner's theory of Operant Conditioning, concisely stated, says: Reinforce what you want the individual to do again; ignore what you want the individual to stop doing. Not concerned with what causes the organism to behave initially, Skinner concentrates his investigations on the impact on behavior of various schedules and types of reinforcements.

---

* Ah ha! A testable theory!

Behaviorism

Skinner starts with the premise that all organisms operate on their environment in an effort to maximize the return from the environment. If some outside structure or individual sets up a situation where greater reinforcement can be gained by changing a behavior, the behavior is changed. Otherwise, the "*operant*" continues as is.

Reinforcement. For Skinner reinforcement is paramount. He discusses two different types of reinforcement: positive and negative. Both of these types increase the likelihood that the reinforced response will occur again in the similar situation. (It is important to remember that for Skinner reinforcement is always contingent upon some response. If the organism never acts on the environment, it never gets reinforced.) Positive reinforcement is what we typically think of as reward. The organism acts and something pleasant to that organism enters the environment. Negative reinforcement is in a way, the opposite. Something unpleasant is occurring in the environment. When the organism acts, that unpleasant event is terminated. A positive reinforcement might be a word of praise, a piece of candy, a raise in pay. A negative reinforcement might include the buzzer on a seat belt, or a ringing alarm clock. Most of us tend to do what we can to eliminate these aversive stimuli from the environment. Reinforcement always leaves the learner in a better situation than he started. He either goes from neutral to pleased (positive reinforcement) or from discontent to neutral (negative reinforcement).

Individuals frequently confuse negative reinforcement and punishment. In Skinner's system there is an essential difference. Reinforcement always leads to learning, whereas punishment leads to no learning at all. Skinner decries the use of punishment and sees it only as a last resort when some behavior must be suppressed in order that another behavior may occur and be reinforced.

Schedules of Reinforcement. Skinner and his followers (Ferster and Skinner, 1957) also investigated the effects of various schedules of reinforcement. Skinner looked at both *variable* schedules (seemingly at random to the subject) and *fixed* schedules (occurring at regular instances). Variable schedules lead to consistent behavior while fixed schedules cause periods of work followed by periods of inactivity. Skinner also investigated the different effects of time bound reinforcement (called interval) and response related reinforcement (called ratio). When the reinforcers were based on the interval schedule, subjects tended to work fairly slowly. When, however, the number of responses were counted before reinforcers were administered, individuals tended to work at high rates of speed. Taking the two dimensions of reinforcement together, one can easily conclude that a variable ratio schedule of reinforcement will lead to the highest rate of continuous responding to the environment.

Shaping. Skinner, then, focuses on controlling which of the various responses available to the organism the individual will choose to use in a given situation. But what if the organism does not have an appropriate response in its repertoire. Then Skinner would initiate a process of progressive approximation or shaping. On each succeeding "trial" the individual's response would have to look more like the final desired ability in order to merit a reward.

Skinner, then, sees his theory as a means to long term control over behavior. He has repeatedly demonstrated that his theory has a variety of practical application.

Neo-Behaviorism.

Basic Premise. Neo-behaviorists are true behaviorists, that is, they look for mechanistic explanations of learning and deny the need to discuss conscious thought as an explanation for learning. Neo-behaviorists also come in the same basic traditions, with associationists or functionalists. They differ from other behaviorists in one major way, however. Neo-behaviorists include some aspects of the organism in the theoretical formulation. Neo-behaviorists look for or discover "intervening variables" that affect the impact of the stimulus on the response. The organism in some way modifies the response that is given. It is not an automatic reaction to the stimulus. Neo-behaviorists, for example, attempt to explain why one stimulus in a group of apparently (externally) equivalent stimuli is chosen to respond to while others are ignored or neglected. For this section, the theories of Clark Hull, Frank Logan and D. O. Hebb will be considered.

Hypothetical-Deductive Theory. Clark Hull might properly be called a neo-behaviorist in the functionalist tradition. His hypothetical-deductive theory places great emphasis on the variables within the individual which intervene between the stimulus and response, but he is clearly a functionalist in his basic desire to explain how these intervening variables, together with environment, help the adaptation of the individual. Hull's intention was to build a set of postulates and theorems about behavior. The theorems would be directly deduced from the postulates much as one does in Euclidian geometry. The postulates themselves are not directly observable. The theorems provide the basis for experimentation. If the experiments demonstrate that the theorem holds, the theorem may be said to be true and the postulate from which it is derived gains strength. Hull's original theory underwent some major revisions in the early 50's, but his system of theorizing remained intact.

Hull's theory discusses three major types of events (as outlined in Hergenhahn, 1976, p. 447):

1. Independent variables, which are stimulus events systematically manipulated by the experimenter.

2. Intervening variables, which are processes thought to be taking place within the organism but are not directly observable.

3. Dependent variables, which are some aspect of behavior that is measured by the experimenter in order to determine whether the independent variables had any effect.

Independent Variables. The independent variables that Hull addresses are: Work, that is, the amount of effort already expended; the number of prior reinforcements already experienced by the individual; the total drive of the individual, that is, how deprived or needy is the organism for a specific item in the environment such as food or water; the amount of reward available to the individual and the intensity of the stimulus. One can see that all the independent variables are essentially a function of the environment. Although drive and work reside in the individual, they result from primary interaction with the environment.

Intervening Variables. The intervening variables in Hull's system are more numerous and interact in specific ways to arrive at a probability of a specific reaction to a given stimulus: Inhibition, including reactive inhibition or fatigue and learned inhibition or avoidance, combine to work against the likelihood of a given response. Habit strength or amount of prior practice, internal drive, drive stimulus or salience of that stimulus to the drive (water is a salient stimulus for thirst but not as salient for hunger), motivation resulting from the prior experience of reward in this situation and the strength of the stimulus, combine to increase the likelihood that the response will be given. These two potentials, inhibition of the response and likelihood of the response, are combined in intricate ways with a variable called oscillation (meaning chance occurrences) to predict response of dependent variables.

Dependent Variables. The dependent variables in Hull's system include the response amplitude or level of response (how much), response latency (how long did it take?), resistence to extinction and finally probability of response, the true variable of interest to Hull.

Hull, therefore, has developed a sophisticated system of deductions and interactions from his postulates. His great emphasis on what happens to the stimulus within the organism that effects prediction of a response moves him away from the more traditional behaviorists. Hull's meticulous pursuit of evidence to support his deductive theory serves as a model to researchers.

Incentive Theory. Frank Logan goes still beyond Hull in his efforts to explain why certain responses follow certain stimuli because of the characteristics of the learner. According to Logan (1971) the "critical difference between a reinforcement theory and an incentive theory is the role ascribed to rewards and punishments." (p. 46) Reinforcement theory, such as Thorndike, examines a learning process in which the strength of the learning depends on the number of times the response has occurred in the presence of the stimulus, as well as, the consequences of that response. Incentive theory adds the notion "that people learn to expect emotionally significant events that have previously followed a response and that this expectation motivates the performance of that response according to the value of the consequent events." (p. 47) According to incentive theory, then, when several stimuli of equal weight occur in the environment of the individual and when drive is not specific, response is not merely a result of habit strength, but also an effort to maximize the reward and minimize the punishment in the situation. Although habit is recognized as important, in fact habit can become the total reason for engaging in certain behaviors, still, incentive is seen as the single most important control of selection of behavior in a given circumstance.

Incentive theory is in some ways more akin to associationisms S-S connection than to functionalisms S-R connections. What is learned from the incentive theorist's point of view is a connection between the response and the expectation of the consequence stimulus. A further distinction is that "habit is a gradual cumulative process which is relatively permanent and can only be supplanted by a stronger habit; incentive can increase or decrease rapidly as a result of changes in contingencies." (p. 48)

Higher Mental Processes. In addition to Hull, who looks at complex interactions of intervening stimuli, and Logan, who sums up the intervening variable as incentive related to contingencies, Hebb (1972) can also be considered a kind of neo-behaviorist. Hebb attempts to explain "higher mental processes." In order to do this he posits a neurological system in which repeated excitation of a given neural pathway leads to a physical change in the neurons (nerve cells) so that subsequent stimulation will flow through the system very easily. One can use the analogy of water flowing over some porous substance. Initially the water may slowly find a path. Subsequent streams of water, however, quickly flow through the channel that the first water created. As the channel deepens, the flow becomes easier. Hebb called these combinations of neurons in a ready pathway "cell assemblies." He further suggests that when several well-learned cell assemblies are active together through some combination of stimuli, they form a rather complex system called a phase sequence. Once it is well-established, a relatively simple stimulus may initiate this intricate system. Hebb's proposal of a theory makes a rather cogent explanation of the data but a full test of his ideas awaits a better understanding of the human neurological workings.

All the Neo-behaviorists attempt to explain some of the phenomena that the more traditional theories ignore. They take into consideration the elements of the organism which affect the probability of a response. Hull, Logan and Hebb and their co-theorists, however, remain behaviorists. They emphasize the importance of the environment and in the final analysis the environment including all other people and organisms control the behaviors of the individual, not some mechanism within the individual, himself.

SUMMARY

In this chapter, we have reviewed the behaviorist tradition in its three major divisions: Associationism, Functionalism and Neo-behaviorism. These are brief overviews of the various theories, some more abbreviated than others. For more complete descriptions of these theories the reader is referred to introductory learning texts including Hergenhahn (1976), LeFrancois (1972), Houston (1976), Snelbecker (1974) and Schwartz (1978).

REFERENCES

Ferster, C.B. & Skinner, B.F. Schedules of Reinforcement. Englewood Cliffs, New Jersey: Prentice Hall, 1957.

Guthrie, E.R. The Psychology of Learning (Revised ed.). New York: Harper & Row, 1952.

Hebb, D.O. Textbook of Psychology (3rd ed.). Philadelphia: Saunders, 1972.

Hergenhahn, B.R. An Introduction to Theories of Learning. Englewood Cliffs, New Jersey: Prentice-Hall, 1976.

Houston, J.P. Fundamentals of Learning and Memory, Second Edition. New York: Academic Press, 1981.

LeFrancois, G.R. Psychological Theories and Human Learning: Kongor's Report. Monterey, CA: Brooks/Cole, 1972.

Logan, F.A. Incentive Theory, reinforcement and education. In The Nature of Reinforcement edited by R. Glaser, New York: Academic Press, 1971.

Schwartz, B. Psychology of Learning and Behavior. New York: Norton, 1978.

Skinner, B.F. Science and Human Behavior. New York: Macmillan, 1953.

Snelbecker, G.B. Learning Theory, Instructional Theory, and Psycho-educational Design. New York: McGraw-Hill, 1974.

Thorndike, E.L. Educational Psychology, Vol. I. The Original Nature of Man. New York: Teachers College, 1913.

The Cognitive theorists, considered in Chapter Five, look within the individual for the cause of learning. Following the introduction and a contrast with the Behaviorist tradition, the chapter includes descriptions of Gestalt Psychology, Information Processing Theories, Learning as Transfer and Schema Theory.

1. In what ways are all cognitive theories similar?

2. Describe Gestalt Psychology, Information Processing, Learning as Transfer, Schema Theory. In what ways do they differ from one another?

CHAPTER FIVE

COGNITIVISM

INTRODUCTION

Cognitive psychology has roots going back to the Greek philosophers who examined their own thoughts in the epistemological search. Basic to cognitive theory is the principle that individuals give meaning to their experiences. While environmental influences are not discounted by cognitive psychologists, the environment is seen as being acted upon rather than causing human behavior.

Meaning. Cognitivists point out that the potential environmental stimuli at any point in time are infinite. How is it that some stimuli are effective while others are ignored? Cognitive theory posits that the individual selects from the available stimulation on the basis of the individual's internal structure. Imposing internal structure on the external world reduces ambiguity and creates a world in which there is order and stability. Attention to one stimulus rather than another is the result of utilizing available internal structures in order to make sense of experience. The ongoing process of interacting with the environment in this selective fashion modifies the internal structure in ways that affect future interactions. As penned by the poet: "The child is father of the man."

Perception. The interaction between person and environment takes place through the senses. Cognitive psychologists, therefore, continue to be very interested in *perception*. Early perceptual studies demonstrated that *the whole is greater than its parts*. Broken lines are seen as connected if the person perceiving has an already formed internal structure of the pattern.  is seen as a triangle, for instance. The study of perception has become very precise and, in some instances, esoteric, as technical advances have made it possible to measure aural and visual sensations. Other trends in the study of perception include imagery research and levels of perception.

Structure. The nature and function of the internal psychological structure which guides the individual in interactions with the environment is the object of much cognitive research. What is the structure? How does it function? How and in what ways is it modified?

Psychological structure, according to cognitivists, is a symbolic representation of past experience potentially available to interpret future experience. Many different models of this structure have been suggested. Early cognitive theories hypothesized an isomorphic (one-to-one) relationship between the environment and cognitive structure. Cognitive theories of the 1960's advance the filing cabinet mode; prior experience is filed and cross-filed. More current cognitive theories talk about schemata; complex organizations of prior experience that are semantically or procedurally linked.

Cognitive theories describe the *functions* or *processes* of psychological structure. Early theories inferred an unconscious process in which elements previously unconnected became joined and emerged to consciousness as insight. More recent theories stress the influence of existing structure on the perceptual process. Flow chart models are utilized to illustrate the paths of incoming stimuli and outgoing responses. Current theories hypothesize dual processing or simultaneous processing of selected stimuli.

Modification of structure is the process of *learning*, according to cognitive psychology. When new experience alters existing structure, learning has occurred. The conditions under which such structural transformations take place is of great interest. Two principles are generally accepted by cognitive psychologists. One is the principle of disequilibrium. If existing structure is unsuccessful in its attempt to process selected stimuli, structural balance is lost. In the struggle to recreate balance, structural change occurs. The second principle is that new structure is always appended to and controlled by old structure. It is this second principle which leads some cognitive psychologists to the position that all learning is transfer.

Contrasted with Behaviorism, cognitive theory approaches the question of how one learns from the opposite side of the skin to the Behaviorist. The environment has control over learning only in the sense of providing or not providing potential stimulation. Whether provided stimulation is attended to and processed will depend upon the internal psychological structure of the learner. Klahr (1976, p. 325) writes: "In all but the most elementary situations, learning is under the learner's strategic control of attention and memory." The emphasis of cognitive theories is on the learner, rather than on the learning task.

One theorist, Edward Tolman, straddles the Behaviorist-Cognitive, fence. Hergenhahn (1976) calls his purposive behavior theory a "behavioral Gestalten" theory. Tolman expressed the reductionist position that behavior could be broken up into small S-R units for study but at the same time he allowed stimuli to be signs or symbols to the learner rather than simply the "cause" of response. Rather than a simple S-R bond the individual learns "what leads to what." One stimulus leads to the next stimulus rather than immediately to a response. In this stimulus-to-stimulus (S-S rather than S-R) system, confirmation replaces reward. Confirmation occurs when the learner's hypothesis that a given sign means another sign will subsequently emerge is validated by the events. The learner retains a validated hypothesis and abandons invalidated or unconfirmed ones. Tolman demonstrated his theory through a series of ingenious experiments which indicated that even subhuman species give meaning to signs rather than merely responding to stimuli.

Theory and research on the learner over the last 100 years have provided significant contributions to learning theory. The following sections of this chapter will cover (1) Gestalt Psychology, (2) Information Processing Theories, (3) Learning-as-Transfer Theories and (4) Schema Theories.

GESTALT PSYCHOLOGY

The classical Gestalt position, initiated by _Max Wertheimer_ and his students, _Kurt Koffka_, _Wolfgang Kohler_, and _Kurt Lewin_, arose in opposition to the "Reductionism" of the behaviorist system. "The whole is greater than the sum of the parts" became a sort of Gestalt battle cry. They claim that the human mind is not simply a passive exchange-terminal system where the stimuli arrive and the appropriate response leaves. Rather, the thinking person interprets sensations and gives meaning to the events that impinge upon his consciousness. Much of the original theory relied on two pillars: the study of perception and an analogy to the field theory of physics. Perception lent the _Law of Pragnanz_, the fundamental law of Gestalt learning, which claims that the human system is dissatisfied until it can "make sense" out of, give meaning to, the stimuli to which it attends. Unfamiliar stimuli unbalance the system and cause it to work to restore balance. The field theory suggests that no stimulus ever acts in isolation. The human person is at the center of the field and responds, not to a single stimulus event, but rather to the push and pull of the several interacting stimuli in the experience. Learning, for the Gestalt theorist, is a special case of perception. Some unfamiliar event or stimulus occurs causing _disequilibrium_ in the system. The individual goes through a sort of mental trial-and-error procedure. An observer would see no activity or "learning" at all during this process. When the correct solution emerges an "_insight_" or "ah ha!" experience occurs. The response to the disequilibrium comes forth fully learned. No practice is needed. Given the same situation again, the individual will use the same insightful solution until it no longer "works." Then disequilibrium will reinitiate the entire process. Theoretically, if one existed in a totally controlled environment, that is, no new disequilibating stimuli ever occurred, one would never learn anything. No new insights would be needed. Fortunately, this type of consistency rarely, if ever, occurs in the "real" world. The Gestalt tradition, then, depends on the continuous "natural" effort of the organism to make sense out of incoming data.

Anyone familiar with the basic outlines of Jean Piaget's theory can see the relationship here. As a learning theorist, Piaget posits the same need for unbalancing the system. Further, his process of adaptation with its dual assimilation-accommodation experiences holds many similarities to the Gestalt position.[1]

INFORMATION PROCESSING THEORIES

How can data from a material world be transformed into an idea or thought which can be associated, manipulated, understood, recalled, responded to and myriad of other possibilities? This question of *transformation* is the basic inquiry of information processing. Although the inquiry has a long history in philosophy and psychology, information processing, itself, demanded the appropriate combination of such diverse disciplines as neurophysiology, psycholinguistics, the psychology of perception, and computer science (Travers, 1971).

While a complete understanding of information processing might require exploration into several of these fields, for the present purpose an overview of information theory will be followed by a delineation of one of the various models of the human as information processor.

Information Theory. While communication models and theories are familiar to students of the present era, it was not until the late 1940's that *information theory* provided a model to account for what occurred when a sender transmitted a message to a receiver (Shannon, 1948). According to the model both the sender and the receiver are terminals at the ends of a channel through which the message is transmitted. If the vocabulary of the sender and receiver is relatively small and common to both, and if the channel is clear of noise, information travels freely from one terminal to the other. Increasing the vocabulary of the termi-

---

[1]Although the theories of Jerome Bruner and David Ausubel would fit neatly into this discussion, their ideas are more appropriately left to later chapters.

nals or introducing noise into the channel inhibits successful communication. According to information theory, successful communication depends on the <u>reduction of uncertainty</u>. In a theoretically perfect communication, then, the receiver progresses from having no notion of the sender's intent to complete possession of the entire message. A telephone conversation can provide a straight forward though somewhat oversimplified, example of information theory. Imagine that a highly skilled surgeon calls a worried husband about his ailing wife. When the husband picks up the phone he has little idea who will be on the other end. When the surgeon identifies herself, the husband has a significant piece of "information" that he lacked a moment before. The surgeon's name, however, evokes further anxiety in the husband. If the doctor can alleviate some of this anxiety and can explain the wife's condition in a clear voice and relatively simple terms, allowing the man to ask clarifying questions, the message will be noise-free and well understood. If, on the other hand, the doctor uses very technical language which makes no sense to the poor man, she does nothing to allay the man's fears for his wife, allows no time for questions and speaks quietly into a poor phone connection, the man will know little more of his wife's health after the call than before. Clearly in the first example, the surgeon reduced the "noise" of anxiety and used a common language over a clear mechanical connection to achieve a "good" communication. In the second example all of this was missing.

Although not all psychologists agree that information theory aids in understanding cognitive processes (Shearer, 1954) a parallel can be made between the model outlined above and the human organism. If the sender equals the world and the receiver equals the human conscious thought, the channel represents the receptors and processors of the human system. If the individual's world is circumscribed and his receptors and processing system are perfect, he finds it easy to reduce the uncertainty of his world. Increase the complexity of the world or decrease the efficiency of the "channel" and the level of uncertainty rises. For example, if someone with well-functioning senses is in a familiar environment, say the dining room of her home, it is easy for her to recognize shadowy shapes in the dark as tables, cabinets, etc. If, however, she visits in a large unfamiliar house and her vision blurs because she has lost her glasses, each shadowy item takes several shapes, benign or terrifying. The world is complex, the receptors and processors often imperfect; yet uncertainty reduction occurs. Humans "make sense" out of their worlds. Information processing offers an explanatory model.

Computer as Model. Computers entered along with information theory as another critical factor in the creation of Information Processing Models. Initially, sophisticated high-speed computers were employed as artificial intelligence, that is, the use of a computer to do things of which the human mind is incapable, for example, direct the guidance system of a space capsule in split-second, minute variations of course and altitude. Computers are still used in this way but psychologists soon saw the possibilities of combining Information Theory and computer technology in an attempt to better understand the cognitive processes of humans. The parallels presented themselves clearly: the computer was made up of an input-output component, a processing unit, a memory; Information Theory posited a sender, a channel, a receiver; and the human had receptors, some transformational ability and a memory. The computer, then, could be a simulated intelligence, doing the same things the human does. Psychologists could program a computer which hypothetically processed "input" the same way the human system did. If the "output" looked similar to human answers, psychologists could assume that the computer "thought" as a human. The obvious advantage to this process was that unlike the human system in which much goes on "behind the scenes," all the steps of the computer system were available to the psychologist. With the initial attempts of researchers such as Newell, Shaw and Simon (1958) and Doyle (1960), the study of Information Processing began.

Distributed Memory Model. Although several different models of Information Processing exist (Broadbent, 1958; Norman, 1968; Newell, Shaw and Simon, 1958; Raulerson, 1971), Hunt's (1971) theory will be used in the present discussion. This model, the Distributed Memory model, contains all the basic components contained in a "typical" Information Processing Model. Briefly, the environment enters through a sensory buffer where environmental data are translated into code. This code is then transmitted through several intermediate (iconic) buffers until it reaches the conscious thought level where it progresses through Short-Term Memory (STM), Intermediate-Term Memory (ITM) and finally is stored in Long-Term Memory (LTM). The model suggests that the buffer stages work in parallel, that is, the conscious mind can simultaneously monitor several sensory input channels. Further along, conscious memory processes work with one item of information at a time. Time is measured in milliseconds. Also, the beginning of the process occurs automatically unless the sensory system is severely damaged or "shut down," for example, blind or closed eyes.

Template Hypothesis. Hunt (1971) hypothesized that the role of the buffers is to reduce the data from the environment to a manageable amount without losing any essential information. For this buffer process some writers (Norman & Lindsey, 1972) discuss a template system in which the individual's memory store contains a file of patterns. The template system compares new data to stored patterns to check on "fit." The template hypothesis lacks parsimony. The inefficiency of such a system easily surfaces. Only one pattern can be tried at a time. More importantly, consider, for example, the number of templates the individual would require to recognize all the possible chairs in the world from a variety of perspectives. The number rapidly rises so that the burden to memory becomes unwieldy. If one multiplies this one item by all the "events" which are recognized in a typical day, one can begin to see the huge set of templates required for such a system.

Feature Detector Hypothesis. A feature detector, a more sophisticated hypothesis, does seem more practical. Such a detector catalogues various components of the item to be recognized into a list of critical features. The individual features can be combined and recombined to become parts of a larger system much as the letters of the alphabet function in different words. This limits the memory load needed for recognition. Further, feature detectors can work in parallel as opposed to the "one at a time" serial process of trying templates. Guzman (1969) and Bongard (1970) have shown that machines can react appropriately when programmed with a feature detector. Several researchers (Lettvin, et. al. 1961; Pomeranz and Chung, 1970; Hubel and Weis, 1959, 1968) found evidence of feature detectors in the visual receptors of frogs, cats and monkeys. One can surmise that some form of feature detector occurs at some level in the human not only in the visual but also the other receptor systems. The initial sensory buffer, then, recodes and begins to organize the environmental data.

At the next level in Hunt's model, the <u>intermediate buffers</u>, the true interpretation of the data begins. Each intermediate buffer is in communication with the buffer before and beyond it in the line-up. A buffer receives input from the lower buffer. This input activates a "<u>store and fetch</u>" unit in the buffer which delves into the "records" of an area of Long-Term Memory (LTM). The buffer processes the information extracted from LTM, selects the most similar record of recognition and compares it with the data already in the buffer. Now the buffer no longer contains the original information but rather a record of the comparison. If the contrast data suggest a close match, the buffer indicates one level of recognition. Feedback from the LTM record is stored in the buffer involved and is sent to the buffers before and beyond the present buffer in the sequence. The process repeats itself at the next buffer but on a progressively "deeper" level. For an example of the process thus far, suppose someone is looking at a chair. The sensory buffer would recode into a binary code and the feature detector might catalogue a list such as "four legs, horizontal surface on top of the four legs, vertical surface above one quadrant of the horizontal surface." The sensory buffer passes this on to the first intermediate buffer which might compare this item with other items in the area of LTM activated by the first intermediate buffer. At this level it might match with an indiscriminate category "furniture" (although the conscious mind would not yet be "aware" of the word). This comparison is passed up and down the buffer sequence and at the next intermediate buffer a new area of LTM would be activated. This time the synthesis might recognize "furniture to sit on." The process would continue until eventually the conscious mind would answer "chair" to the question, "What are you looking at?" Remember, all this occurs in but a few milliseconds.

The interaction between the "store and fetch" and LTM is not static. Unlike the sensory buffer system which responds virtually automatically, the intermediate buffer system "learns" more efficient ways to interact with incoming data. This learning takes the form of programs stored in LTM which regulate the interaction of the intermediate buffer system and LTM. These programs change as the individual gains more and more experience with his/her world. At the same time, the intermediate buffer elicits from LTM increasingly "deep" content data. Each new experience of incoming data has the power (through conscious memory) to change the record stored in LTM. For example, a child's initial stored experience of "dog" may be one black and white, spotted, furry animal. This presumably differs widely from the depth of data stored for this word in the LTM of most adults. Although the process of interaction in the buffer system remains constant throughout life, the way in which that process operates on specific data changes over time as the incoming data "taps into" the LTM. LTM answers with increasingly rich data and, perhaps more importantly, programs for increasingly efficient interaction with that data.

If for some reason, a mismatch occurs in some intermediate buffer, that is, nothing in LTM corresponds closely to the present incoming data, two possibilities exist: either this item represents truly new information or a mistake has occurred. The mismatch causes the system to send a request to the central processor for more processing power. (Whether or not the central processor sends power depends on what else the processor is involved in at the time. Obviously possible life-threatening items are treated by the central processor first, followed by lesser items of value to the person, etc.) The buffer also sends a signal back down the buffer system toward the initial receptors to request a recheck of the data as it has been processed thus far.

Eventually the buffer system ends at the conscious thinking stage. Here the data enters Short Term Memory (STM) which selects a relatively small number of discrete items from the possible information presented by the buffers (Miller, 1956). Unlike earlier buffer stages, all the items in STM are recognizable to the individual, that is, if asked the person <u>could</u> name or describe all the items. This short-term holding space passes information to Intermediate Term Memory (ITM) which is a more general store than STM; that is, some of the fine detail is disregarded at this point unless there is some particular reason to focus on fine detail. The ITM uses the new data to modify previously recognized information. Hunt (1971) states that "since the manner in which new information is to be incorporated with old may be quite complex, the construction of the ITM data structure will have to be under the control of a program for analyzing situations" (p. 80). These programs are stored in LTM. Finally the ITM passes the new data to LTM for storage. The LTM, then, has two roles: it stores both what the individual has seen before and the rules for interpreting data.

Distributed Memory Theory can account for much of the experience that persons encounter daily. Hunt (1971) discusses language, concept identification and problem solving. Although the case may be somewhat overstated, the ideas are thought-provoking. Consider an ordinary example such as a startle reaction. Hunt's model suggests that people are startled when a mismatch or non-recognition occurs at the intermediate buffer stage. This buffer would demand more power for recognition and reanalysis. Recognition occurs and the system "settles down." Since the system works so rapidly, the recognition appears to come almost immediately after the startle. A second example: It is usually easier to recognize something in context than to identify the same item in isolation. Since Hunt's system indicates a variety of interrelationships between the buffer system and LTM and a parallel processing in the buffers, context would aid in recognition because it would create more information in the system, more simultaneous "store and fetch" and better feedback in the system. Further examples can be generated easily but the writer will leave that task to the reader for the present.

Current Trends in Information Processing Theory. The focus of Information Processing Theories on the transformation of input into output has led to very detailed, precise analyses of both the learner and the task. Task analyses by cognitive psychologists are undertaken so that computer programs can be generated to simulate human behavior.

Analyses of learner behaviors continue the search for adequate descriptions of cognitive structure and cognitive processes. Structure is researched by contrasting how experts and novices organize information, or by trying to describe what it means for a person to know something. Processes are studied by minute analysis of behavior as complex tasks are performed (Klahr, 1978).

Posner and McLeod (1982) offer a taxonomy of mental operations which combines structure and process. In a 2-by-2 matrix model, they combine (1) specificity of function and (2) endurance of components. Functions may be either very specific transformations or general cognitive processes. Endurance may be temporary or stable. When specific transformations are stable (enduring), the mental operation is called a structure. Temporary, specific transformations are termed strategies. General cognitive processes which are enduring are traits, while those which are temporary are states. An interesting feature of this model is that it attempts to include personality, as well as more traditional cognitive domains. Whether subdividing the usually more generic term "structure" into four narrower categories will stimulate productive information processing research remains to be seen.

LEARNING AS TRANSFER

Some current cognitive theories of learning center on the phenomenon of transfer. Voss (1978), Royer (1979), and Wittrock (1977) are theoreticians whose work exemplify this trend.

Cognitive Theory of Learning. Voss (1978) hypothesizes that learning is transfer, almost always. According to Voss, traditional research on transfer, by ignoring the skills and knowledge the learner brings to the learning situation, has very limited application. Voss's theory has three principles: (1) Learning is transfer. (2) "When learning is viewed as transfer, the primary factor influencing learning is the knowledge the individual brings into and uses in the particular learning situation." (p. 19). (3) "When learning is viewed as transfer and when the most important factor in learning is taken to be the knowledge of the individual, learning is a function of the degree to which the structure of the input information is related to the memory structure of the individual." (p. 20).

Voss cites an experimental test of his theory in which subjects were pre-assessed on their knowledge of baseball. They demonstrated that high knowledge individuals had concepts about baseball that were more fully discriminated. They assume that high knowledge individuals therefore have more interrelationships among their concepts. One part of the experiment tested recall of sentences about baseball. High knowledge individuals "learned" more from the sentences than low knowledge individuals. Voss's analysis of such results is that high knowledge individuals can identify knowledge-related stimuli more easily and accurately, leading to better encoding and storage than that available to low-knowledge individuals. Since encoding and storage processes determine ease of retrieval, high knowledge individuals experience better retrieval. Voss feels these processing differences are semantic and involve encoding uniqueness. A memory structure with more differentiated concepts and more interconnections among those concepts allows high-knowledge individuals to make better use of context-contingent relationships. All new information has potentially more probability of being related to something the individual already knows (Principle 3). While the low-knowledge individual is processing almost every separate concept in the experimental sentences, the high-knowledge learner is processing the meaning of the complete sentence and placing it in the appropriate storage slot at a higher semantic level.

Glaser, Pellegrino, and Lesgold (1978) agree with Voss that traditional (Behavioristic) transfer models fail to characterize much cognitive learning because these earlier models studied very narrow knowledge domains (often paired-associate lists of words) and then assumed their experimental results generalized to a broad spectrum of learning outcomes. They emphasize that the Voss theory is based on knowledge specific conceptual relationships, rather than common elements of learning or transfer experiences. The individual who experiences optimal positive transfer in acquiring new baseball information may not have such positive transfer for acquiring new information about World War II.

Voss's theory is parsimonious and clear, offering interesting hypotheses to be tested. The comprehensiveness of the theory is debatable. Could one predict new learning in domains of outcome other than verbal information based on these three principles? Is a cognitive unitary theory of learning-as-transfer the best explanation of all learning?

Generative Model of Learning. Wittrock's (1977) answer to the last question seems to be "maybe." He writes: "Cognitive theory implies that learning can be predicted and understood in terms of what the learners bring to the situation, how they relate the stimuli to their memories, and what they generate from their previous experiences." (p. 628). However, Wittrock's Generative Theory does not assume that new learning is tied to a specific knowledge base, as Voss's Theory does. The term "generative" emphasizes the role of the active learner in a learning situation. Wittrock hypothesizes that learners generate associations between their prior learning and new stimuli. "Learning with understanding...is a process of generating semantic and distinctive idiosyncratic associations between stimuli and stored information." (p. 623). In support of his theory, Wittrock refers to research on retention of word hierarchies. Learners told to create their own mediating hierarchies among words (both conceptually related and random lists) had better retention for the target words than learners given hierarchies of words.

While such mediating studies do illustrate the facilitative effects of learner generation of associations, they raise other questions. How does one explain the learning, albeit less, of the learners given hierarchies? Does one assume they generate associations between the given hierarchy and one they create or already possessed? What exactly is generated and how is it generated? Are there characteristics of stimuli that affect the process of generation, or is it solely under the influence of prior experience?

Wittrock heralds the relatively new research area of Aptitude Treatment Interactions (ATI) as an avenue to address the difficult questions of interface between learner characteristics and stimulus characteristics. ATI research assesses learners on specific characteristics and then exposes them to differential instructional paradigms hoping to discover the specific interrelationships between what the learner brings to the learning situation and the parameters of the nominal stimuli. In essence, then, ATI research hopes to describe the functional stimuli in a learning situation, relating them to learner characteristics. The disappointing lack of definitive answers from ATI studies to date is perhaps related to the above questions. ATI studies have tended to assume that learner characteristics brought to the learning situation are static and interact with stimulus dimensions that are static. However, generative processes by definition are dynamic. For ATI research to be productive, it would appear that description of generative processes must be a precursor.

Schema Theory of Transfer. In an excellent article, Royer (1979) surveys the history of Behavioral and Cognitive theorizing on transfer. He concludes that transfer of learning is neither transfer of training in specific stimulus-response elements, nor learning itself. Based upon his analysis of both historical viewpoints, he offers his own Schema Theory of transfer and its role in learning.

Royer traces the evolution of environmental theories of transfer from the early "identical elements" theory of Thorndike and Wood in 1901 to the current attempts to describe the similarities and differences in observables in the learning situation. He asserts that such theories do describe the parameters of near transfer, offering explanations for transfer in specific and/or vertical transfer situations. However, since it is not possible to describe the parameters of future situations in which an acquired skill or knowledge might be used, prediction of future behavior is impossible. Far transfer, therefore, cannot be explained by environmental theories of transfer.

Cognitive theories, according to Royer, have been developed upon a relatively static concept of knowledge structure. The principles of cognitive theories of transfer include: (1) The essential step in transfer is retrieval. (2) Human memory is analogued by the filing cabinet model. (3) Connections among the elements filed are not evenly distributed. (4) Comprehension is a necessary, but not sufficient condition for transfer except in the case of rote learning. (5) Retrieval is a process of sequential search through the memory "file cabinet" until the particular skill or list of knowledge is accessed. (6) The probability of retrieval is a function of the number of cross-references (interconnections) in the system.

Your ability to comprehend and thus "learn" the experimental sentences of Bransford and McCarrell reported in Chapter 3 would depend upon how interconnected (cross-referenced) your concepts were, according to the above principles. If "trip" was not cross-referenced to "ship"; "notes" not cross-referenced to "bag pipes"; "haystack" not cross-referenced to "break fall"; retrieving the appropriate prior learning in order to learn the new statements meaningfully would be difficult if not impossible. The cue words "ship launch," "parachute," and "bag pipes" redirect your memory search and access the right interconnections to build meaning.

Royer writes that far transfer is probably almost totally dependent upon comprehension. Unless prior information and/or skills are meaningful, they cannot be accessed unless new and old information have identical elements, an increasingly unlikely circumstance over time. Although identical elements may help in retrieval, identical elements can never explain all transfer unless semantic meaning is considered an identical element. Consider syllogistic reasoning. Mary is taller than Jane. Sally is shorter than Mary. Who is tallest? Who is shortest? How do you know? Consider a similar example within a far transfer paradigm. During Tim's childhood his family raised pigs and Tim learned that swine have split hooves. Somewhat later Tim learned that the Old Testament forbade eating the flesh of animals with cloved hooves. He deduced (learned on his own) that Old Testament peoples could not eat pork. Or consider the transfer value of analogy, metaphor, simile. All of you have prior information about filing and file cabinets. Using the analogy of a filing cabinet to describe how memory is structured has powerful positive transfer value although no one actually believes in a one-to-one identity between the two constructs.

The inadequacy of earlier cognitive transfer theories lead Royer to develop his Schema Theory of transfer. Royer postulates that transfer is either literal or figural. In literal transfer very specific prior learning facilitates new learning. It is probably accessed as proposed by earlier cognitive theories. Figural transfer, however, cannot be explained in similar ways. Figural transfer involves using interconnected segments of prior learning simultaneously.

Using "file cabinet" as an effective analogy for memory structure requires simultaneously accessing all the information you have about file cabinets: What they look like, how they are used, the processes for filing and cross-referencing, the fact that things get lost if they are mis-filed, and so forth. Royer would call this body of information your "world knowledge" about file cabinets and their uses. World knowledge has great potential for figural transfer, for learning through metaphor and simile.

However, figural transfer cannot be adequately explained within a file cabinet model of memory structure. File cabinets can only be accessed one file at a time. Figural transfer requires that several drawers, as well as multiple file folders, be opened simultaneously. Royer therefore bases his theory of transfer on a model of memory in which prior experience is encoded and stored in schemata: interconnected, semantically linked skills and/or bits of information. A particular schema might be activated either by an identical element or by semantic similarity.

Royer suggests the possibility of two different kinds of schemata. One type is a hierarchically organized generic structure for often experienced/accessed events. Details are subsumed under broad categories on the basis of frequency as well as generality. For example, a "going shopping" schema would include, high in the hierarchy, generalities like "driving to the city," "taking the bus," "clothing stores," "grocery stores." Lower in the hierarchy would be more specific details like "Sears," "Price Chopper," "open from 10 to 10." Even lower in the hierarchy would be "where I bought the blouse," "I like peas better than corn." The second kind of schemata contain procedural information for acquiring new information. These schemata would involve things like "How can I use knowledge/skills I used in starting my standard transmission car to learn to start my new automatic transmission car?"

Both kinds of schemata can be activated at the same time. For example, deciding to go shopping for new living room wallpaper in my new automatic transmission car may activate several schemata. The general schema I have for shopping and the details subsumed under shopping for where and when would be retrieved. Another schema related to wallpaper, probably subsumed under something generic like home decorating would also become active. But I also must activate procedural schemata for starting my new car, for how to manage my time in order to be home for dinner, and so forth.

An interesting theory of knowledge transfer in learning from texts (Thorndyke, 1978) supports Royer's distinction between literal and figural transfer. Thorndyke's research on memory for textual content supports a distinction between two different kinds of knowledge in a narrative text: content and narrative structure. Utilizing a traditional experimental paradigm for studying transfer, Thorndyke exposed one group of learners to two stories which had the same narrative structure but different content (e.g., characters) and another group of learners to two stories with the same content but different structures (e.g. settings, goals of main characters). Testing for transfer effects from story one to story two, he demonstrated that the group exposed to two stories with the same structure had better recall for story two than those exposed to two stories with the same content. In terms of literal and figural transfer, learning narrative structure (organization of events, setting, goals of main character) appears to be learning a generic schema for how stories are formed that has high potential for positive figural transfer. After reading several detective stories, for example, the next detective story is read with greater ease and a wider view of what detective stories are. Reading a story about how Tom overcame his fear of snakes does not provide figural transfer for a story about how the same Tom solved the mystery of the missing chicken eggs.

The schema of memory as filing cabinet appears to have positive transfer value for understanding literal transfer, but little utility for comprehending transfer in a wider context. For instance, could a filing cabinet memory figure out that the provided data are insufficient to tell who is shortest?

SCHEMA THEORY

> Cognitive psychology contrasts with behaviorist theory in assuming that knowledge can be wrested from the purpose for which it was acquired and cast into more general symbolic form, thus rendering that knowledge applicable

> to a much wider range of problems.
> (Olsen, 1976, p. 119)

Olsen echoes the sentiment of those psychologists who view transfer as the basic issue in learning and behavior. He also suggests that the mechanism for learning and behavior has a representative structure -- "general symbolic form." Not all cognitivists would agree that transfer tells the whole story of learning. However, like Royer, many current cognitive psychologists attempt to explain learning and thinking (and thus to some extent, behavior) in terms of internal mental structures. The form of that internal structure is the schema.

Schema. Jean Piaget, the late, great Genevan genetic epistomologist, fathered the current trend in cognitive psychology. Observing his own children and working for Binet, who was developing an intelligence test for the French school system Piaget began a search for knowledge about the path of mature, logical, thought structure.

Noticing that neonate reflex behavior was flexible and modifiable, Piaget hypothesized that mental structure was an organization of plans for action. Further, he hypothesized that new behavior was organized through and around old organizations of behavior. The term schema encapsulates within Piagetian theory that "organization of behavior around which new behavior is developed" (Travers, 1977). The notion of schema has been elaborated and re-defined by many psychologists. Royer (above) for one and Norman, Gentner and Stevens (1976) for some others.

Schemata (plural for schema) are defined in terms of their structure and function. Norman, Gentner, and Stevens (1976) write:

> A schema provides a framework on which to interrelate different elements of information about a topic into one conceptual unit. A schema consists of statements about the important features of the unit, the functions of the unit, rules for selection and rules for use (p. 183).

The Structure of a Schema. Beyond its functions, can

we describe what the structure of a schema is? Piaget proposed the idea of an internal representation of an action or event. Posner and McLeod (1982) offer a taxonomy of mental operations. Another candidate is the semantic network, a schemata of relationships between concepts (Norman, Gentner & Stevens, 1976). Dorner (1978) theorizes that cognitive structure is a dual system. Epistemic structure contains models of reality and heuristic structure operates on epistemic structure, modifying it when necessary. According to Dorner, one can come to understand the nature of epistemic structure by utilizing the Norman concept of semantic network. Heuristic structure operates somewhat like Hunt's model. When input creates a mismatch with located stored information, cognitive strategies are brought into play to reanalyze input and restructure the epistemic (semantic network) structure. Therefore, heuristic structure is a cognitive "bag of tricks."

Imagery is yet another proposed description of structure. Tolman's (1932) work on cognitive maps demonstrated the capacity of infrahuman subjects to find new paths to goals when previously learned paths were blocked. The logical explanation was that laboratory rats had developed "maps" of the mazes, allowing them to select new routes to goals. Paivio (1969) demonstrated that imagery is a powerful aspect of mental structure that mediates a good deal of human learning and behavior. Yuille and Catchpole (1978) compared the learning of preschool children when imagery was encouraged versus when semantic elaboration was encouraged. They concluded that imagery was just one form of elaboration. Neisser (1976) agrees with that point of view, stating that only concrete things can be structured as images (p. 140). He qualifies that, however, by saying that images are not necessarily tied to reality wholistically. Persons can imagine nonexperienced entities, such as "little green men." However, such structures are combinations of concrete experience. On the other hand, one apparently can not image "democracy."

The answer to "what is the structure of a schema?" is barely beyond the point of learning what questions to ask. Unless neurophysiology uncovers a yet undiscovered answer, structure will have to be inferred from function.

The Influence of Schemata on Learning. Few cognitive psychologists would disagree with the Piagetian position that cognitive structure sets the limits of learning. Unless schemata exist with which to perceive stimulation, experience is severely limited. Of the five major perceptual systems, only basic orienting (e.g., balance) appears to be innate (Gibson, 1966). (Robinson's 1979 report of teaching a child motor skills which overcame the child's propensity to fall suggests that even basic orienting requires learned structure.) The four other perceptual systems (visual, auditory, haptic and taste-smell) have been repeatedly demonstrated to depend upon prior experience. Chickens raised in the dark have difficulty learning to see. Persons with surgically created hearing or vision have extreme difficulty learning to see and hear. Unless prior experience has contributed to the development of appropriate schemata, new learning is impossible or difficult. The cycle, say cognitive psychologists, is schemata permit perception, perception builds schemata which then permit expanded perception. So schemata define the limits of learning.

Schemata also direct perception. Neisser (1976) points out that attention is an active progress. Many information processing theories hypothesize that some perceptual buffer zone screens out unwanted stimulation. The assumption is that all stimulation is processed at some basic level, with selected input advancing to higher levels of processing. Neisser advances his "Theory of apple picking" (p. 87) to discredit this view. He says we actively choose what juicy apple we want from the tree. Just as we do not need a mechanism to keep unwanted apples out of our mouth, we do not need a buffer to keep unwanted stimulation out of our minds. We decide in advance what percepts we want and then actively set out to find them.

According to Neisser, the cycle of perception is anticipation, exploration, information pick-up. The schemata provide a plan for deriving information from the environment. The schemata provide expectations about what will be perceived; they direct the search for that information, and they assimilate the information discovered.

The influence of schemata on perception has been demonstrated in many clever experiments. Primed to see either glasses or barbells, students in our classes shown a simple line drawing of O-O regularly reproduce a more detailed drawing in line with their internal schemata. Subjects told to look for state capitals in a list of words insist they have seen Albany when Atbury flashes on the screen (Travers, 1977). Schemata are chosen according to similarity to the situation (Norman, Gentner, & Stevens, 1976). If the similarity is slight, based on too little information from the environment or too inadequate a schema, misperception can occur. Surely you have had the experience of seeing a "friend" across the room only to discover a total stranger at closer inspection.

Schemata influence learning by setting the limits of what can be perceived and by directing that perceptual process.

How Schemata Change or How Learning Takes Place. Piaget's work again sets the stage. Only by looking at developmental stages can we fully understand how schemata change and what those changes are. The neonate has a number of schemata, usually called reflexes, ready to anticipate survival components of the environment. These early schemata, however, are barely fleshed out. Most often cited as the sucking reflex. The neonate has the rudiments of a sucking behavior but little detail for when and where. Activating the sucking behavior, the neonate interacts with the environment in anticipation. Anticipation leads to exploration in which information is received and added to the sucking schema. Each sucking experience enriches the schema and builds a consistent internal representation (or memory) of reality. Eventually the sucking schema probably includes anticipatory plans for things that can and can't be sucked, what they taste like, when and where and how, and so forth.

From the modest beginning of reflex/action schemata, interaction with the environment directed by gradually enriched schemata leads to even more enriched, consistent and stable schemata. Piaget described and researched this evolution of mental structure within the framework of a stage theory of cognitive development. Sensori-motor schemata develop into pre-operational structures which develop into concrete operational structures. For some individuals a further refinement into formal operations ensues. (Many excellent books on Piagetian theory are available, and the reader unfamiliar with the theory is urged to read at least an introductory text.)

"The human being can be regarded as a system that engages in a continuous process of redesigning his behavior as he lives and experiences" (Travers, 1977, p. 25). Although the control is within the individual, mediated by extant schemata, the environment is not unimportant. The neonote who experiences the breast develops a different sucking schema from the infant who experiences a bottle. The preschool child who is exposed to a variety of peers, adults and media develops different pre-operations than the preschool child unexposed to such variety. A child of China develops different schemata than the child of New York.

The universals of cognition across culture and time reflect similarity of experience as a function of species-specific behavior (Furth, 1974). The ways we can interact with the environment are biologically and genetically limited. No infant can view the environment from a vertical position without the intervention of another person. No adult can see through brick walls or hear sounds of certain wave lengths. No infrahuman species has a thumb as clever as ours. The similarities of cognitive structure that humans share are extractions from idiosyncratic experience/schemata by the common denominator of species-specific capabilities expressed in an environment with certain similarities.

The exact process by which interaction with the environment changes schemata is under intensive investigation. Most cognitivists believe in some variation of a match-mismatch theory. Piaget writes about equilibration, the simultaneous action of assimilation and accommodation. Using whatever schemata available, individuals actively receive environmental information (assimilation) and try to make sense out of it. Since experience is never identical to a previous experience, the prior structure is not going to be a perfect match. Therefore the structure will be modified in whatever ways necessary to accommodate the new information.

Schemata conceived as plans-for-perceiving have expected attributes for which to search in the environment. Norman, Gentner & Stevens (1976) write that schemata are modified by "relaxing the restrictions of arguments of a schema" (p. 184). To the extent that the learner is willing or able to operate in an open system, the schema can be modified. How do we know when to "relax" the restrictions for our schema of circle to include a four-sided figure? Well, what if the schema is shapes? Difficult theoretical questions that await empirical answers.

The fact that normally functioning humans <u>can</u> "relax" the boundaries of their existing schemata <u>and</u> therefore modify cognitive structure is obvious. The importance of this capability is also obvious. Neisser (1976) writes: "The ability to divide, detach, and manipulate our own anticipations (schemata) is immensely important...the fundamental operation in all so-called higher mental processes" (p. 133). Royer writes about figural transfer (world knowledge); Piaget about operations; Dorner about heuristic structure; Olson about wrestling general symbolic form; Travers about redesigning self. I have often remembered the message of a short story I read in high school. The author and title are irretrievable. The message was that every person is responsible for her/his own facial appearance after the age of forty. During childhood genes and nutritions determine how we look. By forty the life we have lived and the attitudes we hold have overpowered those weaker genetic influences. Cognition is much like our faces. Nature gives us species-specific schemata. By forty years of age those "givens" have been overpowered by self-construction. The environment we expose ourselves to, the rigidity with which we cling to old schemata, the culture in which we immerse ourselves determine the schemata available for future growth.

SUMMARY

Cognitive psychology attempts to explain learning by understanding the learner. What mental structures mediate learning, how is information processed, how are mental structures modified? The answers to these questions are not fully known. The underlying principles of cognitive psychology theorize that

1. persons construct their own meaning

2. cognitive structure develops in

interaction with the environment

3. prior structure directs perception and therefore determines the limits of learning

4. there are species-specific influences on learning

REFERENCES

Bongard, M. Pattern recognition. New York: Sparton, 1970.

Broadbent, D.E. Perception and communication. London: Pergamon Press, 1958.

Dorner, D. Theoretical advances of cognitive psychology relevant to instruction in Lesgold, A.M., Pellegrino, J.W., Fokkema, S.D. & Glaser, R. Cognitive Psychology and Instruction. New York: Plenum Press, 1978.

Doyle, W. Recognition of sloppy-hand-printed characters. Proceedings of the Western Joint Computer Conference. New York: IRE, 133-142.

Furth, H.G. Two aspects of experiences in ontogeny: development and learning in Advances in Child Developmedt and Behavior, Vol. 9. New York: Academic Press, 1974.

Gagne, R.M. Analysis of Objectives in Briggs, L.J. (Ed.) Instructional Design. Englewood Cliffs, N.J. Educational Technology Publication, 1977. pp. 115-146.

Gagne, R.M. The conditions of learning. (3rd ed.) New York: Holt, Rinehart and Winston, 1977.

Gibson, J.J. The senses considered as perceptual systems. Boston: Houghton Mifflin, 1966.

Glaser, R., Pellegrino, J.W. & Lesgold, A. Some directions for a cognitive psychology of instruction. In Lesgold, A.M., Pellegrino, J.W. & Fokkema, S.D. & Glaser, R. (Eds.) Cognitive Psychology and Instruction. New York: Plenum Press, 1978.

Guzman, A. Computer recognition of three-dimensional objects in a visual scene. MIT Artificial Intelligence Laboratory, Project MAC-TR-59. Cambridge.

Hubel, D., & Wiesel, T. Receptive fields of single Neurons in the cat's visual cortex. Journal of Physiology, 1959, 148, 574-591.

REFERENCES CONTINUED

Hubel, D., & Wiesel, T. Receptive and functional architecture of monkey striate cortex. _Journal of Physiology_, 1968, _195_, 215-243.

Hunt, E. What kind of computer is man? _Cognitive Psychology_, 1971, _2_, 57-98.

Klahr, D. Designing a learner: some questions in Klahr D., (Ed.) _Cognition and Instruction_. New York: John Wiley & Sons, 1976.

Klahr, D. _Information Processing Models of Cognitive Development: Potential Relevance to Science Instruction_. Paper presented at annual meeting of American Educational Research Association, Toronto, 1978.

Lettvin, J.Y., Maturana, H.R., Pitts, W.H., & McCulloch, W.S. Two remarks on the visual system of the frog. In W.A. Rosenblith (Ed.) _Sensory Communication_. Cambridge, Mass.

Merrill, M.D., & Kowallis, T. _Instructional Design in Transition_. Paper presented at annual meeting of American Educational Research Association, Boston, 1979.

Neisser, U. _Cognition and Reality_. San Francisco: W.H. Freeman & Co., 1976.

Newell, A., Shaw, J., & Simon, H.A. Elements of a theory of human problem solving. _Psychological Review_, 1958, _65_, 151-166.

Norman, D.A. Toward a theory of memory and attention. _Psychological Review_, 1968, _75_, 522-536.

Norman, D.A., Gentner, R. & Stevens, Albert L. Comments on learning schemata and memory representation in Klahr, D. (Ed.). _Cognition and Instruction_. New York: John Wiley & Sons, 1976.

Olson, D.R. Notes on a cognitive theory of instruction in Klahr, D. (Ed.). _Cognition and Instruction_. New York: John Wiley & Sons, 1976.

REFERENCES CONTINUED

Paivio, A. Mental imagery in associative learning and memory. Psychological Review, 1969, 76, 241-263.

Pomeranz, B. & Chung, S.H. Dentritic-tree anatomy codes formvision physiology in tadpole retine. Science, 1970, 170, 983-984.

Posner, M.I. & McLeod, J. Information processing models, in search of elementary operation. In Rosensinug, M.R. & Porter, L.W. (Eds.). Annual Review of Psychology. Palo Alto: Annual Review, Inc., 1982.

Robinson, R. Paper in requirement for the course Theories of Learning, 1979.

Royer, J.M. Theories of the transfer of learning. Educational Psychologist, 1979, 14, 53-69.

Shannon, C.E. A mathematical theory of communication. Bell System Technical Journal, 1948, 27, 379-423, 623-656.

Thorndyke, P.W. Knowledge transfer in learning from texts. In Lesgold, A.M., Pellegrino, J.E., Fokkema, S.D. & Glaser, R. (Eds.). Cognitive Psychology and Instruction. New York: Plenum Press, 1978.

Tolman, E.C. Purposive Behavior in Animals and Men. New York: Appleton-Century-Crofts, 1932.

Travers, R.M. Essentials of Learning, Fourth Edition. New York: Macmillan, 1977.

Travers, R.M.W. Human information processing. The Encyclopedia of Education edited by Lee C. Deighton. New York: Macmillan and the Free Press, 1971, 5, 435-441.

Voss, J.F. Cognition and instruction: towards a cognitive theory of learning. In Lesgold, A.M., Pellegrino, J.W., Fokkema, S.D. & Glaser, R. (Eds.). Cognitive Psychology and Instruction. New York: Plenum Press, 1978.

REFERENCES CONTINUED

Wittrock, M.C. Learning as a generative process in Merlin C. Wittrock (Ed.). Learning and Instruction. Berkeley, Calif.: McCuthan Publishing Corporation, 1977, 621-631.

Yuille, J.C. & Catchpole, M.J. Imagery and children's associate learning in Lesgold, A.M., Pellegrino, J.W., Fokkema, S.D. & Glaser, R. (Eds.). Cognitive Psychology and Instruction. New York: Plenum Press, 1978.

Theoretical explanations of motor learning and performance discussed in Chapter Six encompass Behavioristic reinforcement theories and cognitive, internal, anticipatory, patterning theories. A meta-theory is emerging which integrates the findings of both Behaviorists and Cognitivists.

1. Is motor learning the same process for children and adults?

2. Do early stages of learning a motor skill resemble the later stages?

3. What effect does speed of performance during learning have on final performance?

4. Can mental rehearsal be used in motor learning?

5. How can we explain the marvelous flexibility of motor responses in the presence of novel stimuli?

CHAPTER SIX

MOTOR LEARNING AND PERFORMANCE

INTRODUCTION

Marilyn is a twenty-year old college student who wants to become a music teacher. She is skillful on the guitar, but does not play the piano. To be certified as a music teacher, Marilyn must learn to play the piano. She resists this requirement for two reasons: she feels the guitar is an adequate substitute and she is blind.[1]

Ronald is a kindergarten student, 5.7 years old. Extensive medical examinations have determined that he is normal for his age in every way. His family is typical middle

---

[1]This true case history from a graduate student has been modified to protect the privacy of the student. Used by permission of the author, Margaret A. Byrnes.

> class and he has had all the usual benefits of a middle class home: loving parents, jungle gyms, older sister, swimming, skating and skiing experiences. In spite of this, Ronald falls down at least twice a day. The falling began when he started to walk at eleven months. He falls, both walking and standing still.[2]

What do Marilyn and Ronald have in common? Marilyn and Ronald both lack a motor skill that is essential for their future successful lives.

DEFINITION

Gagne (1972) defines motor skills as those "capabilities that mediate organized motor performance." Marilyn needs a set of capabilities that she can organize into the performance of a musical composition on the piano. Ronald lacks some capability essential to the motor performance of maintaining balance.

Gagne's definition of a motor skill is similar to what Fleishman (1967) terms a "motor ability": an underlying general trait that is relatively stable and difficult to change once learned. Fleishman reserves the term "skill" to define levels of proficiency on specific motor tasks. Lack of agreement on definition of terms is one manifestation of different theoretical approaches to the study of motor learning and performance.

The study of motor learning and performance has been undertaken by behaviorists and cognitivists. Within each approach discrete aspects of motor learning and performance have been studied, revealing differences between acquisition and performance, between description and explanation, between adult learning and child learning. To help Marilyn or Ronald, the instructor will need to be aware of and use several theoretical models.

---

[2]This true case history from a graduate student paper has been modified to protect the privacy of the child. Use by permission of the author, Rochelle Robinson.

THEORETICAL PERSPECTIVES

This chapter will review, respectively, behavioristic and cognitive viewpoints on adult learning and performance of motor skills, followed by theory and research on the development of motor skills in children. Behaviorism encompasses the psychometric approach and functionalism.

BEHAVIORISM

Psychometric Approach: Common Abilities. The psychometric approach to the study of motor learning and performance has been to identify individual differences in the acquisition and performance of motor tasks. Utilizing many individuals and many tasks, the psychometrician looks for correlations among individuals over tasks. If performance on tasks 1, 5, and 6 are highly correlated, a common underlying ability or capacity is hypothesized. Within this approach, Fleishman (1967) has identified eleven motor abilities that mediate motor performance on tasks. These abilities are such things as multi-limb coordination and aiming. Eight physical proficiency factors (e.g., trunk strength) have also been delineated. Fleishman hypothesizes that these underlying abilities are over-learned during childhood and adolescence and thus become enduring traits. The rate of learning and final level achieved on a specific task (skill) is limited by these previously acquired basic abilities. Some abilities may be more important in initial attempts to master a skill, while other abilities may be more important later in the learning process.

Marilyn's teacher determined that she had not overlearned some of the basic underlying motor abilities essential to learning to play piano. She did not have a left, right aiming orientation and could not easily locate notes on the keyboard. Marilyn needed large motor movement activities using the whole arm to establish this basic underlying ability.

Practice Effects. The psychometric attempt to describe acquisition of a new skilled response in a mature learner led to a fruitful area of research on practice effects. The distribution of practice (massed vs. distributed) affects performance, but not learning. In general, distributed practice is better than massed, and short practices between long rests produce better performance (Irion, 1969). These research findings suggest that Marilyn will make faster progress with two or three short practices a day, than with one long practice period. As practice continues, the combination of abilities mediating performance changes in a gradual and lawful way and finally becomes stabilized in specific patterns appropriate only to the task being learned. As this unique pattern is evolving, contributing non-motor abilities, such as the ability to understand directions, decrease in importance (Fleishman, 1967).

The speed of practice is also hypothesized to contribute to the final performance (Logan, 1963). Logan postulates that the speed of practice becomes part of what is learned. He suggests that if speed is sacrificed for accuracy during practice, what is learned is slow accuracy. Since rate of performance is so critical to many motor responses, instruction and practice must take this into account. If Marilyn learns to play an eighth note at a tempo that is closer to a whole note in typical performance, she is learning misinformation. Note instruction, then, should be presented in whole notes and time instruction should initially be on one note and up to typical speed. Another example of the importance of speed of practice is typewriting. Successful typing instructors stress speed from the very beginning of a course, ignoring errors. Accuracy can be acquired later; speed is not so easily learned later.

Retention of a well-practiced skill is very high. Fleishman (1967) cites a study on retention of a complex, perceptual-motor skill. Different groups of subjects matched on degree of original learning were retested at 1, 4, 9, 14, and 24 months. Retention was as good for those tested at 24 months as for those tested at 1 month. Examine your own experience in retention of a motor skill: swimming, riding a bicycle, playing a musical instrument. What differentiates the skills you retain from the skills you have lost or find seriously diminished?

Interference between two tasks is also related to practice, the greater the amount of practice, the less the interference (Irion, 1969). Motor skills seem to be unique in that transfer of training is almost always positive. Prior training facilitates later training on a new skill, but rarely hinders (negative transfer). The best explanation for this is probably that basic abilities underlying skill acquisition have a large measure of commonality, while specific tasks have very unique patterns of movement. Different motor skills that share patterns of movement not common to other motor tasks are subject to interference, however. Water or snow skiing, for example, or ice and roller skating, or tennis and racquetball are reported as motor skills interfering with each other in initial learning experiences. In such cases, instruction must stress the differences in the organization of the motor patterns in order to be successful.

The psychometric approach has contributed much descriptive data which identifies the variables involved in the acquisition and performance of motor skills among adults, and it does offer strong predictive validity (the Armed Forces and industry have made good use of predictive tests for motor skills developed by psychometricians). However, as theory, the psychometricians seem most comfortable with behavioristic explanations of the performance they describe.

<u>Reinforcement Theory</u>. <u>Reinforcement theory</u> directed research efforts to the effects of feedback (knowledge of results) on motor learning and performance. Traditional learning theory, following Thorndike's Law of Effect, postulated that new responses are substituted for old responses when the contingencies of reinforcement reward the new response. Such a theory requires external control of the reward system that is difficult to reconcile with observational data in human skill learning. It is relatively easy to demonstrate changes in performance as a function of operant conditioning, but less easy to explain changes in performance when no external reward system is observable. Therefore, feedback or knowledge of results is hypothesized as a reinforcer present in the learning situation.

<u>Knowledge of Results</u>. Irion (1969) summarizes a body of research on the effects of <u>knowledge of results</u> in skill acquisition. Practice without knowledge of results does not improve skill, but delay of knowledge of results is not harmful to skill acquisition so long as the learner does not make other responses of similar nature during the delay. The absolute frequency of

knowledge of results is an important factor, with 100% feedback producing the fastest acquisition rates. Reporting results of greater or lesser error than the learner actually performed affects performance, demonstrating again the importance of feedback. The group of studies reviewed by Irion (1969) conceptualizes feedback as a unitary variable operating as a reinforcer (shaper) in an operant conditioning paradigm. McKeachie (1974), however, suggests that reinforcers are not unitary variables, but rather a combination of informational and affective feedback differentially reinforcing learners according to motivational levels. This distinction may be critical in teaching a resistant learner, such as Marilyn.

Cybernetic Theory. Cybernetic theory also takes issue with a simple operant conditioning explanation (Smith and Sussman, 1969). Cybernetics concerns the guidance and control of behavior. Cybernetic theory makes a distinction between dynamic feedback and static feedback. Static feedback is what is commonly called knowledge of results or reinforcing after-effects. Dynamic feedback is the concurrent "reactive, instrumental and operational effects of movement." In swimming, for example, staying afloat or reaching the end of the pool would be static feedback. The way your body feels to you when you float as opposed to when you sink would be dynamic feedback. Cybernetic theory holds that dynamic feedback is the critical variable in motor learning. According to Smith and Sussman, the direct sensory effects of movement are sufficient to guide and control behavior. Static feedback has small and less important effects on learning. Miles and Evarts (1979) agree that static feedback contributes little to motor learning, but expand the concept of dynamic feedback. Reporting research on laboratory animals, they demonstrate that the central nervous system coordinates excitability in both the afferent and efferent systems to effect movement. Afferent feedback is the direct sensory feedback of movement (sometimes called proprioceptive feedback). Surgically blocking afferent feedback did not block excitation of learned motor systems in laboratory animals, demonstrating that the efferent system (messages going out from the central nervous system) is sufficient to control movement. This suggests that once a motor pattern is learned, it is controlled by the central nervous system, and only modified by sensory feedback.

Miles and Evarts (1979) state that feedback modifies motion by indicating when the performer should switch from one motor pattern to another pattern (e.g., from playing softly in the treble cleft on the piano to playing loudly in the bass cleft) and by indicating need for change within a single motor pattern (e.g., from playing softly to playing loudly in the same hand positions).

Social Learning Theory. Yet another "feedback" theory of motor learning is the social learning theory of Albert Bandura (1969). The feedback component of this theory is affective in nature: vicarious reinforcement. Bandura's research indicates that when an observer identifies with a model, that observer will imitate the behavior of the model and be reinforced vicariously through that identification. What is pleasurable to the model will be rewarding to the observer; what is punishing to the model will have negative affect on the observer. This process of vicarious reinforcement supports the learning of behaviors from models through imitation. Because the observer is not usually an overt learner -- not concurrently practicing the act -- the lesson must be symbolically stored in memory to be run-off later. The accuracy of the actual performance will then be a function of the availability of the pre-requisite skills necessary for performance. For example, we can all symbolically store a representation of Sugar Ray Leonard throwing a punch, but few of us have the pre-requisite skills necessary to accurately imitate it.

Marilyn, a blind learner, cannot learn to play the piano by the visual demonstration of a model -- a technique typically used in piano instruction. Does this mean Social Learning Theory has no application for blind learners? Marilyn's instructor thought that identification with a model might be a powerful instructional tool for her if properly extended. Marilyn could feel the model's movements, could store that aural/movement image for later retrieval. Her instructor suggests the use of two models -- her instructor and a peer practice partner. If Marilyn finds it difficult to identify with her instructor, perhaps identification with a classmate will be easier. The classmate will also be available on a daily basis. Marilyn's ability to imitate her models will, of course, be dependent upon her available repertoire of pre-requisite skills. The model must be careful to demonstrate skills within Marilyn's reach at each point in her progress. Marilyn's success in imitating her models will reinforce both the skill being learned and the future desire to identify with the models.

Behavioristic theories, then, rely upon some variation of the reinforcement theme to explain and predict motor behavior. The reinforcement may be internal feedback, informational feedback, vicarious reinforcement, or food pellets, depending upon the theorist. Cognitive theorists relegate reinforcement to the back burner and attempt to explain and predict motor behavior on the basis of cognitive processing.

COGNITIVE THEORIES

Bolles. Bolles (1972) takes issue with the behavioristic assumption that what is learned is a response. Expanding Tolman's (1932) earlier theorizing, Bolles hypothesizes that what is learned is an expectancy that anticipates a response. He would supplant the Law of Effect with his Primary Law of Learning: "What is learned is that certain events, cues (S) predict certain other, biologically important events, consequences (S*)." This stored information about the environment becomes a prediction formula for the future. If one smells hotdogs cooking, one predicts hunger will be assuaged.

Bolles' Secondary Law of Learning describes response-consequences (R-S*) expectancies that reflect R-S* contingencies in the environment. Certain responses are followed by specific consequences. If one bites into a hotdog, one tastes hotdog. S-S* and R-S* prediction formulas are thus conceptually stored, ready to be used when appropriate. They constitute what is learned in a learning experience.

To explain performance, Bolles hypothesizes that two expectancies (S-S* and R-S*) are combined when S becomes a cue in the environment. This Law of Performance explains both response flexibility and the effectiveness of reinforcement. Different combinations of S-S* and R-S* are potentially performable. Persons have many stored R-S* expectancies concerning food. In addition to the one mentioned above, one might have "eat-hunger assuaged," "eat hotdog -- bad taste in mouth," et-cetera. One might also have other food related S-S* expectancies, for example "smell steak-steak hunger assuaged." At different times, these S-S* and R-S* expectancies will be combined in different ways. If one is starving and smells hotdogs cooking, she will ignore "bad taste in mouth" consequence and utilize "hunger assuaged" response. If one smells both hotdogs and steak, she will probably combine "smell steak -- hunger assuaged," "smell hotdog -- hunger assuaged." "eat hotdog -- hunger assuaged," "smell hotdog -- hunger assuaged," "eat hotdog -- bad taste in mouth," "eat steak -- hunger reduced," and and head for the steak.

While a behavioristic theory has trouble explaining those instances where external reinforcement doesn't control behavior, Bolles' cognitive theory is strong. The Law of Prior Expectancies says that a strong S-S* expectancy may be combined with a previously learned or innate R-S* expectancy, circumventing any concurrent contingencies of reinforcement. This explains the difficulty of training a new response that has to compete with an innate response or previously learned strong expectancy, such as the food-washing of the raccoon, or the difficulty humans experience trying to change a habit, such as smoking behavior. The food washing behaviors of raccoons are innately associated with hunger reduction. Attempts to teach raccoons to engage in other behaviors, such as bar pressing, to receive food are over-powered by the prior food-washing -- eat R-S* expectancy. Likewise, the learned R-S* expectancy of reduced nicotine tension is strong competition for any substitute response when smoking cues are present.

Bolles believes that the simplistic S-R patterns hypothesized by traditional behavior theory are operative only in very simple reflex behavior or in over-learned skill behavior. An interesting speculation concerns the possibility that the shift in observed behaviors from initial learning trials to final performance recorded by the psychometricians may be a reflection of a shift from information processing combining S-S* and S-R*) to simple S-R patterns. (This speculation gains some support from the work on development of motor skills in children to be discussed below.)

Very few researchers of motor learning using mature subjects have been of cognitive orientation. Tolman (1932) was a pioneer in the exploration of cognitive determinants of motor behavior. Bolles (1972) is a current proponent of this theoretical view. The mature subjects of both researchers, however, have been rats. This does not negate their work. Nevertheless, it does mean that the external validity of their work must be examined. Does expectancy in rats generalize to expectancy in humans? That is an empirical question and researchers like Lindquist (1970) are beginning to explore the information processing approach to skill learning. Lindquist (1970) trained a college student to serve a tennis ball and recorded an oral account of the subject's on-going discussion with herself as she learned. This account suggests that a great deal of information processing was going on. More such studies will contribute to a cognitive theory of motor skill acquisition in adult humans.

Adult Learning. The preceding review has reflected the study of performance and acquisition of motor skills primarily with adults. There is little evidence to suggest that children respond in similar ways. Quite the contrary, what evidence there is suggests that adult response patterns are built on top of an underlying ability structure that is developmental in children (Fleishman, 1967). In other words, adults approach a motor skill learning task with a number of well-established sub-routines that can be simply recombined to specifics of the task at hand (Kay, 1969). Therefore, the process of acquiring a new motor skill is distinctly different for adults than for children.

Interestingly, while research on mature learners has been dominated by the behavioristic viewpoint, research on children's acquisition has grown mostly from cognitive hypotheses. This is, of course, partly the result of the assumption of behaviorism that reinforcement theory has unlimited generalizability as a law of learning. Therefore, the study of motor learning has been for Behaviorists a vehicle for studying reinforcement theory rather than to discover the laws governing motor learning.

DEVELOPMENTAL THEORIES

Researchers interested in the acquisition of motor

skills in children have been forced by their data to abandon a simple reinforcement theory of learning. Infants acquire a number of behaviors (feeding, attending, manipulating, locomoting, interacting with others) that have not been successfully explained by reinforcement theories (Bruner, 1973).

The maturational processes involved in skill acquisition: senses, muscular, and central nervous system must be taken into account (Kay, 1969). Attempting to separate the contributions of nature and nurture to learning is a time-honored pursuit of psychologists. Motor skill learning research in the 1930's (Hilgard, 1932) seemed to indicate that, at least with motor skills, maturational factors were either pre-requisite to learning or strongly affected the rate of acquisition. Twin studies in which one twin was given earlier training on bicycle riding or stair climbing than the other twin demonstrated that physiological development was more important than length of training in acquiring these basic motor skills. More recent research, however, (Dubose and Folio, 1977; Halverson, Robertson, Sofrit & Roberts, 1977; Schnabl and Dickey, 1977) indicates that the nature/nurture differential may be quite task specific. While no one would suggest that a three-month old infant could be taught to walk, instructional variables such as task analysis and maternal attitudes have been shown to affect motor learning in young children.

To help Ronald overcome his falling problem, it was important to assess his physiological development. If he had been found to lack essential maturation, motor skill training would create no improvement in balance, but would create frustration, and a sense of failure, a greater feeling of incompetence.

Information Processing Theory. In the initial stages of learning a motor skill, when the responses are under external control, they are hesitant and intermittent. The speed and flexibility of skilled performance, such as running or playing the guitar, reflect an internal system that can anticipate cues and respond with little processing of external criteria. The anticipation of cues is essential. Kay (1969) points out that the human physiological system has a built-in limitation; the delay of reaction time. Such a limitation requires that the organism learn the "probability of signals" and "pre-set its responses" for smooth and rapid performance. This sounds very much like Bolles' (1972) cognitive expectancy theory. The necessary serial ordering of events and responses in skilled performance suggests a necessity for information processing more compatible with cognitive than behavioristic interpretation.

Kay (1969) suggests that the amount of information that can be processed, the level at which it is processed, and the amount of practice are the limiting factors in skill acquisition. When cues are known and anticipated, and pre-set responses are available, those cues can be processed and responded to with a minimum of conscious attention. The remainder of the processing system can attend to other cues. If you had to concentrate on moving your eyes from left to right across this page, you would have little processing "space" left to decipher and comprehend the message. The weakness in using adult subjects to study motor skill acquisition is that adults subjects have many well-practiced pre-set responses for anticipated cues (S-S* and R-S* expectancies) that are transferred to new skill learning. Marilyn's piano instructor recognized the potential importance of Marilyn's previously learned guitar routines. To the extent that these prior learnings could be related to learning the piano, new combinations of responses could be formed which required less information processing than trying to teach totally new responses. For example, Marilyn knew the "I" and "V7" chords on the guitar. She could anticipate their sound. This could be related to the same chord sounds on the piano. For the adult learner, skill acquisition is frequently just a reorganization of old sub-routines (new combinations of S-S* and R-S*). Using adult Ss, therefore, tells us about the flexibility of reorganization of the sub-routines, but tells us little about the acquisition of the sub-routines, or the process of initially learning to flexibly combine sub-routines in the face of stimulus cues and limited information processing space. Thomas, Pierce and Ridsdale (1977) used a model to teach children of different ages a motor skill. They found great differences in learning as a function of age and explain those differences in terms of information processing space and previously learned sub-routines. Their younger subjects performed better on trial and error experiences than with a model demonstrating the skill. The researchers suggest that the model provided more information than the young subjects could process, leading to confusion. The older children not only had greater information processing space, but they also had previously learned sub-routines which would be used by the model and recombined in the new pattern with new routines.

Recognizing the limits of information processing space and the lack of previously learned sub-routines is essential to successful motor skill training with young children. The human neonate is a helpless miracle. "It is genetically programmed with the capacity for the *arousal of an intention*, desire to reach a goal," (Bruner, 1973) and for the *coordination of intersensory systems* (Kay, 1969). Phylogenetically, humans are very superior in the capacity for complex interrelationships among the senses. Touch, taste, sight, smell, hearing, etc. can be combined in a myriad of ways to interpret and interact with the environment. Neonate reflex behavior becomes goal related after the infant has experienced the results of her own acts (Bruner, 1973). All her senses contribute to the growing realization of the connections between means and ends (S-S* and R-S*).

Bruner's Theory. Bruner (1973) delineates the progression of a skill in human infants. Stimulation is responded to by the desire to achieve a goal (an "intention"). The nervous system discharges both a motor volley to the effectors and a signal to related senses. After the arousal of an intention, a loosely ordered sequence of *sub-routines* is performed. At this point the sub-routines are not serially ordered in a way that will be successful. The infant, may, for example, chew, wave arms in direction of object, and clench fists. Eventually, the infant coordinates these sub-routines in a serial order that successfully brings the object to her mouth. Each of the sub-routines is probably genetically and maturationally determined. The combination into successful routines, however, is due to trial and error practice.

Once a series of sub-routines is arranged in a successful combination, aspects of the sub-routines begin to alter to better perform the routine; for example, clenched fists will be replaced by open palm. It is at this point, Bruner (1973) believes, that reinforcement effects become important. Success brings about increased anticipatory patterning, the routine becomes rapid and smooth (Bruner calls this "modularization"), and the routine becomes a sub-routine in a more complex action.

Like Kay (1969), Bruner (1973) hypothesizes that as sub-routines are modularized into new routines, information-processing space becomes available for attending to new input. A child learning a motor skill (e.g., walking) has to concentrate on all the sub-routines (balance, locomotion, direction, etc.). Since it is difficult to process all that information at once, the skill is poorly performed (Kay, 1969). Mentally retarded persons have great difficulty learning motor tasks that require their simultaneous attention to several details at once. Similar to young, normal children, they lack sufficient information processing space (Davis, 1977). Over-learning sub-routines greatly facilitates motor learning among retardates. The over-learned routines can be called forth with little effort, leaving the bulk of information processing space free to attend to what is new in the instruction (Chasey, 1977).

As the sub-routines become modularized into a single routine, the child can easily process the cues, anticipate the response, and perform -- all without conscious attention. Ronald's inability to maintain balance suggests that some sub-routine or routines are not properly modularized into his motor routines. His instructor determined that he did not properly distribute his weight, consequently losing his balance and falling. Further diagnosis revealed that Ronald's head stance and shoulder alignment were uneven and that he did not visually fixate on a target in front of him. Remediation, then, had to involve the over-learning of these sub-routines taken for granted by those of us over three years of age who ambulate without conscious effort.

Ronald repeatedly practiced walking toward a visual target. Other sub-routines included balancing an object on his head as he walked and holding a yardstick at shoulder level in his extended arms as he walked. As these sub-routines were over-learned, they were combined in the more complex task of walking a specialized balance beam.

The construction and consolidation of such serially ordered motor sequences is the play of infancy and childhood. New objects are assimilated into as many old routines as are modularized and new routines are tried out on as many different objects as possible. This play stabilizes the routines, making them fully available for later use in more complex routines. Ronald's instructor recognized the "play" element of basic motor learning and presented all the practice activities as play routines. Different visual targets could be presented; different objects could be balanced on the head, etc. Play is much less anxiety-producing than practice -- failure without penalty is part of play; therefore over-learning is much more likely to occur. This is the basis of flexibility (Bruner, 1973). Schmidt (1975) agrees that the observed flexibility of motor responses humans perform cannot be explained in terms of a simple stimulus-response learning paradigm. He hypothesizes that cognitive motor schemes are learned and tied into cognitive motor programs that can be run-off under appropriate stimulation. These motor schemes are similar to other cognitive schemes in that they are sets of rules for classification which produce a concept -- in this case a motor response concept. These schemes can be combined in novel and flexible ways. Such theorizing has important implications for instruction (McKinney, 1977; Schmidt, 1975). Motor skill teaching should involve encouraging a wide range of responses; trial and error practice in which movement error expands the repertoire of motor schemes would be beneficial for children. Ronald needs to learn which motor responses throw him off balance, as well as those responses which help him maintain balance. Circus clowns make skillful use of their knowledge of which motor responses make them fall!

SUMMARY

Bolles' cognitive theory of S-S* and R-S* expectancies is a parsimonious explanation of the novelty and flexibility of skilled motor performances. Behaviorist reinforcement theories explain how some of the responses are learned and/or modified. Bruner's study of infants points toward a meta-theory of motor skill acquisition which would encompass prior research and theory from all the viewpoints discussed so far in this chapter.

Three forms of feedback are hypothesized by Bruner (1973) to be important in early skill acquisition: internal feedback, feedback proper, knowledge of results.

Bruner's "internal feedback" is feed forward that signals an intended action within the nervous system. Such internal feedback suggests an internal system of available expectancies. His "feedback proper" is feedback from the effector system during action. This is what cybernetic theory calls dynamic feedback. It is proprioceptive and travels the afferent nervous system. His "knowledge of results" is consequences of the completed act. This is traditional reinforcement theory.

Formerly discrete areas of research and theory on motor learning are beginning to interrelate. A larger picture is emerging that encompasses the work of behaviorists and cognitive psychologists.

MEMORY

Retention of a well-learned motor behavior is extremely strong. Well-learned motor skills not practiced over long periods of time are easily performed once again. The level of proficiency may deteriorate, but the basic moves involved are remembered. Motor abilities acquired developmentally become part of the motor repertoire, ready to be assimilated as a subroutine in new and/or more complex motor behaviors.

TRANSFER

Transfer of motor learning occurs frequently and is usually positive. As the basic, underlying motor abilities are acquired in the developing child, these abilities are transferred to an ever-increasing variety of motor skills. In the adult, well-learned motor routines are combined and re-combined in a myriad of new motor performances. Although motor routines with very similar sub-routines occasionally elicit negative transfer, most motor learning transfer is positive.

EVALUATION

Evaluation of motor skills depends largely upon observation techniques, although self-observation and task analysis procedures may also be useful. Anecdotal records, rating scales and checklists are probably the most useful formats.

Anecdotal records are objective descriptions of performance, sometimes followed by an interpretation of the observation. It is important that the description itself be devoid of interpretation. Anecdotal records should only be used if the behavior cannot easily be evaluated by rating scales and checklists: instances where the "whole picture" is needed in order to adequately evaluate progress. When the learner has a handicapping condition or attitude problems, for example, a series of anecdotal records might be very helpful.

Rating scales structure an observation so that precise evaluation is potentially possible. You are all familiar with the Olympic experience when judges rate performances on a zero to ten scale with very fine discriminations. The behavior being observed must be carefully defined and the judges must know what to look for. As with anecdotal records, objectivity is essential. When Russian judges give American performers lower ratings than the other judges do we ascribe the rating to judge bias, not to the quality of the performance. Rating scales are probably most useful when a total performance must be evaluated. Many motor skills are too complex and fast-paced to be evaluated any other way.

Checklists also structure an observation. The observer simply indicates whether a behavior was performed, without judging its quality or frequency. Checklists are very useful when the behavior can be broken down in some way. Task analysis is frequently used to develop a checklist. The list will then clearly define the steps in the task, telling the observer what to look for. For example, using a checklist to evaluate a bowler, the initial items would list preparation and positioning of body and ball, followed by items on approach, delivery, and finally, success rate.

Formal evaluation of motor skills is less frequent than formal evaluation of other domains of learning. Outside of athletic competitions, minimum competency at a motor skill is usually considered adequate to acclaim successful learning. We then say "He learned to skate...ski...bicycle...use the microscope." In facilitating the learning of difficult motor tasks, however, evaluation can provide vital information for both learner and instructor. This is true whether the task is difficult for everyone or just difficult for this particular learner. Developing evaluation instruments that are valid and reliable measures of motor learning is a challenge for the instructor, but has positive payoff for the learner.

REFERENCES

Bandura, A. *Principles of Behavior Modification*. New York: Holt, Rinehart and Winston, 1969.

Bolles, R.C. Reinforcement, expectancy, and learning. *Psychological Review*, 1972, *79* (5), 394-409.

Bruner, J.S. Organization of early skilled action. *Child Development*, 1973, *44*, 1-11.

Chasey, W. Motor skill overlearning effects on retention and relearning by retarded boys. *The Research Quarterly*, 1977, *48* (1), 41-46.

Davis, M. Movement and cognition. *Theory into Practice*, 1977, *16* (3), 207-210.

Dubose, R., & Folio, R. Investigation of short-term gains in motor skill achievement in delayed and non-delayed preschool children. *Peabody Journal of Education*, 1977, *54* (3), 181-184.

Fleishman, E. Individual differences and motor learning. In R.M. Gagne (Ed.), *Learning and Individual Differences*. Columbus, Ohio: Charles E. Merrill, 1967.

Gagne, R.M. Domains of learning. *Interchange*, 1972, *3* (1), 1-8.

Halverson, L., Robertson, M., Safrit, M., & Roberts, T. Effect of guided practice on overhand-throw ball velocities of kindergarten children. *The Research Quarterly*, 1977, *48* (2), 311-318.

Hilgard, J. Learning and maturation in school children. *Journal of Genetic Psychology*, 1932, *41*, 40-53.

Irion, A. Historical introduction. In E.A. Bilodeau (Ed.). *Principles of Skill Acquisition*. New York: Academic Press, 1969.

Kay, H. The development of motor skills. In E.A. Bilodeau (Ed.). *Principles of Skill Acquisition*. New York: Academic Press, 1969.

REFERENCES CONTINUED

Lindquist, E. An information processing approach to the study of a complex motor skill. Research Quarterly of the American Association for Health, Physical Education, and Recreation, 1970, 41, 396-401.

Logan, R. Micromotor behavior theory and performance speed in education. Harvard Education Review, 1963, 33 (2), 157-283.

McKeachie, W.J. The decline and fall of the laws of learning. Educational Researcher, 1974, March, 7-11.

McKinney, E. ...But can game skills be taught? Journal of Physical Education and Recreation, 1977, 48 (7), 18-20.

Miles, F.A., & Evarts, E.V. Concepts of motor organization. In Rosenzweig & Porter (Eds.). Annual Review of Psychology, 30, 1979.

Schmidt, R. A schema theory of discrete motor skill learning. Psychological Review, 1975, 82 (4), 225-260.

Schnabl, J. & Dickey, E. Relationships between parents' child-rearing attitudes and the jumping and throwing performance of their preschool children. The Research Quarterly, 1977, 48 (2), 382-390.

Smith, K.U. & Sussman, Harvey. Cybernetic theory and analysis of motor learning and memory. In E.A. Bilodeau (Ed.). Principles of Skill Acquisition. New York: Academic Press, 1969.

Thomas, J., Pierce, C., & Ridsdale, S. Age differences in children's ability to model motor behavior. The Research Quarterly, 1977, 48 (3), 592-597.

Tolman, E.C. There is more than one kind of learning. Psychological Review, 1949, 56, 144-155.

This chapter covers the expanded definition of cognitive structures/cognitive strategies; Furth's theory of learning which integrates Piagetian and Behaviorist approaches; the theory of Pascual-Leone, which integrates Piagetian and Field Independence research; and Flavell's concept of metacognition. The impact of cognitive structures/cognitive strategies on learning is discussed within the scope of several different theoretical perspectives.

1. Can cognitive structures or cognitive strategies be taught or only learned?

2. What aspects of cognitive structure/cognitive strategies are genetically determined? Environmentally determined?

CHAPTER SEVEN

COGNITIVE STRATEGIES/COGNITIVE STRUCTURE

INTRODUCTION

Gagne (1977, p. 116) defines <u>cognitive</u> <u>strategies</u> as "skills by means of which learners regulate their own internal process of attending, learning, remembering, and thinking." He suggests that Rothkopf's mathemagenic behaviors (Rothkopf, 1970) and the executive control processes of information processing theories are attempts to describe and explain these regulatory skills. However, a broader conception of cognitive strategies seems advisable in the light of research on cognitive development and cognitive styles. Therefore, the domain of cognitive strategies has been expanded in this work to the domain of cognitive strategies/cognitive structures (CS/CS). This broader conception of CS/CS includes (1) cognitive developmental level as described within a piagetian theoretical framework, (2) the cognitive style construct field independence -- field dependence, (3) executive -- management strategies that control thinking and other behavior at a particular point in time, and (4) metacognition variables.

This chapter will present theoretical position on (1) the characteristics and development of structures and strategies, (2) developing instruction in tune with developmental structures, and (3) teachable strategies. Remember that theories may be descriptive, prescriptive or a combination of both (see chapter 1). Since descriptive theories tell what phenomena exist, deriving instructional models directly from the theory is challenging. Prescriptive theories, in attempting to answer the "why" questions, suggest potential intervention strategies. In combined theories as well, instructional strategies most profitably emerge from "why" aspects. "What" aspects increase our understanding of the potentials and limitations of learners; "why" aspects help us to develop intervention techniques.

The Development of CS/CS. Humans develop and learn with great adaptive flexibility. This flexibility seems directly related to the underlying CS/CS which determine the scope and emphasis of personal interaction with the environment. For example, what and how a younger, wholistic student learns in a given situation may be quite different from what an older, wholistic student learns. This, too, will be different from what an older, analytic student learns. All are in the same situation, yet their CS/CS regulate what they learn in that situation. How these regulatory systems develop (are learned?) is the focus of much empirical research and theory building. Behaviorists have traditionally adhered to a unitary reinforcement theory: CS/CS are skills learned through the cumulative force of contingent reinforcement. At the opposite end of the theoretical spectrum, ethologists (nativists) have posited that underlying CS/CS are predetermined for each specie through the evolutionary survival process. The classic nurture-nature debate continues.

Furth (1974) points out that neither the behaviorists nor the nativists successfully explain the unique adaptability of the human. He uses Piagetian Theory to suggest a logical and pragmatic formulation that bridges the gap between the nature side of the debate (phylogenetic or innate explanations of knowing, e.g., ethological/nativistic theories) and the nurture side (individually learned explanations of knowing, e.g., Behavioristic/Empiricist theories). Furth's model includes (1) phylogenetic determinants, things that are true of all members of a species; (2) individual species-specific common experience, experiences that all members of a species typically have; and (3) individual particular experience, experiences unique to one member of a species. All of these elements interrelate as sources of knowledge for the individual.

Phylogenetic Determinants. Phylogenetic determinants appear to set the limits of interaction with the environment and therefore provide the basis for a common, normal experience. For example, walking on two limbs and having a thumb provide the opportunity for a common normal experience of humans not shared by any other specie. Other potentially phylogenetically controlled characteristics include the development of the neurological aspects of cognitive abilities that are under maturational control. For example, myelinization of the nervous system in humans is different from that of the great apes. Another, more detailed example of neurological development is found in a body of research reviewed by Case (1975, 1974). His work indicates that the human capacity to simultaneously process units of thought (schema) develops at a consistent rate. One additional schema can be simultaneously processed for every two years of chronological growth, culminating in late adolescence with a seven unit capacity. This correlates positively with research on short-term memory (Miller, 1956) which indicates 7 ± 2 capacity for adults. No evidence is currently available which indicates that environmental intervention can modify this information processing space capacity.

Cognitive Style. Another candidate for innately controlled cognitive characteristics is what is called "cognitive style." Cognitive style describes a characteristic way of interacting with the environment. A number of cognitive style variables have been hypothesized; e.g., impulsivity-reflectivity; focusing-scanning; conceptual style; field independence-field dependence. Most cognitive style variables are conceptualized as an individual difference continuum, i.e., some persons have more, some have less, of the characteristics defined by the construct. Some style variables, e.g., impulsivity-reflectivity, have been demonstrated to be modifiable by specified intervention (Kagan & Pearson, 1966) and therefore would not qualify as an innate determinant of behavior. Since, to date, there is no evidence that intervention can change field independence-dependence, it may qualify.

Cognitive Strategies/Cognitive Structure

The characteristics of field independence-dependence are displayed in a continuum described by the ability to analyze and differentiate the components of a stimulus array (field independent) on one end to responding to the total Gestalt or to an exceptionally salient aspect of the array (field dependent) on the other end. Since they are adept at analyzing, field independent persons would find working on a jig-saw puzzle easier and more enjoyable than field dependent people would. Because of their propensity to deal with their environment in a wholistic manner, and to be caught by one most salient aspect of the stimulus array, field dependent persons would find it difficult to analyze the "holes" in the puzzle and match a given color and shape of a piece to that hole. On the other hand the wholistic style of the field dependent individual serves him well in a situation where interaction with the whole group is important. Social situations, then, are usually more enjoyable for field dependent, than field independent, persons.

While children as a group tend to be more field dependent than adults, relative status within their year of birth (cohort) tends to remain stable. The more field dependent children are still more field dependent than their peers when they become adults (Witkin, Goodenough, & Karp, 1967). This cognitive style variable has been demonstrated to be an important mediating factor in both species-specific common experience and individual particular experience, as will be discussed later in the chapter.

<u>Individual Species-Specific Common Experience</u>. As suggested above, innately programmed characteristics influence both specie and individual experiences. Furth (1974) postulates that ontogenetic development (that is, the development of regulatory structures in individuals) is the result of species-specific interactions with a common environment. For example, the human ability to manipulate objects makes the ordering of objects (from biggest to smallest, tallest to shortest, etc.) a possible and common way for humans to interact with the environment. The <u>individual</u> who interacts with the environment in this common way abstracts from the experience the strategy or structure of "ordering." Once abstracted, such cognitive structures become a basis for future interactions with the environment. For example, if I have several different-sized dolls

and several sets of doll clothes, I must figure out some method to fit the clothes to the doll. Eventually I may find the strategy of ordering dolls and clothes from biggest to smallest. As a result of such experiences, I can more easily order the plastic storage containers in the kitchen from biggest to smallest. Other ordering tasks, such as ordering sets of objects in my math book from biggest set to smallest set, should also be easier. Piaget calls such experience "logico-mathematical," to distinguish it from "physical" experience. Physical experience translates directly into knowledge, logico-mathematical experience does not. By sensory-motor feedback, the learner comes to "know" physical qualities of the environment. Color, shape, texture, then, result from physical experience. The CS/CS of "ordering" cannot be known in such a direct way. Only reflection upon one's actions on the environment produces this kind of "knowing." To learn to "order" from my experience with my dolls and their clothes I must reflect on my experience and abstract the process of ordering. Logico-mathematical experience which contributes to the development of CS/CS is a reflective abstraction of actions on the environment that are possible within the phylogenetic limits of the human specie. The number of schemata which can be simultaneously processed and the degree of field independence-dependence probably affects the capacity for reflective abstraction. So, although reflective abstraction is possible for all humans, it is usually easier for older or for more field-independent learners.

Insight into the importance of individual species-specific common experience for the development of CS/CS comes from Reuven Feuerstein (1980). Confronted with abandoned children of World War II who had not had typical adult/child relationships, he developed a theory of mediated learning. The cognitive deficiencies of these learners reflected a passive approach to environmental interaction. They seemed not to understand that their own intellectual efforts could contribute to problem solution. The deficiencies they exhibited included impulsivity, not reacting to inconsistency appropriately, failure to see relationships among events and objects, and failure to make comparisons. Feuerstein hypothesizes that these deficiencies are not due to lack of interaction with the environment, but rather to a lack of instruction about what these interactions mean. These children had had many and various experiences but had no adult around to model for them such things as what was normal or surprising, how objects and events inter-related, how things were alike or different. Instruction mediates experience. A more knowledgeable person intervenes between the individual and the environment, transforming, reordering, organizing. The learner is exposed to the "reflective abstraction" of a viable model. The learner/observer gains insight into the thinking processes of a more sophisticated learner. An example of mediated learning may be as simple as a parent cooking in the presence of a child. The child watches the adult search for a special cup for measuring. Such an experience may be one of many that lead to conservation of volume. Or another parent explains to a youngster why the cat and the cow, so different in outward appearance from us, need water like we do. This may lead to comparison and classification. Both examples are simple, everyday common experiences.

According to Feuerstein, the World War II children had too few mediated experiences to learn adequate thinking skills. His proposed remediation is to provide varied experiences which aid deficient learners to learn how one goes about solving problems and acquiring information. In terms of the Furth model, learners are put in situations which require _reflective abstraction of actions on the environment_. In Piagetian terms, they encounter a _logico-mathematical experience_.

Karmiloff-Smith and Inhelder (1976) report studies of children engaged in what Furth (1974) might call species-specific common experience. Children were asked to balance weighted blocks on a metal rod. To be successful, the child has to recognize that the fulcrum (the metal rod) must be adjusted in relation to where on the block extra weight has been added. The children demonstrated the construction, overgeneralization, and refinement of what the experimenters call "theories-in-action."

The children's theories were dynamic and general processes that represent their cognitive strategies in approaching the balancing problem. A common theory used by the children was "Place the midpoint of the block on the rod." When the midpoint theory failed to balance the block because of hidden weights placed inside the block, other theories were tried, such as "Push down hard on the higher side," or "Slide the block toward the higher side." To be successful in balancing the block, the child must be able to discover relevant and irrelevant dimensions, keep those dimensions in mind, and plan and execute a hypothesis-testing action. The child's capacity for and success at reflective abstraction (logico-mathematical learning) on his current "theory-in-action" seems likely to be mediated by both information processing space and field independence-dependence. CS/CS are important to consider in solving such a problem. For the child whose developmental age constrains information processing space to two units, a highly improbable lucky sequence of trial and error moves would be necessary to develop a consistently successful strategy. The child who is highly field dependent would also experience difficulty. Unlikely to analyze the situation into relevant and irrelevant dimensions without prompting, the child could engage in endless reflective abstraction without discovering an appropriate rule.

Karmiloff-Smith and Inhelder (1976) reported a cross-sectional developmental pattern in this research with weighted blocks. Older children were more successful at deriving workable hypotheses than younger children. This suggests that this is an example of ontogenesis (development of regulatory systems in individuals) of a species-specific interaction with a common environment. Given the characteristics of the human family which allow manipulation of the environment and many things in the environment which can and should be balanced, most individuals will develop a balancing scheme.

Individual Particular Experience. The third component in Furth's model is individual particular experience (Furth, 1974). The contribution of this source of knowledge is the abstraction of knowledge from physical experience that is unique to the individual. Such experience is hypothesized to be mediated by phylogenetic determinants, by cognitive structures developed from species-specific experience (ontogenetic development) and by the reinforcement contingencies of the particular environment (ontogenetic learning). Individual particular experience is therefore subject to forgetting (extinction) and has limitations related to the particular environmental experiences. Ontogenetic learning as defined by Furth (1974) appears to coincide with a behavioristic conception of learning.

For example, one individual may experience breast feeding while another experiences bottle feeding. One individual may wear moccasins while another wears only hard-soled shoes and yet another never wears shoes at all. One individual may be exposed to trees and open sky while another sees only concrete and tall buildings. One individual may always be punished for reading while another is always praised. Individual experiences will always be within the limits of inherent human characteristics (phylogenetic determinants) and the limits of possible environmental contexts (individual, species-specific common experiences), but the possibility of endless unique individual variations in experience exists.

<u>Interdependence of Components</u>. The inherent interdependence of phylogenetic characteristics, specie-specific experience and individual particular experience is a crucial concept. While phylogenetic characteristics set limits, specie and individual experience contribute to evolutionary changes. For example, once mills started belching black smoke in England, black moths gradually outnumbered white moths. In like manner, while CS/CS mediates individual particular experiences, it is only through these unique individual experiences that reflective abstraction can take place. Therefore, Furth is positing a totally dynamic system in which all of the parts are at the same time separate entities and yet totally interdependent.

A study by <u>Case</u> (1975) illustrates the dependence of individual particular experience on available cognitive structure. Elementary school age children were asked to find the shortest route in a maze problem. Less mature children chose a route that had the shortest segment rather than the overall shortest route. Didactic instruction on the shortest route was not successful in improving the children's performance. What was successful was requiring reflective abstraction on the experience. In this experiment, the teacher put pegs through the maze and then wound strings along the pegs on each route. If a child could identify the shortest string, then he could identify the shortest route through the maze. Some of the children persisted in identifying the shortest route with the shortest segment in any route. The teacher would then refer back to the strings and ask the child how the shortest segment related to the shortest route. When forced to reflect on their experience in this way, the children developed better strategies of finding the shortest route in other mazes.

Intellectual skills (being able to find the shortest route) appear to be developed through a combination of particular experiences and underlying cognitive structures that support that interaction at an appropriate level for learning. However, particular experiences contribute to the development of new cognitive structures only when those interactions induce reflective abstraction. For example, children who were not asked to reflect on the difference in length of strings as well as the difference in length of segments would not develop better strategies as quickly or easily. When reflective abstraction does not take place, the learning is dependent solely on reinforcement contingencies, is easily forgotten and is narrowly applied (little horizontal transfer). When reflective abstraction is built into the instructional process, underlying cognitive structures are modified, reinforcement contingencies are irrelevant, the newly acquired structure is never forgotten and transfer is broad.

<u>Transfer Related to Underlying Structure</u>. The extent of transfer of learning, then, is related to characteristics of the domain of learning in which the transfer is expected to take place. Since CS/CS development involves structural change, <u>all</u> future learning will be affected -- the broadest possible transfer. Breadth of transfer is another way to think about difference between cognitive strategies/cognitive structure and intellectual skills. Wohlwill (1970), who conceptualizes learning as a combination of horizontal and vertical transfer offers insight into this distinction. He believes that <u>what</u> a child is capable of learning depends on, first, the "vertical distance" between what the child knows and what is to be learned. This vertical distance is specified in terms of how many steps up a Gagne-type hierarchical model the application example is. The second condition is the breadth of horizontal transfer desired, i.e., how different does the application problem look from the original learning problem? For example, if I learned to categorize cats as mammals, it is a close transfer step to categorize dogs

as mammals. It is a considerable farther transfer experience to see whales as mammals. Or if I learn the rule, "Be respectful to parents," it is a near step to "Be respectful to other adults," but a further transfer to "Be respectful to other children, even younger children."

Wohlwill hypothesizes an inverse relationship between vertical distance and horizontal transfer. The greater the distance between known and to-be-learned, the less the horizontal transfer. Wohlwill believes that horizontal transfer has the greatest ultimate payoff. He sees it reflecting underlying cognitive structure, while vertical transfer remains tied to specific content (intellectual skills, verbal information).

As an example of this inverse relationship between vertical and horizontal transfer, suppose that the learning task is conservation of continuous substance (that is, substance such as water or clay) and there are two learners. Chris, at age four, can handle one unit of thought at a time and is highly field independent (that is, analyzes easily, organizes efficiently). Jean, at age six, can handle two units of thought simultaneously and is moderately field dependent. Chris has had countless baths, has a kiddie swimming pool, and has been drinking from a glass for two years. Jean has had even more baths, more swimming experiences, and more glass-drinking experience.

Learning about conservation has to do with recognizing what elements stay the same in a situation while other elements are changing. Although Chris is field independent and therefore prone to analyze situations, she can only hold one element in her thoughts at a time. She cannot, therefore, compare situations before and after change. To teach Chris to conserve water (that is to recognize that 2 ounces of kool-aid in a tall, thin glass is equivalent to 2 ounces of kool-aid in a short, fat glass) is virtually impossible. One could train Chris to say that the amounts were the same by concentrating on a specific element such as always using the same two glasses and by rewarding Chris for making the appropriate response (This would be physical experience under the contingencies of reinforcement.). There would be vertical transfer from Chris's earlier experience with drinking to equate amounts of kool-aid in those two specific glasses. But, there would not be horizontal transfer to glasses of other dimensions holding 2 ounces of kool-aid. The distance between the skills and knowledge Chris has and the to-be-learned concept is too great. She cannot engage in the necessary reflective abstraction.

Jean, on the other hand, can compare before and after. Since she is field dependent, her instructor or her life experience will have to help her isolate the relevant elements from the irrelevant ones. Once these significant elements have been recognized, Jean can compare before and after simultaneously and learn to conserve continuous quantity. She needs some mediation, but has the capability for the essential reflective abstraction. She will recognize two ounces of kool-aid are equivalent to any other two ounces of kool-aid no matter what shape the container may be. In other words, the learning will have broad horizontal transfer. The distance between where Jean was before instruction and the instructional goal was relatively small.

The lack of horizontal transfer when vertical distance is large may be a function of innate capacities such as information processing space and field independence-dependence. When capacity demands of a problem are high, species-specific limitations (e.g., information processing space) may force attention only to physical experience under the contingencies of reinforcement, leavning no room for reflective abstraction. Wohlwill's conceptualization, then, clarifies the distinction between intellectual skills and CS/CS, and parallels Furth's (1974) distinctions between species-specific and individual particular experience. Furth's comprehensive formulation of the two aspects of experience in ontogeny, therefore, provides a powerful framework for theory building and hypothesis testing.

<u>Cognitive Theory of Pascual-Leone</u>. Another theoretical formulation gaining increasing attention is that of Pascual-Leone. He, also, utilizes Piagetian theory as a starting place for a parsimonious explanation of the development of cognitive structure. He incorporates information processing theory and field independence-dependence as critical variables.

Case (1974) contrasts Piaget's <u>structural</u> theory with Pascual-Leone's <u>functional</u> theory. Piaget describes human knowledge and competence at different points of development; Pascual-Leone attempts to answer the "how did this knowledge and competency develop?" and "how is this knowledge and competency used?" questions. As discussed above, Furth proposes a trichotomy of "sources of knowledge"; Pascual-Leone hypothesizes a trichotomy of units of thoughts which are responsible for behavior. Following the Piagetian tradition, he calls these units of thoughts "schemes." The three categories of schemes hypothesized are figurative, operative, and executive. These categories are somewhat analogous to Gagne's distinctions between verbal information, intellectual skills, and cognitive strategies.

Figurative Schemes. Figurative schemes are internal representations of items of information familiar to the learner or a perceptual configuration which is recognizable. The internal representation is a code similar to Miller's conception of "chunk" or a weighted set of features and cues, not a simple response bonded to a stimulus. The subject transforms sensory input into a network of features already associated with a conceptual or class response (Case, 1974). Information processing conceptions of "sensory buffer" and "search and fetch" processes seem analogous (see Chapter Five).

Operative Schemes. Operative schemes are representations of rules (functions) which when applied to one set of figurative schemes results in a new set of figurative schemes (Case, 1974). An operative scheme for same-different might be "Same requires that all important attributes be shared." This operative scheme could be applied to two figurative schemes: one for Mary and one for Suzy. A new figurative scheme resulting from this operative might be "Mary and Suzy are both female." Reorganization of internal structure might then be a recoding of "Mary" and "Suzy" representation under "female" -- a chunking. New verbal information available for future reference is then stored as a result of applying an operative (an intellectual skill?).

Executive Schemes. Executive schemes are internal representations of procedures available to reach an objective. Executive schemes determine what operative schemes will be used on what figurative schemes (Case, 1974). Executive schemes appear to be conceptually close to Gagne's "cognitive strategies," those skills which regulate internal processes. The executive scheme for recoding "Mary" and "Suzy" as "female" must include some plan for invoking the operative same-different rule scheme.

Scheme Commonalities. Figurative, operative and executive schemes are alike in that they (1) are "active," not just responses triggered by stimula; (2) are mechanisms by which humans acquire and utilize knowledge -- "functional units"; (3) have both an initial component and a subsequent component (a "releasing" and an "effecting" component) (Case, 1974).

The Development of Structures. Schemes develop from an innate set of sensorimotor reflex/instinctive schemes. New schemes develop through modification of old schemes over experience and through the combination and consolidation of several old schemes (Case, 1974). Bruner's (1973) concept of "modularization" of sensorimotor schemes is similar (see Chapter Six, Motor Learning and Performance).

The process of thought at any point in development is hypothesized to follow a regular pattern (Case, 1974). The subject first activates a general executive scheme that reflects the nature of (1) the problem constraints, (2) the perceptual field, (3) past experience, and (4) emotional reactions. This activated executive scheme determines the activation of relevant figurative and operative schemes which follow in "discrete mental steps." In order, each operative scheme is applied to one or more figurative schemes resulting in new figurative schemes. These new figurative schemes are rehearsed and made available (stored) for future reference. When the original objective is matched, the general executive scheme orders termination. For example, suppose a high school student must pronounce several unusual names for an oral reading assignment for speech class. As the student does her homework, the executive scheme would identify the problem, the perceptual field would be reading material, past experience would include phonics rules, other reading experiences, name pronouncing experiences, dictionary skills, prior oral reading success, and so forth. Emotional reactions would include such aspects as motivation to do well in speech and fear of reading aloud in public. The operative schemes of appropriate phonics rules, dictionary skills, name-pronunciation rules, motivation rules, avoidance of potentially embarrassing experiences rules would be applied to the task. The result would be new figurative schemes, that is, the pronunciation of new names. These "new" names now become prior experience and become incorporated as part of operative schemes. The process goes on.

The activation of any scheme requires <u>information processing space</u>. Only so many schemes can be simultaneously active, dependent upon the information processing capability of the individual. If the student in the name-reading example were younger, she would not be able to keep the motivation scheme, various phonics rules, the name-pronunciation rules and the dictionary skills all active at the same time. If two conflicting schemes are simultaneously activated, cognitive conflict results (Berlyne's conceptual conflict? Festinger's cognitive dissonance?). If "salience, past reinforcement or emotional involvement" does not interfere, this disequilibration is resolved by an executive scheme to activate all other relevant schemes. The most consistent information among the schemes available produces a new equilibrium.

Whether the outcome of this directed thinking pattern is successful or not depends upon the previous repertoire of schemes developed, the number of schemes the individual is capable of activating at the same time, the individual's tendency to use his/her full capacity and the field independence-dependence of the individual (Case, 1974). Research that supports the criticality of those dimensions is reported by Scardamalia (1977) and by Ehri and Muzio (1974).

Scardamalia (1977) found that if subjects were field independent and task dimensions were structured so that information processing load did not exceed the developmental capacity of the subject, conservation operations (operative schemes) could be developed by children at much younger ages than formerly thought to be possible. Ehri and Muzio (1974) illustrated the crucial factor of field independence-dependence in the successful solution of a problem in logic. Asked to determine the relative speed of horses on the inside and outside of a merry-go-round field dependent subjects were unable to separate the relevant variables even after instruction designed to encourage activation of appropriate schemes.

In summary, Pascual-Leone's answer to his questions "how does knowledge and competence develop and how are they used?" seems to incorporate the Furth-described dimensions of phylogenetic limits, species-specific common experience, and individual particular experience, and suggests an essential interdependence among the Gagne-described domains of learning.

Metacognition. Recent theory and research on metacognition shed some light on the executive function of thought processes. Metacognition refers to knowledge about one's own and other persons' cognitions. Flavell (1976) writes that, in general, metacognition concerns knowledge about how, where, and when to store knowledge; how, where and when to retrieve that stored knowledge. Some specific metacognitions would be (1) knowing what information to store and what to ignore, (2) knowing when to update stored information, (3) learning to do systematic long-term memory searches, (4) knowing how many items one can hold in short-term memory, and so forth.

Developmental studies have demonstrated that young children have limited metacognition, for example, young children believe they understand directions when they do not. This aspect of the executive function appears to develop gradually through adulthood. Flavell (1979) offers a model of cognitive monitoring which describes fully mature metacognition, the developmental goal of the child.

Flavell believes that adults monitor their cognitions through "four classes of phenomena: (a) metacognitive knowledge, (b) metacognitive experiences, (c) goals (or tasks), and (d) actions (or strategies)" (p. 906). Metacognitive knowledge is the world knowledge one has about cognition in general and personal cognitive capabilities in particular. Knowing you can plan and produce a seven course dinner is an example of metacognitive knowledge. Metacognitive experiences are ongoing realizations concerning cognition in progress. An "aha" insight would be a metacognitive experience in which one realizes that a solution has been found. Another example is the realization that you do not understand the instructions for doing a project. Goal or task metacognitions have to do with knowledge about task dimensions. Knowing that a lecture is poorly organized and therefore your task is a reorganization of the ideas would be a task metacognition. Strategy metacognition has to do with knowing what strategy to use when. Recognizing that imagery is a good strategy to use to remember paired-associate words is a strategy metacognition. Since children lack this ability to monitor their cognitions, they need instructors who offer detailed explanations/experiences and on-going evaluation of understanding.

IMPLICATIONS

CS/CS have two major implications for learning theory. One implication is that the potential for new learning is mediated by the extant CS/CS of the individual learner. A second implication is that CS/CS should be identified and, where possible, learned/taught.

Designing Instruction with CS/CS in Mind. Robbie Case (1974, 1975, 1978) draws a parallel between learning cognitive-developmental tasks and learning difficult school subject matter tasks. Recognizing that information processing space capabilities, cognitive style, and operational stage create limits for learning, Case offers a theory of learning which incorporates and overcomes these limitations.

Cognitive-developmental research demonstrates that children attempt to solve problems (to learn) using the logical thought structures they possess. Their strategies are sensible, but wrong. Responses to the classic Piagetian tasks are examples. Shown two rows of six pennies, one spread out into a longer row than the other, most four year olds will maintain that the longer row contains more pennies. The logical structure they are using is "Longer is more." Asked to determine what causes the speed of a pendulum, a fifth grade concrete operational thinker will experiment with a pendulum and pronounce a rule such as "The weight of the ball at the end of the pendulum determines speed." His strategy for discovering the rule is to manipulate the environment and watch what happens.

In both instances the children are using the logical structures they have available. Their strategies are "reasonable" and reflect past experiences where they have worked. In the world of the four-year old, most of the time "longer" is "more." In the world of the fifth grader, most of the time observation is a sufficient strategy. Case (1978) points out that the strategies displayed by children "are not so much incorrect as they are incomplete" (p. 442). He also demonstrates that the incomplete (incorrect) strategies require a smaller information processing space than complete strategies would require.

Successful instruction, therefore, according to Case, must (1) help the learner recognize the inadequacies of the strategies being used, and (2) keep the demands on working memory (information processing space) within the actual constraints of the learner's capability.

Recognizing the Inadequacy of a Strategy. Case's research suggests that learners can recognize the inadequacy of a strategy if instruction follows this procedure:

1. It must provide the student with some meaningful procedure for determining whether or not his or her approach has been successful.

2. It must present the student with problems for which his or her current strategy will not work.

3. It must provide an explanation for why the current strategy will not work...

4. It must provide a demonstration of (or invite the student to discover) the correct strategy.

5. It must explain why the correct strategy works better...

6. It must provide a period of practice with coaching, together with the opportunity to transfer the new strategy to new situations. (pp. 446-7)

Minimize Information Processing Space Needed. Instructional situations frequently overload the working memory of adults. Can you remember right now the elements of Furth's and Pascual-Leone's theories? If you can, have you organized them in such a way that just one or two ideas encapsulated all other theoretical points?

Cognitive Strategies/Cognitive Structure

If the working memory of the learner is severely limited, as with children, instruction must compensate by limiting the number of stimuli to be processed at one time. Task analysis can reveal the essential stimuli and the order in which they must be processed. Instead of presenting the total task to be learned, the learning situation can present small piece after small piece, staying within the confines of individual information processing space.

Other ways to reduce the load on working memory include familiarizing the learner with stimuli and responses that will later be combined, and making sure that all relevant stimuli are salient to the learner.

An Example. Case (1978) demonstrates his model by "The Missing Addend Problem." Given the equation 4 + () = 7, most first grade children cannot supply the missing addend. The strategy they use is the familiar "add the two numbers when you see a + sign." Their answer is thus 4 + (11) = 7. Case uses simple line drawings of faces to help the learners recognize that their strategy is giving them the wrong answer. Keeping the stimuli simple and salient, the instruction focuses on checking to see if two faces are the same. Once they achieve the strategy of comparison, they are confronted with line drawings of faces that are not the same but are connected by an "=" sign. Reminded that = means both sides are the same, they are then asked to combine two half faces, one of which has no features, to = a whole face. The preceding instruction illustrates to the children a situation where their strategy will not work. The children are then told and re-told that the addition paradigm says "put things together so that you get the same thing on both sides of the = sign." Graduating from faces to dots to numbers, the children are offered strategies to find the missing addend while being reminded again about keeping things equal and noticing the position of the + sign.

By designing instruction with CS/CS in mind, the instructor takes advantage of cognitive developmental theory and research to match curricula to realistic learner potential.

Instruction to develop CS/CS. Although there has been some limited success in teaching the operative structures described by Piaget, (conservation, classification, et cetera) the benefits of such learning are questionable. Little transfer beyond the training paradigm has been demonstrated and most children acquire the necessary operations in the normal course of development. In the case of special students, such as those described in Feuerstein or those with learning disabilities or mental retardation, instruction designed to facilitate learning of operations is probably indicated. The above described model of Robbie Case should be effective in achieving CS/CS learning outcomes.

Other researchers (Carroll, 1981; Resnick & Glaser, 1976; Rigney, 1978), within the narrower definition of cognitive strategies, are in the process of describing the various strategies learners use to facilitate their learning. They are also offering suggestions for learning these strategies.

Problem Solving Strategies. Resnick and Glaser (1976) discuss problem solving as a form of invention. Like Gagne, they see the novel recombination of previously learned rules as a key strategy. Their model, which is both a description and a blue print for instructional planning, has three components. Faced with a novel problem the learner must (1) *encode* the problem in some representational form that can be held in working memory, (2) *search* long-term memory for relevant schemes, (3) when no relevant schemes are found, *re-formulate* the problem and *re-institute* memory search. They hypothesize that this procedure explains the combination of prior processes into more complex processes and accounts for the transition from one stage of development to the next. Although an interesting theory, the focus on a narrow range of cognition (problem-solving) and lack of empirical support limits the current utility of the Resnick-Glaser model.

Operations and Procedures. Another theoretical perspective on cognitive strategies is put forward by Rigney (1978). Defining cognitive strategies as *operations and procedures* used "to acquire, retain, and retrieve different kinds of knowledge and performance" (p. 165), he posits that the executive function of learning consists of a cognitive orienting task and one or more *representational*, *selectional*, or *self-directional capabilities*. An orienting task is an instructional method used to elicit particular learner operations. Orienting tasks can be determined by either the learner or the instructional package. And orienting tasks can be independent of the subject matter learned, for example, use a drawing. Or, the orienting task can be embedded in the instruction in such a way that a strategy, e.g., imagery, must be used to complete the task. The orienting task, then, will call upon one or more learner capabilities. Representational capabilities include things like reading, imagery, speech and drawing. Attention and intention are selectional capabilities. The latter are reminiscent of Flavell's metacognitions, but Rigney does not draw the parallel.

Rigney relies upon the Norman model (see Chapter 2) of accretion, restructuring and tuning to suggest instructional interventions. During accretion, learners should be taught how to locate and organize subject matter, how to select useful information and how to best encode for long term store. Since restructuring takes place during retention, strategies for controlling proactive and retroactive inhibition/interference are needed. Tuning requires time and practice. In all stages, Rigney emphasizes the importance of learning to control for both internal and external distractions.

Rigney proposes three different and distinct long term memory stores: semantic (verbal and imaginal), episodic and motor. He feels that each store is unique and that different cognitive strategies are probably more or less effective in facilitating learning as a function of that uniqueness.

Cognitive Strategies Applied to a Given Domain. Singer (1978) agrees that different learning domains interact with cognitive strategies differentially. Working within the domain of motor skills, he focuses upon the involvement of cognitive processes and strategies in the learning of motor skills. The cognitive strategies he lists are not different from other lists of strategies; however, where and when they are appropriately applied is somewhat unique.

Singer discriminates between self-paced and externally paced activities, pointing out that the strategies for each are different. In self-paced activity, e.g., golf, split-second decisions rarely have to be made. In externally paced activity, e.g., tennis, rapid decisions must be made with the performer ready to adjust to circumstances beyond her control. In addition to the pacing dimension, psychomotoric activities may be _open loop_ or _closed loop_. In an open loop system there is insufficient time to process feedback from performance in order to modify ongoing activity. When you hear the wrong note, it is too late to correct it. A closed loop performance is one in which continual feedback is used to modify performance. Ice skating would be a closed loop activity.

The executive management of these dimensions requires cognitive strategies. Singer (p. 91) lists the following areas in motor skill learning where it appears specific cognitive strategies are necessary.

1. To understand goals and to create an internalized image (covert verbalization), a process that could be termed _goal-image formation_.

2. To recognize similarities in the characteristics of the present task and situation with previous experiences (generalizability).

3. To recall related behaviors to the present task (to remember related cue-response associations and procedures; to retrieve information effectively).

4. To perceive the nature of the activity in the context of the environment, with situational demands and costs and payoffs relevant to decision-making.

5. To identify and select at any given time the most relevant and minimal cues to which to respond.

6. To concentrate in a relaxed state, demonstrating the desirable arousal level (the effect of cognitions over emotions).

7. To maintain the ideal motivational state and attitudes for original performance, task preference, and task perseverance (the effect of cognitions over emotions).

8. To establish goals and expectations that are high and specific, but attainable -- a process that could be termed goal-expectancy formation.

9. To make correct response decisions (amplitude, speed, accuracy, direction).

10. To use problem solving, analysis, and adaptive behaviors when required.

11. To rehearse mentally prior to, during, and/or after performance (depending upon the situation and desirability of rehearsal).

12. To adapt to stress (cognitive control over and regulation of emotions).

13. To evaluate ongoing performance to monitor, regulate, and adjust performance, and evaluate the results of performance for future accommodations.

14. To attribute performance outcomes to the appropriate reasons (ability, energy expended, task difficulty, and luck). (p. 91)

Singer notes that the skillful performer may not continue to consciously use the cognitive strategies that she used to learn the skill. Once performance is automated, processing at the higher cognitive level is not only unnecessary but may interfere with smooth performance. For example, the accomplished pianist who begins thinking about strategies for fingering while playing a well-rehearsed piece will probably begin to make errors.

Cognitive strategies, then, play an important role in learning motor skills. That role changes depending upon the dimensions of the motor skill being learned (pacing and looping) and the progress toward mastery of the learner.

Are there cognitive strategies specific to a learning domain? Probably not. However, the application of cognitive strategies (the when, where, how and why) is probably unique within domains. Just as Singer has so skillfully interfaced motor skill learning with cognitive strategies, the instructor in any domain of learning outcome could analyze the cognitive strategies that are essential for success.

Research on teaching cognitive strategies is sparse. Work on memory and on problem-solving has some relevancy. As the job of describing cognitive strategies progresses, theoretical formulations will become more precise. Research interest is currently high. The consumer will need to keep abreast of new developments in this area.

SUMMARY

Cognitive strategies/cognitive structures (CS/CS) are the underlying operations and procedures that mediate learning. They encompass cognitive developmental level, cognitive style, executive functions, and metacognitions. The development of CS/CS is an interaction of phylogenetic determinants, individual species-specific common experience and individual experience. Because of the interdependence of innate and learned aspects of CS/CS, instruction designed to develop CS/CS will be successful in only narrowly confined areas. However, the implications of CS/CS for instruction in other domains are broad and useful. Operational level, cognitive style, metaknowledge and executive strategies mediate all other learning.

MEMORY

To the extent that CS/CS are underlying structural components of thinking, memory is not a relevant construct. There is no evidence to suggest that operations are brought to conscious thought in the typical learning experience, if indeed the learner has any knowledge of her extant operations. Late concrete operations and formal operational thinkers can probably re-construct the process they have used to solve a problem if instructed to do so, however. Some research indicates that memory over time may change in accord with changes in underlying structure. Unclassified events encountered while in a pre-operational stage may be remembered during the concrete operational stage as classified, for example.

Problem-solving strategies, on the other hand, are frequently brought to consciousness; e.g., "I'll try an alphabetical search for that name I can't remember." Since research on retention of such strategies is sparse, no conclusions can be drawn.

TRANSFER

As discussed in the chapter, CS/CS have enormous transfer effects, because all learning is mediated through CS/CS. Transfer will be positive when the match between CS/CS and the learning goal is optimal. Transfer will be negative when there is little or no match.

EVALUATION

Evaluation of cognitive structure, cognitive style, and cognitive strategies is unevenly researched. The typical evaluation of structure consists of Piagetian type tasks. While several paper and pencil tests of logical thinking ability are available, they are still in experimental stages. Other experimental attempts to evaluate structure include measuring semantic networks by word associations, assessing hierarchical arrangements of concepts and so forth.

Cognitive style variables that are of current interest to learning theorists are evaluated by instruments developed by researchers. Several psychological tests are available to measure field independence-field dependence. Tests also exist to measure impulsivity-reflectivity. *Buro's Mental Measurement Handbook* and *Tests in Print* are valuable resources for persons searching for evaluation instruments.

Beyond memory and problem-solving research, assessing cognitive strategies is a new endeavor. For the practitioner, assessing cognitive strategies should be accomplished in the same way all learning outcomes are assessed. Well written, precise, specific objectives lead to assessment instruments that are valid and reliable (see Chapter Three).

Cognitive Strategies/Cognitive Structure

REFERENCES

Bruner, J.S. Organization of early skilled action. Child Development, 1973, 44, 1-11.

Carroll, J.B. Psychometric tests as cognitive tasks: A new "structure of intellect." In Resnick, L. (Ed.). The Nature of Intelligence. New York: Wiley, 1976.

Carroll, J.B. Ability and task difficulty in cognitive psychology. Educational Researcher, 1981, 10, 11-21.

Case, R. Structures and strictures: Some functional limitations on the course of cognitive growth. Cognitive Psychology, 1974, 6, 554-573.

Case, R. Gearing the demands of instruction to the developmental capacities of the learner. Review of Educational Research, Winter, 45, (1) 59-87.

Case, R. Implications of developmental psychology for the design of effective instruction. In O'Neil, H.F., Jr. (Ed.). Learning Strategies. New York: Academic Press, 1978.

Ehri, L. and Muzio, I. Cognitive style and reasoning about speed. Journal of Educational Psychology, 1974, 66 (4), 569-571.

Feurstein, R. Instrumental Enrichment. Baltimore, MD: University Park, 1980.

Flavell, H. Metacognitive aspects of problem solving. In Resnick, L. (Ed.). The Nature of Intelligence. New York: Wiley, 1976.

Flavell, J.H. Metacognition and cognitive monitoring: A new area of cognitive-developmental inquiry. American Psychologist, 1979, 34, 827-833.

Furth, H.G. Two aspects of experience in ontogeny: Development and learning from Advances in Child Development and Behavior, 9. New York: Academic Press, 1974.

REFERENCES CONTINUED

Gagne, R.M. *The Conditions of Learning* (3rd ed.). New York: Holt, Rinehart & Winston, 1977.

Kagan, J., Pearson, L. and Welch, L. The modifiability of an impulsive tempo. *Journal of Educational Psychology*, 1966, 57, 359-365.

Karmiloff-Smith, A. and Inhelder, G. "If you want to get ahead, get a theory." *Cognition*, 1976, *3*, 195-212.

Messick, S. *Cognitive styles in educational practice: Research Report*. Princeton: Educational Testing Service, June, 1982 (RR-82-13).

Miller, G.A. The magical number seven, plus or minus two: some limits on our capacity for processing information. *Psychological Review*, 1956, *63*, 81-97.

Rigney, J.W. Learning strategies: A theoretical perspective. In O'Neil, H.F., Jr. (Ed.). *Learning Strategies*. New York: Academic Press, 1978.

Rothkopf, Z. The concept of mathemagenic activities. *Review of Educational Research*. 1970, *40*, 325-336.

Scardamalia, M. Information processing capacity and the problem of horizontal decalage: A demonstration using combinatorial reasoning tasks. *Child Development*, 1977, *48*, 28-37.

Singer, N. Motor skills and learning strategies. In O'Neil, H.F., Jr. (Ed.). *Learning strategies*. New York: Academic Press, 1978.

Witkin, H., Goodneough, D., and Karp, S. Stability of cognitive style from childhood to young adulthood. *Journal of Personality and Social Psychology*, 1976, *7*, 291-300.

Wohlwill, J. The place of structured experience in early cognitive development. *Interchange*, 1970, *1*, (2), 13-27.

Attitudes are internal states that influence our actions. Chapter Eight looks at several definitions of attitudes, distinguishes them from other similar phenomenon and presents Behaviorist, Cognitive, and Innoculation Theories related to attitude formation and change.

1. What are attitudes? How do they affect the way in which we act?

2. How are all the behaviorist theories of attitude learning similar? How do they differ?

3. In what ways do the cognitive theories disagree with the behaviorists in attitude formation?

5. Do the cognitive theories differ in significant ways from one another?

CHAPTER EIGHT

ATTITUDES

INTRODUCTION

A Chinese couple traveling through the United States in 1934 receive excellent service at several hotels. Later the managers of ninety-percent of these hotels claim that individuals of Chinese descent will not be served (La Piere, 1934, as cited in Gagne, 1977). Junior high school students, when asked about the effect of the bomb on Hiroshima, realize that they have attitudes about the atomic bomb even though they have no information on the subject and no clear support for these attitudes (Barnes, 1972).

How might one account for these phenomena? This chapter attempts to examine how we form and change attitudes, these elusive hard-to-manage aspects of human interaction. Following an attempt to define attitudes and delineate some relationships with other affective phenomena, the chapter will examine some common theories of attitude. The rest of the chapter will look at memory, transfer and evaluation as they relate to attitudes.

DEFINITION

Himmelfarb and Eagly (1974) make a distinction between the operational and construct definitions of attitude. Operational definitions refer to attempts to define a variable through a set of operations which are in some way observable to the experimenter, whereas construct definitions are used in more abstract theoretical delineations. For the most part the present chapter will be looking at the construct definition rather than the operational type. The following are a selection of the definitions used by various theorists. Some theorists define attitude in the sense of some "set" or "readiness" to act. For example, Gagne (1977) defines attitude as "an internal state that influences (moderates) the choices of personal action made by the individual" (p. 44). Several theorists (Allport, 1935, Newcomb, 1950) agree that attitude implies this readiness or set for some action.

Other researchers look at attitudes as some evaluative phenomenon. For example Fishbein (1962) sees attitude as an evaluative response which is implicit, and Krech and Critchfield (1948) relate attitude to the organization of motivation, emotion, perception and cognition about some aspect of the individual's experience. Thurstone (1931) described attitude as the effect for or against a psychological object. Behaviorists, on the other hand, describe attitude as a drive producing phenomenon (Doob, 1947).

Although you can clearly see that there is little agreement in several definitions of attitude, perhaps one of the most widely accepted descriptions of attitudes is that ascribed to by Triands (1971), Travers (1982) and Katz and Statland (1961) which suggests that attitudes include three components: (1) an affective component, a positive or negative feeling, (2) a cognitive component, involving knowledge and beliefs and (3) an action or behavioral component which frequently appears to be independent of the others. While all three components are necessary for a completely formed attitude, any person also holds several partially formed attitudes which might consist only of two of the possible components. Most theorists agree, however, that unless the affective component is present you do not have an attitude but rather a belief or an opinion.

Distinctions. Perhaps we should pause and make some distinctions between attitudes and other aspects of psychological thought/feeling. Interests, like attitudes, have an affective component but attitudes are more basic than interests. For example, my attitude may cause me to have an interest in something. Also attitude implies some kind of commitment to the attitude object whereas interest does not necessarily mean any commitment. I may be interested in frogs but not wish to preserve their habitat or feed them flies. I may even be interested in something that I have a fairly neutral or negative attitude toward. For example, I may have a negative attitude toward totalitarian governments, but have a great interest in how they achieve their goals. Opinion is also a preference. But cognition forms the basis of the opinion, which is not true of attitudes. Opinions to which I have a significant commitment are beliefs. Beliefs may or may not have clear facts to support them. Values are a broader concept than attitudes. Like attitudes they have a strong affective component, but they also tend to imply a greater commitment. Values, for some theorists (Travers, 1982), are the basis of attitudes. My values, then, can predict my attitudes. One can see that the distinctions between attitudes, values, opinions, and interests are not clear cut. This is one of the reasons that operational definitions are so essential.

Functions of Attitudes. Why do people have attitudes? What functions do they fulfill for the individual? Travers (1982) outlines four different functions of attitudes. First, attitudes have an adaptive function. It is adaptive to have negative attitudes toward things that are potentially dangerous to the individual, for example, crossing the street from between cars. At a more sophisticated level attitudes may help us adapt to new situations. A positive attitude toward reading may make graduate school much less painful for the student. Attitudes also have a cognitive function. They help the individual to simplify the world much as generalizations or concepts do. For example, I do not have to have a separate attitude toward every shopping mall I encounter. I can either basically enjoy shopping malls or basically dislike having to shop there. Third, attitudes have a need-gratification function, that is, specific attitude objects are seen as "good" by all humans. For example, all normal humans have a positive attitude toward tasty food. (Of course, what is defined as "tasty" may differ markedly from culture to culture.) Attitudes also have an ego-defense function. Persons hold some attitudes to help them feel good about themselves. For example, a poor student may have a negative attitude toward study, calling it a stupid waste of time so that when he does poorly he has a good excuse. Although the final function is not as clearly delineated, attitudes also seem to have a motivational function. Katz (1960) and Kelman (1958) both cited by Himmelfarb and Eagly (1974) give additional background on the functional theory of attitude change.

Relationship Between Attitudes and Behavior. The relationship between attitudes and behavior is far from clearly defined. Some theorists completely ignore the necessity for attitudes to directly affect behavior, assigning only a set or readiness function to attitudes. Others see fully formed attitudes as needing an action component, while still others, for example, behaviorists, see behavior as the only clear evidence that a particular attitude exists. This relationship will be further discussed as a part of transfer later in the chapter.

This first part of the chapter has demonstrated that there is no universally accepted definition of attitudes, that attitudes perform several different functions for the individual and that there is no clear, well-established relationship between attitudes and behavior.

THEORIES

Many theorists seem to have a clear idea of how attitudes are changed, but few confront the problem of how attitudes are originally formed. Most of the following discussion, then, will deal with the changing of already existent attitudes. Several different theories will be examined. These have been loosely grouped into Behaviorist, Cognitive, Social Judgment, and Innoculation perspectives.

BEHAVIORISTS

Classical Conditioning. In a classic experiment Menzies (1937, as cited in Bem, 1970) demonstrated that Pavlov's work with animals could be applied to humans.

Initially, Menzies used a container of ice water to cause constriction in the blood vessels of the subject's hand. As the hand was plunged into the water a buzzer was sounded. After several pairings Menzies successfully substituted the conditioned stimulus (buzzer) for the unconditioned stimulus (ice water) to achieve the same response (constriction of the blood vessels in the hand). The blood vessels now constricted to the sound of the buzzer. Later researchers (Roessler and Brogden, 1943) used a word instead of a buzzer to show similar results.

It may be difficult to imagine immediately how this research relates to attitudes. Surely every person who has a negative or positive attitude toward some attitude-object has not had a negative or positive event directly paired with each attitude-object. Subsequent experiments throw some light on this dilemma. Bem (1970) cites experimentors who worked with the concept of <u>stimulus generalization</u>:

> For example, with human subjects a GSR (Galvanic Skin Response) conditioned to the sound of a bell may also be elicited by the <u>sight</u> of the bell or by the spoken word <u>bell</u>. If conditioned to the word "bell," human subjects will generalize to the word "gong" (p. 43).

A fine example of this "semantic generalization" is found in the work of the Russian researcher at Volkova (1953, as cited in Bem, 1970). Using cranberry puree as an unconditioned stimulus, she conditioned children to salivate to the word "good." She then demonstrated that children would salivate to sentences such as, "The young pioneer helps his comrade." but not to sentences such as, "The fascists destroyed many cities." Further, Staats and Staats (1958) paired several names of nationalities with consistently positive or consistently negative evaluative terms. After subjects had heard several of these combinations they were asked how they would rate members of each nationality. As might be expected, members of those nationalities paired with positive evaluative terms were rated more positively than those paired with negative evaluative terms.

<u>Fishbein</u> (1961) further delineates the effect of

conditioning. He does not distinguish between attitudes and beliefs, but rather asserts that all concepts elicit some evaluative response. If I have a negative attitude toward dark skin and I believe that Indians have dark skin (even if this is not objectively true) then I will have a negative response to the concept "Indian." Fishbein claimed that any evaluative response to an individual concept was the sum of the evaluations associated with that concept. For example, if I believe, not only that Indians have dark skin (negative for me), but also that they are kind (positive), loving to their families (positive) and loyal to their friends (positive) then I may ultimately arrive at a positive attitude toward Indians. If, however, the importance of "dark skin" outweighs all these other attributes combined, then I will arrive at a negative attitude. For Fishbein, then, attitudes can be changed by associating new beliefs or new weights for already established beliefs about the attitude-object.

Those who hold that attitudes are formed by classical conditioning would also suggest that attitudes are subject to extinction. For example, in the experiment by Staats and Staats (1958) cited above, if pairings between the nationality and the positive or negative terms ceased, and particularly if the nationalities were paired with neutral evaluative terms, the attitudes toward the groups would revert to their pre-experimental level. For the classical conditioning theorist, then, attitudes are learned and unlearned in the same way as other aspects of learning.

Operant Conditioning. Operant conditioning theorists agree with the classical conditioning theorists that attitudes are learned and unlearned in the same way as other aspects of learning. They see attitude formation and change as a specific case of action and reinforcement. Operant conditioning advocates believe that attitudes are observable behaviors, like all other behaviors. According to this theory, if an instructor wishes to change the attitude of her students all she has to do is reinforce any evidence of the attitude tending toward the direction the teacher considers positive. If, for example, a teacher wishes to have students believe that history is an enjoyable discipline to study, the teacher might ask each student to write an essay or present a talk on the positive values of history. The teacher could then rate these assignments with high grades and praise. These high ratings should lead to attitude change. Research (Festinger and Carlsmith, 1959) supports this by demonstrating that expressions of attitude coupled with reward and/or praise result in substantial change in attitude.

Self-Perception. Bem (1970) articulates a closely related theory. In his self-perception theory he states that "attitudes follow behavior" (p. 57). By this Bem means that individuals, in a sense, infer their emotions and attitudes by watching their own behavior. They also notice whether this behavior is "successful" or not by watching other's reactions to them. Further, individuals assume how others must be interpreting their behavior. This interpretation becomes feedback to the learners about who they are, what they like, how they feel. In response to the example of the history teacher and students cited above, Bem would explain that the students saw themselves "through the eyes of the teacher" as positively inclined toward history. The students then begin to perceive themselves in the same way, that is, the way their rewarded behavior indicates that they feel.

Social Learning. Still another theory which relates to reinforcement is Bandura's (1969) theory of human-modeling. Allied to the old moral dictum of "good example," Bandura's modeling suggests that when an individual who is "credible" to an observer acts in a particular way, the observer will tend to act the same way in a similar situation. This effect is modified further when the modeled behavior is either rewarded or punished. Vicarious reward or punishment, that is, reward or punishment applied to the model, affects the behavior of the observer, regardless of whether the observer is rewarded or punished.

Chittendon (1942) found that not only "real life" but also dramatic presentations can serve as modeling situations. Much popular literature purports to indicate that TV serves as a source of models of behavior. Surely advertisers attempt to find "credible" individuals to sponsor their products. Modeling, then, has popular appeal as a theory.

Bandura and his associates (1963, 1965) also showed that once a modeled attitude is learned by the observer it affects not only the modeled situation but generalizes to other situations as well. The human modeling theory, then, provides a relatively sufficient theory to account for incidental learning of attitudes.

Information Integration. While Information Integration theory does not clearly fit in the behaviorist school, it does relate to the modeling theory of Bandura. Information Integration theory hypothesizes that each piece of information which an individual takes in is immediately assigned both *weight* and *position* on a scale with respect to a particular attitude (Anderson, 1973). The information may be given little weight because it is perceived as propaganda or it may receive great weight as the pronouncement of an authoritative source. Also, as the "credibility" of the model affects the success of the modeling technique, so, too, the characteristics of the communicator-of-information affect the attitude change in Information Integration. The individual places this weighted information onto a scale of agreement or disagreement with the present attitude stance. New information which is positive and from a valued source may move a negative attitude more toward the positive. Negative information may move the same attitude further toward the negative end of the scale. Anderson (1973) does not imply that this integration is a conscious process, that is, the person behaves *as if* this assignment of weight and position occurred, whether or not she is aware that she is doing it. Further, the attitude value assignment occurs immediately so that if the specific bit of verbal information is forgotten it nevertheless has already impacted upon the attitudes of the individual. Conversely, communication which comes from a source with low credibility may demonstrate a "sleeper effect" (Aiken, 1980). Once the source is forgotten, the message increases in its effect on the attitude. Fishbein and Coombs (1974); Nosanchuk (1972) and Elam (1974) present research that supports the Information Integration Theory.

COMMUNICATIONS

Since the previous theories have discussed the importance of the model or communicator of information, we will make a slight digression from theory here to present some research about communications. Bersheid and Walster (1979, as cited in Travers, 1982) recognize *three aspects of communication*: the *communicator*, the communication itself and the receiver.

Communicator. Perhaps the most clearly recognized attribute of a "good" communicator is expertness or credibility. As suggested above, however, the effect of this characteristic may fade as the receiver forgets from whom he received his information. Overheard information that relates to the listener appears to have greater influence than communication directed toward the listener. If I overhear you say that I talk too much and that is something I want to work on, I am more likely to change than if you tell me directly to cut down on the amount of chatter I produce. Also there is some evidence to suggest that the greater difference between the attitude of the listener and that of the communicator, the greater the likelihood of a change in attitude of the listener.

Some characteristics of the speaker which have no real relationship to the information still affect the success of the communication. If the speaker is attractive (this is not a direct effect but is mediated by whether or not the listener chooses to listen to the speaker or is there by force), recognized as more competent than his peers, "gregarious, and tends to belong to the top crust of the social class with which he identified" (Travers, 1982, p. 395), he will have greater effect on the listener. Further, the speaker who in some clear way is archtype of the group to which he is allied is a better communicator than "one of the gang."

Communication. The communication itself has a greater effect if it is surprising, that is, contains unexpected information, than if it has nearly all familiar information (Travers, 1982). The other major finding in this research area is that presenting both sides of an argument changes the attitudes of a more intelligent audience but a one-sided argument works better with the less intelligent.

Receiver. The receiver of information also plays a significant part in the success of the communication. In everyday life individuals tend to seek out information which corresponds to what they already believe and therefore leave themselves less open to the possibility of attitude change. Individuals are much more likely to go to a speaker or read an article or subscribe to print media which they believe will support their positions than they are to spend time and money listening to those with whom they are likely to argue. Notice how often people seek advice from those whom they expect to agree with their decisions and may even avoid contact with those who have disagreed before. This effect may be slightly mitigated by a research orientation or those who are highly educated and therefore trained to seek the opposite information. There is, however, no clear cut relationship between intelligence and educational level and suggestibility, that is, how open to attitude change the receiver is. The intelligent are more likely persuaded by information that they had not thought of before, whereas the less intelligent or younger individual may be more easily changed by relatively simplistic arguments. One rather clear finding of the research into characteristics of listeners is that women tend to be more easily persuaded than men. McGuire (1969) suggests that since women are trained to be better listeners, they hear more of the communication which results in greater attitude change. Interestingly, a fairly high degree of modifiability is associated with either very high or very low self-esteem, whereas those in the middle range tend to be almost totally resistent to change.

A final characteristic of the listener which has been well researched is dogmatism or authoritarianism versus egalitarianism. As the labels suggest dogmatic people tend to be very clear in their beliefs and have a very low tolerance for ambiguity. Egalitarian people, on the other hand, find it rather easy to take in and relate to information from opposing sides of an argument. Although they have their own attitudes toward any concept they can still tolerate information and even memorize information which refutes their attitude. Contrary to intuitive belief, dogmatic people are often more easily changed than egalitarian individuals. Apparently, dogmatic people in ordinary circumstances scrupulously avoid contact with those who oppose their views, whereas this is not true of egalitarians. Thus, when dogmatic people cannot avoid this confrontation, for example, when their favorite candidate is not indeed elected, they are more likely to change their perceptions of the candidate than the egalitarian who was initially opposed to the candidate. Since the egalitarian can tolerate opposing information, the need to change is less for him than for the authoritarian individual. The new office-holder is now the authoritarian's leader so cannot also be "stupid" or "corrupt." Thus, the dogmatic individual changes while the egalitarian simply adds this new information to the package.

COGNITIVE THEORIES

Balance Theory. Heider (1946) produced one of the first of the various cognitive consistency theories. He sees the individual as fitting into a system. The person, P, is accompanied in the system by other people, O, and non-human entities, X. Further two basic types of relationships exist in the system: Liking (L) and Units (U). Liking implies all sorts of positive affect; units are things that belong together. Actually the functioning of the system is quite simple. I expect the individual that I like to have similar likes, that is, to like and dislike the same objects that I like and dislike. Conversely, I expect those I dislike to like the things I dislike and dislike the things that I like. The first scenario describes balance in the system and therefore no change is needed. If, however, those persons I dislike like the same things I do or P whom I like dislikes things I like the system is in imbalance. In order for it to reach homeostatis (the desirable goal, similar to equilibrium), I must either change my attitude toward the person or change my attitude toward the concept. For Heider, then, maintaining relationships with other individuals causes me to change my attitudes toward both people and objects.

Congruity. The congruity theory of Osgood and Tannenbaum (1955) extends Heider's model by quantifying the degree of relationship in the model. As in Heider's system, if a valued friend and I have the same evaluation of an object or concept, then, no change is called for. If, however, the valued friend and I have opposite evaluations of the same object, I must either change my evaluation of the object or of the friend. Different from Heider's model, however, the process of semantic differential used in assigning a level of value to the friend and the object quantifies the degree of value. In the earlier model the statement of relationship was either positive or negative. The Osgood and Tannenbaum model allows the experimenter to assign a degree of expected change resulting from a quantified imbalance. For example, each person and concept are assigned a degree of positive or negative assertion from -3 to +3. If the individual values the concept at +3 and is told that the valued friend assigned a -2 to the same concept a greater change in attitude can be expected than if the individual chooses +3 and the friend chooses +1. The closer the two numbers of the person and her friend, the less she is called upon to change. A wide differentiation between the individual's choice and the source's choice, however, usually leads to disbleief, that is, the individual does not change her attitude because she believes that the valued source must have been misunderstood or misquoted or some such. The attempt to change attitudes by presenting nearly opposite viewpoint, then, can ultimately backfire.

Intra-attitudinal Inconsistency. The Intra-attitudinal Inconsistency Theory implies that the cognitive and affective aspects of an attitude which one holds must be consistent or the attitude will become unstable (Rosenberg, 1960). In an effort to return the attitude to homeostasis or equilibrium, the individual either: rejects the communication, or other force, which caused the instability and returns to the original attitude resulting in no change; isolates the affective and cognitive aspects of the attitude and maintains them in a compartmentalized state resulting in no change; or accommodates to the new information, thereby achieving a new stable attitude through attitude change. Some individuals, for example, egalitarians, may be more successful at maintaining compartmentalization than others, for example, authoritarians. Both groups, however, have two avenues for resistence to change and only one for change.

Cognitive Dissonance. A well-researched consistency theory is that of Leon Festinger's (1957) Cognitive Dissonance. Festinger (1957) holds that an individual cannot possess simultaneously two attitudes which are logically inconsistent. If the individual attempts to assimilate these two inconsistent attitudes, dissonance occurs. Dissonance causes the greatest "discomfort" when commitment to an attitude is high and the individual's self-esteem is on the line. For example, Carlsmith, Collins and Helmreich (1966) asked subjects to lie about an issue either face-to-face or in an anonymous essay. The researchers also manipulated the incentive for lying (either high, $5.00, or low, $.50). They found that face-to-face lying for low incentives produced more attitude change than face-to-face lying for high incentives. With anonymous essays, however, the reverse was true, that is, high incentives caused more attitude change. Being perceived as a liar is rather ego-damaging for most people. Since the low incentive people could not blame their lying on incentive, they had to change their attitude to prevent the "punishment" of being liars. Another related type of research (Jones and Brehm, 1967) shows that listeners who voluntarily listen to lecturers who hold views opposite to their own are less likely to change their attitude if the speaker is perceived as likeable. Again, the one who listens to the unpleasant speaker has no "excuse" for his behavior, whereas the likeable speaker is enjoyable regardless of what he says. Insko, et. al., (1975) implies that dissonance is related to locus of control. With a large reward/incentive the subject can claim, "The experimenter made me do it." The subject with a small reward/incentive must take responsibility for her own actions. Cognitive Dissonance, then, puts the individual in discomfort. In some situations the only way to allay that discomfort is through a change in attitude.

INOCULATION

Inoculation theory relates more clearly to resistance to attitude change than it does to attitude change itself. A religious establishment sending out missionaries or a nation sending out a diplomat wants to assure that their emmisaries will maintain their attitudes toward the "parent" organization and resist the influence of those opposing its views. Inoculation theory is analogous to the biological system where one receives a vaccine containing a small amount of a given disease so that the natural immune system will build-up appropriate antibodies and prevent a full-scale bout with the threatening germs. McGuire (1964) hypothesized two steps in the inoculation process. A person needs both mild attacks on the original belief system and refutational arguments against the attacks. The mild attacks purportedly motivate the individual to build a defense system and the arguments supply the information needed to combat the attacks. McGuire has also examined the results of forewarning the individual that an attack will happen and threats to the person if he does not defend the original belief as well as reassurances that he can, indeed, be a competent defender. While some of the intervening variables in the system need better definition, the theory has generated some interesting research.

SUMMARY

Several theories, then, arising from various schools of psychology suggest methods of helping people control or change their attitudes. While the research is still largely in its infancy, the practitioner can glean some principles with high probability of effectiveness to aid students in attitude formation and change. The remainder of the chapter will discuss memory, transfer and evaluation as they relate to attitudes.

MEMORY

Since attitudes are not well-defined and tend to be largely unconscious, specific formulations of attitudes are not well remembered. One cannot often say, for example, how she responded to specific questions on an attitude survey a year ago whereas, if the questions involved adequately learned verbal information it would be fairly simple to remember. Also, since attitudes are not typically in conscious thought we do not recognize when our attitudes are changing, therefore, we assume that the attitudes that we have today are the attitudes we have always had toward a particular attitude-object.*

Given this state of lack of awareness of our own attitudes, three theories of memory explain how we remember or forget attitudes: subsumption, interference, and construction.

Subsumption. Subsumption helps explain how we remember

---

*Attitudes may be in conscious thought if we specifically set out to change a particular attitude within ourselves, for example "I am going to learn to enjoy mystery novels."; or if we set out to expose ourselves to situations in which our attitudes are likely to be changed, for example, consciousness-raising seminars.

specific information related to attitudes. In fact we do not remember the specific information, rather it is subsumed into the attitude that we have already established about a specific attitude object. The specific bit of information or the particular instance in which we acted upon the attitude is frequently "forgotten." The memory of the attitude, that is the global category of "attitudes about X," is expanded and "remembered."

Interference. Interference applies to attitude memory in terms of new information interfering with old attitudes. We no longer remember the old attitude but rather remember the new attitude. Again, this may all happen with no conscious awareness. Retroactive interference perhaps better represents what happens in attitude memory. The prior attitude is so well "remembered" or established that new information and experience is blocked by the old information. If I have a negative attitude toward American Indians, because I believe they are lazy, an experience of one hard-working Indian or even a whole group of hard-working Indians will not extinguish my belief that Indians are lazy. Or if I believe that most people on welfare are on welfare because they do not wish to work and believe that the system "owes" them something, one situation in which I develop a positive attitude toward specific welfare recipients who either desire to work or are physically unable to work will not cause me to forget my general attitude toward the welfare system. Well-established attitudes, then, seem to interfere with the learning of new attitudes. The old attitudes are well-remembered and the new attitudes are "forgotten."

Construction. Constructive memory seems to explain the process that occurs when someone says, "What is your attitude toward oregano?" Unless we are grocers, gourmet cooks, allergic to oregano or some other similar category we probably do not have a ready answer to the question. Rather we construct our memory out of past experience of interactions with oregano. In a sense we look over these past interactions; e.g., we typically choose dishes from a menu that are heavy on oregano; I always have enough oregano readily available for cooking in my own home. From this "evidence" we construct a memory of our attitude toward oregano. Do not imagine that this process is clearly and carefully considered. Rather, a very rapid search of our prior experiences occurs. The questioner may not wait long at all for our answer. We appear to have an immediate response. The process of construction works quickly. Further, since attitudes toward food are often made conscious through questioning we might find the oregano question simpler to respond to than a question that explored our attitude toward books with plastic covers or green filing cabinets. It might take us a little longer to construct a memory of our attitude toward these.

Little empirical research into memory for attitudes exists. This results partly from the emphasis of memory research in the verbal information area and partly from the difficulty of assessing attitudes clearly in order to ascertain that they are remembered at a later date.

EVALUATION

In Chapter Three the authors pointed out the difficulty of achieving validity and reliability in attitude measures. In addition, any measures that use rating scales or outside observers for evaluating attitudes can run into serious problems in _objectivity_. The observer herself has an attitude toward every attitude object as well as every learner. The attitudes within the observer can significantly limit the objectivity with which the observer observes. This problem is especially prevalent among untrained observers.

Measurement Tools. In spite of all these pitfalls there are some tools that have been developed in an attempt to measure attitudes. They must always be used with the above limitations in mind. _Observation_ is certainly one way in which educators infer attitudes. We watch what our students do and make some decisions about what attitudes must be mediating their behavior. If, for example, students groan, shuffle their feet and move slowly when I announce that it is time for arithmetic class, I may infer that they have a negative attitude toward arithmetic. This observation can be enhanced in objectivity somewhat by use of a _checklist_ so that we have some structure to the observation. Also if we make the observation as unobtrusive as possible we are likely to record behaviors that demonstrate typical attitudes rather than attitudes the student wants us to believe she has. _Structured inter-_

views can also assess attitudes. In such an interview I ask all the students the same questions, and frequently a clarification or explanation question follows up on the original question. For example, I might ask a student, "How much do you like the dance class that you are taking?" I follow up with "What specific elements do you like and/or dislike?" A further refinement of this may involve either an interview or a paper and pencil test where I ask the student to scale her response. So I say "On a scale of one to ten where ten is high, how much do you like your dance class?" Then I give the specific elements and the student rates each on the same scale, e.g., "How much do you like the teacher? the techniques? the practice?, etc. The student scales each one.

One recent measurement tool looks not at the individual student's attitude toward the learning situation, but rather at the social climate that has been created in the learning situation. Walberg and Moos (1980) describe the dimensions of social climate as revolving around three major categories: relationships, personal growth, or goal orientation and system management or system change. The relationships category examines how people in the environment interact with each other, what kind of communication they use and how interdependent they are. Personal growth refers to measures of the basic goals. How does personal enhancement occur in this setting? System management or change is concerned with how orderly the situation is, how clear the goals and rules are made to the participants and how innovation occurs. Walberg and Moos have investigated and delineated how measures in each of these areas can help the instructor look at instructional systems that enhance learner attitudes toward achievement of the goals of the setting and thereby produce a greater likelihood that learners will achieve successfully.

Evaluation, then, is rather nebulous in attitude domains. Validity, reliability and objectivity are at risk and the tools for measurement are in their infancy.

TRANSFER

Most attitude researchers and theoriticians agree that attitudes do transfer laterally from one situation to another. How broad that transfer is relates in part to the breadth of the attitude object. It may be a relatively specific attitude object, e.g., "I like to travel on Amtrak from Albany." Or the attitude object may be more global. "I hate to travel on trains," or even, "I hate to travel." Obviously the broader the attitude object the broader the transfer that results.

As in all transfer the similarity of attitude objects for the individual causes transfer to occur when the external observer might not expect that it would. For example, if I know that a certain of my acquaintances dislikes associating with immigrants, I would expect him to avoid circumstances that would lead to interaction with persons of a lower social class. The basis of his negative attitude toward immigrants is their frequent poverty. From the outside, however, this basis for transfer is not readily apparent. Attitudes, then, do transfer, but not always in predictable ways.

Attitudes and Motivation. For the practitioner one relevant aspect of transfer of attitudes is how attitudes relate to motivation. For example, if a teacher decides to change his students' attitudes toward arithmetic, it is probably not for any particular need to have every one love arithmetic. Rather he attempts to change the attitude toward arithmetic in order to make his task of motivating his students to do arithmetic activities and therefore succeed in arithmetic classes. Walberg and Moos (1980) showed that attitudes do correlate with student performance. Positive attitudes among the classroom group correlated with success in the learning situation, whereas, negative attitudes related to lower performance among the students. It is intuitively satisfying to assume that the positive-attitude dimensions of the social climate "motivated" the students to perform differently in those situations.

Attitudes and Behavior. A related topic to the attitude-motivation connection, and one more typical in the attitude literature, is the relationship between attitudes and behavior. Clearly there is some relationship. The very definition of attitudes used by many investigators suggests that attitudes mediate behavior, meaning that attitudes make some behaviors far more likely to occur than others. For those who hold a three-component definition of attitudes, behavior is one of the components. In this definition, when behavior is not directly related to the attitude the attitude is incomplete.

Several of the theories that were considered above discuss or imply a relationship between attitudes and behavior. Ajzen and Fishbein (1980) theorize that attitudes together with norms (or the beliefs that an individual holds that others think he should or should not do something) combine to form an intention (read motivation?) to perform specific behavior.

Social learning theory indicates that individuals will do the modeled action in a similar situation. Do the observers of the model seek out the similar situations to try out the behavior? Are they "motivated" to find opportunities to perform the modeled behavior? The advertisers who use social learning theory as a basis of their campaigns, probably assume that this motivation exists.

Certainly the Balance theory of Heider (1946) suggests that disequilibrium in the system motivates individuals to change some attitudes and expressions of those attitudes toward other individuals and objects in the system.

Inoculation theory aims at motivating the individual to maintain specific attitudes and further to develop clear behavior (argumentation skills) to preserve those attitudes.

Although the above discussion addresses the question of whether attitudes affect behavior, the opposite hypothesis (behavior affects attitudes) can also be explored. Surely the Intra-Attitudinal consistency theory and the Self-Perception theory would suggest this as the correct direction of the relationship between attitudes and behavior.

In this section we have looked at the relationship between attitudes and behavior, especially as it relates to the motivation problems of practitioners. A good review of the relationship can be found in Calder and Ross (1974).

Attitudes, then, clearly do transfer from one

situation to another. The "jury is still out," however, on the question of how broadly these attitudes transfer. Do they in fact directly or indirectly transfer to the behavior of the individual and cause different behavior or is it the behaviors that transfer to the attitudes?

REFERENCES

Aiken, L.R. Attitude measurement & research. In D. Payne (Ed.). _New directions in testing: Recent developments in affective measurement._ San Francisco: Jossey-Bass, 1980, 1-24.

Ajzen, I. & Fishbein, M. _Understanding attitudes and predicting social behavior._ Englewood Cliffs, N.J.: Prentice-Hall, 1980.

Allport, G.W. Attitudes. In C. Murchison (Ed.). _Handbook of social psychology._ Vol. 2. Worcester, MA: Clark University Press, 1935, 798-884.

Anderson, N.H. Information integration theory applied to attitudes about U.S. Presidents. _Journal of Educational Psychology_, 1973, _64_, 1-8.

Bandura, A. _Principles of behavior modification._ New York: Holt, Rinehart & Winston, 1969.

Bandura, A. & McDonald, F.J. The influence of social reinforcement and the behavior of models in shaping children's moral judgements. _Journal of Abnormal and Social Psychology_, 1963, _67_.

Bandura, A. & Mischel, W. The influence of models in modifying delay of gratification patterns. _Journal of Personality and Social Psychology_, 1965, _2_, 698-705.

Barnes, A.C. Attitudes: Positive changes through the study of literature. _The Clearing House_, 1972, _47_, 25-29.

Bem, D.J. _Beliefs, attitudes, and human affiars._ Belmont, CA: Brooks/Cole, 1970.

Calder, B.J. & Ross, M. _Attitudes and behavior._ Morristown, N.J.: General Learning Press, 1973.

Carlsmith, J.M., Collins, B.E. & Helmreich, R.L. Studies in forced compliance: I. The effect of pressure for compliance on attitude change produced by face-to-face role-playing and anonymous essay writing. _Journal of Personality and Social_

REFERENCES CONTINUED

Psychology, 1966, 4, 1-13.

Chittendon, G.E. An experimental study in modifying assertive behavior in young children. Monographs of the Society for Research in Child Development. 1942, 7, (Serial No. 31).

Doob, L.W. The behavior of attitudes. Psychological Review, 1947, 54, 135-156.

Elam, S. Attitude formation: Direct experience best. NASSP Bulletin, 1974, 58, 50-53.

Festinger, L.A. A theory of cognitive dissonance. Stanford, CA: Stanford University Press, 1957.

Festinger, L. & Carlsmith, J.M. Cognitive consequences of forced compliance. Journal of Abnormal and Social Psychology. 1959, 58, 203-210.

Fishbein, M. An investigation of the relationships between beliefs about an object and the attitude toward that object. Human Relations, 1963, 16, 233-240.

Fishbein, M. & Coombs, F.S. Basis of decision: An attitudinal analysis of voting behavior. Journal of Applied Social Psychology, 1974, 4, 95-124.

Gagne, R.M. The conditions of learning. (3rd Ed.) New York: Holt, Rinehart and Winston, 1977.

Heider, F. Attitudes and cognitive organization. Journal of Psychology, 1946, 21, 107-112.

Himmelfarb, S. & Eagly, A.H. Readings in attitude change. New York: Wiley, 1974.

Insko, C.A. Worchel, S., Folger, R., & Kutkus, A. A balance theory interpretation of dissonance. Psychological Review. 1975, 82, 169-183.

Jones, R.A. & Brehm, J.W. Attitudinal effects of communicator attractiveness when one chooses to listen. Journal of Personality and Social Psychology, 1967, 6, 64-70.

REFERENCES CONTINUED

Katz, D. The functional approach to the study of attitudes. Public Opinion Quarterly, 1960, 24, 163-204.

Katz, D. & Stotland, E. A preliminary statement of a theory of attitude structure and change. In S. Koch (Ed.), Psychology: A study of a science (Vol. 3). New York: McGraw-Hill, 1959, 423-475.

Kelman, H.C. Compliance, identification, and internalization: Three processes of attitude change. Journal of Conflict Resolution, 1958, 2, 51-60.

Krech, K. & Crutchfield, R.S. Theory and problems of social psychology. New York: McGraw-Hill, 1948.

McGuire, W.J. Inducing resistance to persuasion: Some contemporary approaches. In L. Berkowitz (Ed.), Advances in experimental social psychology. Vol. 1. New York: Academic Press, 1964, 191-229.

McGuire, W.J. The nature of attitudes and attitude change. In G. Lindzey and E. Aronson (Eds.), The handbook of social psychology. (2nd ed., Vol. 3). Reading, MA: Addison-Wesley, 1969, 136-314.

Newcomb, T.M. Social psychology. New York: Dryden, 1950.

Nosanchuck, T.A., Mann, L., & Pletka, I. Attitude change as a function of commitment, decisioning and information level of pretest. Educational and Psychological Measurement. 1972, 32, 377-386.

Osgood, E.G. & Tannenbaum, P.H. The principle of congruity in the prediction of attitude change. Psychological Review, 1955, 62, 42-55.

Roessler, R.L. & Brogden, W.J. Conditioned differentiation of vasoconstriction to sub-vocal stimuli. American Journal of Psychology, 1943, 56, 78-86.

Rosenberg, M.J. An analysis of affective-cognitive consistency. In C.I. Hovland and M.J. Rosenberg

REFERENCES CONTINUED

(Eds.) Attitude organization and change. New Haven, CT: Yale University Press, 1960, 15-64.

Staats, A.W. & Staats, C.K. Attitudes established by classical conditioning. Journal of Abnormal and Social Psychology, 1958, 57, 37-40.

Travers, R.M.W. Essentials of learning. 5th Ed. New York: MacMillan, 1982.

Triandis, H.C. Attitude and attitude change. New York: Wiley, 1971.

Walberg, H.J. & Moos, R.H. Assessing educational environment. In D. Payne (Ed.), New directions for testing: Recent developments in affective measurement. San Francisco: Jossey-Bass, 1980.

This chapter covers the hierarchy of skills subsumed under intellectual skills, presenting the theories and models of both Gagne and Merrill. Task analysis procedures which contribute to good instructional planning and which assure prerequisite skills are presented.

1. What distinguishes intellectual skills from verbal information?

2. What role does practice play in the acquisition of intellectual skills?

3. How generalizable are intellectual skills?

4. What theoretical frameworks inform instructional techniques?

CHAPTER NINE

INTELLECTUAL SKILLS

INTRODUCTION

Gagne (1972) defines intellectual skills as capabilities the student acquires that enable him to deal with his environment symbolically. Intellectual skills are potentials for applied behaviors. They need to be distinguished from verbal information, the capability to tell about something, and from cognitive strategies, the underlying management system for thought. Gagne (1968) believes that positive transfer from subordinate pre-requisite intellectual skills is the key to learning new intellectual skills. Pre-requisite skills are delineated in terms of a learning hierarchy that orders eight different, increasingly complex kinds of learning. Most curriculum developers are now utilizing a Gagne-like analysis to derive learning hierarchies for sequencing instruction. Research in the area indicates that some success is probable if developers are cautious about differentiating between specific and general transfer and between content and task analysis.

<u>Distinctions between Intellectual Skills and other Domains</u>. Gagne (1968) carefully discriminates between intellectual skills and verbal information. The former

are things the individual can do; the latter are things the individual can tell. The ability to define "pie crust" reflects verbal information; the ability to read a recipe and make a pie crust reflects intellectual skills. Being able to use a definition to determine if an item is a member of a class or concept is an intellectual skill. (According to Markle (1975), an intellectual skill many students have not learned and which is poorly taught!). Other examples of intellectual skills are formulating propositions in syllogistic form, noting effects of factors, constructing predictions, making and testing hypotheses, distinguishing salient features (Gagne, 1968).

The following are not intellectual skills: knowing that 2+2=4; that hot air rises; that people come in different shapes; feeling sad; loving your neighbor; approaching problems impulsively, wholistically, or analytically; hiring a pre-operational thinker or a formal operational thinker. Intellectual skills are rules used to interact with the environment. They are not as content free as cognitive strategies, not as specific as verbal information and attitudes. Being able to verbalize an intellectual skill (rule) is not an indication or necessity of possession of that capability. Performance is the key. Intellectual skills are performed on and with verbal information, however, and in that sense are not content free. Being able to compute sums requires some knowledge of the numbers and signs being manipulated. The important distinction is that summing (an intellectual skill) can be performed on a variety of numbers and objects (verbal information).

Intellectual Skills Hierarchy. Intellectual skills are learned as a result of positive transfer from other relevant intellectual skills (Gagne, 1977, 1973, 1968). Unlike verbal information, intellectual skills are related to each other in a sub-ordinate to super-ordinate pattern. Very specific, vertical transfer is involved. Within a neo-behaviorist theoretical framework, Gagne seems to be explaining intellectual skill learning as a cumulative associative network reinforced by success. This logical progression from simpler to more complex skills makes analysis of learning hierarchies possible and worthwhile. Instruction can then be structured so that the appropriate associations and the reinforcement of success will occur. (See Gagne, Mayor, Garstens and

Paradise, 1962, for an example of a learning hierarchy for the summation of numbers.)

Gagne (1973, p. 21) notes the following characteristics of learning hierarchies as he and his colleagues have defined them.

1. They are descriptions of successively achievable intellectual skills, each of which is stated as a performance class (e.g., "Given columns of two-place numbers and the instruction to add, solves to find the sum"). Each specific skill thus described is placed in a hierarchy in such a way that the skills subordinate to a given skill are hypothesized (or at some point empirically demonstrated) to contribute substantially to the learning of the given skill, in the sense of exhibiting positive transfer to it.

2. Learning hierarchies provide descriptions <u>only</u> of intellectual skills, not of verbal information, cognitive strategies, motivational factors or performance sets. All of these latter variables are acknowledged to contribute to the learning of any of the intellectual skills described in the hierarchy, but the intention is not to describe them specifically.

3. In essence, then, what each "box" of the hierarchy describes is only <u>those prerequisite skills that must be recalled</u> at the moment of learning so that this critical "internal" component of the total stimulus situation will be present.

4. In theoretical terms, a hierarchy is not intended to be a description of an entire sequence. It indicates to the designer of instruction: Whatever else is present in the learning situation (verbal instruction, sets, etc.), these particular pre-requisite intellectual skills <u>must</u> be available to the learner. This usually means they are recalled by the learner at the time the new learning occurs. Accordingly, a reasonable sequence of instruction can be designed to insure that these subordinate skills are successively

> mastered. There is nothing fundamentally immutable about such a sequence, in a theoretical sense; it is basically only a matter of convenience, and some hierarchies (or instructional sequences based upon them) may indeed be found to "work" better than others, on the average. The theoretical requirement is only that the stated pre-requisite skills for any given skill must be available to the learner as a part of the stimulus situation at the time learning occurs.

In developing a learning hierarchy for a to-be-learned intellectual skill (terminal behavior), the developer repeatedly asks "What must the learner be able to _do_, before he can perform this skill?" The heuristics of hierarchy development demand that the developer start with the desired terminal performance and work backwards -- just the opposite of developing an instructional plan. Following this procedure produces a diagram with one or more skills on each level of the hierarchy sub-ordinate to a skill on the next higher level. The process is regenerated until "a level is reached for which all behaviors in subsequent levels are, without instruction, possessed by the learner" (Eisenberg and Walesser, 1971, p. 245).

Gagne's well-known hierarchy model encompasses four of what Gagne (1977) calls Basic Processes of Learning and four levels of intellectual skills. Signal learning, stimulus-response learning, chaining, and verbal association learning are hypothesized to be basic to all forms of learning. These are low-level processes that regulate the learning of discrete pieces of information, specific motor acts, and emotional association. As such they contribute to the learning of intellectual skills as basic building blocks. The four upper-level processes (discrimination learning, concept learning, rule learning, and problem solving) are intellectual skills reflecting rule-governed behavior. Problem solving involves learning to combine rules into higher-order rules that address novel situations (a cognitive strategy). Consequently, rule following is pre-requisite. Rules involve the combination of concepts to effect a relationship. Therefore, classifying is a pre-requisite. Using a concept, classifying, requires responding to things or events as a class of things or events. To perform this skill, a learner must first be able to discriminate.

Prerequisites. Rule-governed behavior demonstrates a prerequisite acquisition of concepts and discriminations. A rule is a prediction of a relationship between two or more concepts. A concept is an organization of environmental input. The organization is dependent upon similarities and differences among the inputs. Recognition of those same-different dimensions is a discrimination. To learn a rule, one must first learn to discriminate, then to form concepts, then to combine concepts in relational patterns that consistently predict reality.

INTELLECTUAL SKILL PRE-REQUISITES

Use relationships to interact with environment -- Problem Solve

Combine concepts in meaningful way -- Make Rules

Organize into classes or categories -- Create Concepts

Discriminate salient features

Receive sensory stimulation

Figure 1. Skills hierarchy

Gagne and Briggs (1979) reiterate the essential condition of prerequisite learning to the learning of intellectual skills (see fig. 1). The prerequisites for discrimination learning are the abilities to receive sensory stimulation and to respond. The prerequisites for concrete concept learning are the abilities to make appropriate discriminations. Prerequisite to rule learning is the ability to organize input into concepts. The essentiality of prerequisites makes evaluation of learning at each step crucial.

Evaluation. Imagine that you are teaching the rule "Put your shoes under the bed." This rule contains the relationship among five concepts. Each concept must be learned prior to the rule, and each concept requires discrimination learning. Let us use the concept "bed" to illustrate the evaluation of prerequisite intellectual skills. At the discrimination level, the learner must be able to make same-different judgements on attributes of beds and non-beds. Shown flat surfaces and curved surfaces, the learner must be able to indicate that these attributes are different. If she cannot make this difference judgement, she cannot learn to organize environmental input into "bed" and "not-bed" categories. Thorough evaluation at the discrimination level would assess the ability of the learner to make same-different judgements on all relevant attributes of the concept "bed."

Success of the discrimination learning would enable concept learning to ensue. Exposure to many instances of the class of beds, noticing which attributes are always present and which vary from instance to instance should lead to concept learning. To evaluate whether the concept has been learned, assessment must require the learner to identify several instances of the concept which vary on irrelevant dimensions. A valid test for our concept of "bed" might include these instances: a brass twin bed, a wooden bunk bed, a water bed, a velvet sofa, a leather recliner, a kitchen stool, a table, a pile of blankets, two pillows, a bedspread. The successful learner should be able to identify the beds and reject the non-beds.

When the learner can demonstrate mastery of all five concepts in the rule "Put your shoes under the bed", she has the prerequisites for learning the rule. At this point verbal instruction or demonstration that illustrates the correct order or pattern of relationships among the concepts will promote rule learning. Evaluation of rule learning should consist of identifying and/or showing instances of correct relationships. To assess mastery of our shoe rule, we could place a pair of the learner's shoes, a toy, a blouse, two apples and a pair of shoes not belonging to the learner on a table in a room that also contains a dresser, a closet, a bed, a toy chest, and a chair. To be really thorough in our assessment, we would repeat this evaluation with different prompts in a different room.

Our shoe rule is relatively easy to learn once the prerequisite concepts are known. The relationships among the concepts are quite straightforward. It would be quite difficult to confuse the order by "Putting the bed under your shoes," or "undering the put shoes your bed." Not all rules reflect an obvious order of things, however, The rule to "open air vents before opening the door of your wood stove" is not so straightforward. In this instance, the instruction and the assessment must take into account the effects of altering the order or pattern of relationships among the concepts. Truly successful learning may be dependent upon building a network of rules (a schema). Learning that "Higher heat increases chimney draw" and that "Smoke is made up of small particles that can be combusted" and that "Increasing the air supply increases the speed of combustion" would all increase the likelihood that the rule "Open air vents before opening wood stove door" would be remembered with the concepts in the correct order.

Procedural Bugs. Brown and Burton (1978) have done some very interesting work on evaluating intellectual skill errors in math learning. Using computer terminology, they call rule errors "bugs." Their research reveals that most math errors (bugs) are the result of using inaccurate or incomplete rules in a systematic way. By studying student errors, instructors can deduce the incorrect rule being used and thus supply appropriate remediation. An example they provide (p. 157) is this:

$$
\begin{array}{r}
41 \\
+\ 9 \\
\hline
50
\end{array}
\qquad
\begin{array}{r}
328 \\
+917 \\
\hline
1345
\end{array}
\qquad
\begin{array}{r}
989 \\
+\ 52 \\
\hline
1141
\end{array}
\qquad
\begin{array}{r}
66 \\
+887 \\
\hline
1053
\end{array}
\qquad
\begin{array}{r}
216 \\
+\ 13 \\
\hline
229
\end{array}
$$

Deduce the incorrect rule and predict the answers the student would give to these problems.*

$$
\begin{array}{r}
446 \\
815 \\
\hline
\end{array}
\qquad
\begin{array}{r}
201 \\
399 \\
\hline
\end{array}
$$

They caution that instructors should not be quick to come to a conclusion about what the bug is because several different bugs may result in the same incorrect problem answer. They suggest that the instructor

*1361 and 700. The student continues to "carry" beyond appropriate column.

should generate at least two different bugs that could be causing the errors, then create a set of problems that will reveal which bug is actually causing the problem. This approach will prevent improper remediation on a procedural error that does not exist.

A diagnostic evaluation tool not suggested by Brown and Burton but used by others is to ask the learner to "talk" her way through several problems. A careful listener can often deduce the inappropriate rule being used. The remediation strategy suggested by Case (1978) and discussed in Chapter Seven addresses the problem of inappropriate or incomplete rule use.

A learning hierarchy for an intellectual skill is not an instructional plan. It is an analysis of the conditions that must be present if learning is to take place. The actual instruction may be inductive or deductive or random so long as it assures prerequisite skills are present. (This may include cues to recall prerequisite skills, instructions, or a prior teaching of prerequisite skills.) Of course, if a learning hierarchy is used by a curriculum developer to sequence a series of instructional units, logic would dictate an inductive approach. This would not preclude, however, using deductive, discovery instructional techniques for lessons within the sequence. It would preclude offering lessons in problem-solving prior to lessons in discriminating.

Merrill's Model. David Merrill (1971) has approached learned capabilities in a somewhat similar way. He identifies ten categories of learned behavior, adding "naming" and "complex skills" to the eight categories identified by Gagne. Merrill's paradigm is well-presented in his 1971 article. Behaviors in this model are organized from less-to-more complex in two dimensions. Merrill divides all learned behavior into four domains: Emotional, Psycho-motor, Memorization, and Complex Cognitive Behavior. These domains appear on the vertical axis of the model. Emotional behavior precedes and colors all other behaviors. The other three domains are conceptualized as progressive developments from a simple single unit learnings through combinations of single units to synthesis of larger units used differentially in different situations. Moving from Emotional Behavior through Psycho-motor Behavior and Memorization Behavior to Complex Cognitive

Behavior involves a progression from global, involuntary responses to consciously determined transfer responses. A second, horizontal dimension of the paradigm orders behaviors within each domain from less-to-more complex.

Merrill believes his hierarchy is more useful than Gagne's because it specifies observable performances. For example, classification behavior (concept learning) is defined as correctly identifying the class membership of a never previously experienced object or event. Such an approach, suggests Merrill, is conducive to developing more effective instructional sequences. Rather than starting with an objective implied by the subject matter, Merrill endorses starting with a desired behavioral level outcome, stating the psychological conditions for achieving that outcome, and then creating those conditions within the context of the subject matter.

Relationship between the Merrill and Gagne Paradigms. Merrill's paradigm seems an interesting mix of Gagne's domains of learning, types of intellectual skills and instructional theory. It echoes the five domains, but places them in a hierarchical relationship incompatible with Gagne's formulations. Gagne is quite clear in his later writings (1973, 1977, 1968) about limiting the hierarchical relationship to intellectual skills. He especially excludes verbal information learning from hierarchical patterning and makes a clear distinction between verbal association learning and meaningful verbal learning. In contrast, Merrill suggests that all memorization behavior is hierarchically ordered. As discussed in Chapters Three and Ten (Memory and Verbal Information), that supposition is not well supported by research. Merrill's Complex Cognitive Behavior appears to combine Gagne's concepts of intellectual skills and cognitive strategies. Since Merrill is primarily concerned with observable performance, the exclusion of underlying mental structure in his paradigm is consistent.

Combining different domains of learning in umbrella categories, however, makes utilization of the above Merrill model difficult. Since different instructional strategies are required for different domains, a task analysis based on this model would not provide a clear guide for developing instruction. Part of the difficulty lies in disengaging specific transfer from general transfer (Gagne, 1973) and content analysis from task analysis (Gagne, 1978). Specific transfer involves the direct influence of one intellectual skill on the acquisition of another specifically identified intellectual skill. For example, in Gagne's model, "Performing addition and subtraction of whole numbers" directly influences "Supplying other numerals for whole numbers, using the associative property." There are also general transfer influences on acquiring an intellectual skill that involve such things as intelligence, cognitive strategies, age of learner, etc. The confusion between content and task analysis arises from mixing analysis of what the learner must <u>tell</u> and what the learner must <u>do</u>, the distinction Gagne makes between verbal information and intellectual skills. A more recent model, that of Paul Merrill (1982), appears to overcome this problem.

The Paul Merrill model attempts to make the combination of content and process more usable to the nonvisually oriented practitioner. Using a rather traditional outlining technique, Merrill sets up three dimensions (See Fig. 2 & Fig. 3). The top-to-bottom dimension records the "when" or sequence of instruction. This dimension is not strictly hierarchical but rather occurs in the actual sequence that the behavior will take place "on the job." For example in the picture hanging model (Fig. 2) the student would learn to attach the wire before she learned to attach the bracket to the wall. The left-to-right dimension suggests "how" the instruction should take place. Thus, in order to make certain the wire is evenly attached (Fig. 2: IA) I would instruct the student to measure and mark. The left-to-right dimension answers "why" each step in the process should occur. In other words, the reason I teach my students to select the appropriate length and circumference screws (Fig. 2: I, B, I, a) is so that the student will not crack the frame when she attaches the screw. When the teacher uses such a model, the items farthest to the right of the outline (In Fig. 2 & 3: the small a's and b's) within each category are taught first and then the next set of items to the left and so on until one whole category (or Roman Numeral) is completed. Then the teacher moves to the next category lower on the page (Fig. 2: Roman Numeral II) and begins again at the farthest to the right. Merrill believes that this process works

HANGING A PICTURE

I. Attach a wire to the frame

A. Make certain that the wire is evenly attached.
1. Measure down both sides of frame.
2. Mark an even distance from the top and about one-third of the way down the frame.

B. Screw the eye-screws into each side of the picture frame at the marked spots.
1. Screw so that the screw does not crack the frame.
a. Select an appropriate length and circumference screw for the job.
b. Start the screw properly.
2. Screw directly into the wood so that there is no slant on the final placement.

C. Select an appropriate length and type of wire.
1. Select an appropriate weight for the picture.
a. Weigh the picture
b. Read the wire packages to determine the amount of weight each type will hold.
c. Select the type of wire which will support the measured weight of the picture.
2. Select a wire longer than the distance between the two eye-screws and shorter than the arc formed by tracing a circle between the two eye-screws and the top of the frame.
a. Measure these distances
b. Measure a length of wire between these two distances.

II. Attach the bracket to the wall

A. Decide at what height the picture will be hung.

ETC.

Figure 2. An example of the Merrill Model.

Intellectual Skills

READING A MAP

Task: Calculate the shortest distance along the fastest roads between two cities on a standard Road Map

I. Find the two cities on the map.

   A. Find the alphabetical listing of cities on the map
      1. Know that an alphabetical listing exists
      2. Use a search strategy to find the list.
   B. Find each of the cities in the alphabetical listing
      1. Use alphabetical-order skills (Not necessary but useful)
      2. Read the city names
   C. Note the location indicators on the alphabetical listing
      1. Recognize location indicators after city names
      2. Remember or write down the location indicators
   D. Find the intersection of the two location indicators on the map
      1. Recognize that location indicators match a matrix on the map
      2. Use the matrix system
         a. Find each location indicator on the edge of the map
         b. Visually or manually find the intersection of the two location indicators
         c. Visually or manually circle the "search area" of the intersection
   E. Find each city within the specified "search area"
      1. Visually scan the search area
      2. Recognize the name of the specified city

II. Locate the fastest roads between the two cities

   A. Realize that major roads (i.e. larger, better-paved roads) are usually faster roads than secondary roads (i.e. narrower, less-well-surfaced roads)
      1. Discriminate larger/smaller
      2. Discriminate well-paved/poorly paved

3. Discriminate fast/slow
4. Discriminate limited access/unlimited access

B. Read the map legend to find the road-type symbols
   1. Find the map legend
      a. Know that a map legend exists
      b. Know that map legends are <u>usually</u> found at the bottom edge of the map
      c. Use a search strategy to find the legend
   2. Read the road-type symbols on the map legend
      a. Discriminate between road-type symbols and other map legend information
      b. Discriminate major road markings from secondary road markings
      c. Find the hierarchy of road types among the secondary roads
         1. Know that a hierarchy of road-types exist based on road surface type and width of road
         2. Be able to order good, better, best

C. Find roads between two cities that are of the desired type

III. Estimate which road combination would be the shortest between the two specified cities.

A. Discriminate shorter from longer

B. Choose all the roads necessary to get from one city to the other
   1. Recognize that more than one road may be necessary to get from one city to the other
   2. Recognize that all chosen roads must intersect at some point
      a. Recognize an intersection of two roads
         (1) read the map legend to find the intersection symbols
            (a) discriminate intersection symbols from other information on the map legend
         (2) store intersection symbols in memory

b. Check to make sure that all roads intersect before selecting final route

The outline would continue in like manner considering such major headings as:

IV. Read the map legend to find the mileage symbols

V. Find the mileage symbols along the chosen route

VI. Add up the numbers between the mileage indicators on all the chosen roads between the two cities.

VII. Compare mileage to alternative routes

Figure 3. An exmaple of the Merrill Model

well because learning occurs in a logical sequence both hierarchically and in terms of content organization. The teacher uses the top-to-bottom schema not because category I is a necessary prerequisite for category II, but rather because it is the sequence in which the behavior will be used when carrying out a task. Within each category the behaviors farthest to the right are necessary prerequisites to those left of it. Figure 3 is another example of the model. Notice that with a more complex learning objective the dimensions are not as categorical. For example, in Figure 3 there is a much greater intrusion of Verbal Information as well as a greater reliance on very basic intellectual skills (Fig. 3: II B, 2, C, 2).

This model is easier to construct for most teachers than the Gagne hierarchy because it is a more familiar format. The process, however, is the same. Within each category the instructional designer breaks down the behavior by asking, "What does the individual need to be able to do to complete this task?" He continues asking this question moving farther to the right with each prerequisite behavior until a behavior may be assumed as an entering behavior of the learners. Just as in Gagne's system, the designer and teacher work in opposite directions. In Merrill's system, the designer works from left to right in construction while the teacher teaches from right to left.

Transfer. Vertical transfer is the key to intellectual skill learning. The use of specific or identical elements from prior learning is a necessary condition for intellectual learning. The relationship between rule learning and higher-order rule learning (problem-solving) also has elements of vertical transfer. Successful problem-solving depends upon the availability of prerequisite rules and information in addition to the cognitive strategies which control and direct a novel combination of those prior learnings.

Other categories of transfer are not so neatly tied to the domain of intellectual skills. Some discriminations, concepts and rules have great lateral and far transfer; others appear to have only vertical transfer, if they are retained at all. Since intellectual skills can be learned in isolation from other learning within the narrow confines of a task hierarchy, the opportunity to connect the skill to other potentially relevant learning may not occur. Analogous to the difference between rote verbal learning and meaningful verbal learning, some intellectual skills may end up as rote learning in a sterile schema weakly connected to other schemata.

Retention. Retention of practiced intellectual skills over a long period of time is poor. Jonathon got $20 off on a $43 shirt. What percentage was the discount? *Comemos una comida sabrosa*. Figure the area of this plane .

Speculation about the cause of poor retention of intellectual skills invokes the ideas of insufficient initial learning, isolated learning, specific or vertical transfer, and associative learning. Probably all of these are involved to some extent. Intellectual skills are usually learned as isolated performances within a hierarchy of skills that are related only to the prerequisite skills and the skills that follow. Too often instruction does not provide lateral transfer experiences and rarely are intellectual skills taught within a carefully thought out network of skills and information.

An interesting study by Beeson (1981) explored the effect of providing a knowledge network on the acquisition and retention of intellectual skills. Using Ausubel's theory of meaningful verbal learning, he provided high school students with an *advance organizer* relating electrical circuits to water flow under pressure prior to lessons on electricity. He hypothesized that anchoring intellectual skills to a prior schema would increase the meaningfulness of the intellectual skills, would provide more retrieval cues for the intellectual skills and would promote conditions conducive to lateral transfer of the intellectual skills.

Task and content analysis of the to-be-learned material on electricity revealed a hierarchy with 14 intellectual skills (discriminations, concepts and rules) and 6 verbal information elements. Three experimental conditions for learning the new material were tested. Condition 1 (Isolated Elements) presented the material in hierarchical order with minimal verbal communication. Condition 2 (Verbal Instructions) presented the material in hierarchical order with verbal instructions that included stimulation of prerequisite skills and guidance about the direction of thinking that should take place. Condition 3 (Advance Organizer) not only presented the material in hierarchical order and included the advanced organizer; it also included frequent references to the water analogy and four other short advance organizers for sections of the hierarchy. Controlling for relevant student ability, Beeson demonstrated significantly better retention of the intellectual skills among learners in Condition 3 seven weeks after instruction. Embedding the intellectual skills in a larger network -- a schema -- effectively increased the retention of these intellectual skills. He was not able to demonstrate increased lateral transfer, however. He believes his failure to demonstrate lateral transfer was methodological, not theoretical. Future research on the use of advance organizers for intellectual skill learning should prove interesting.

MEMORY

Retention of intellectual skills is dependent upon overlearning a frequent repetition. Since a rule is a unique combination of concepts, proactive and retroactive interference are a possibility each time one of the concepts is combined in a different rule with different concepts. Providing an embedding context that allows for generalization should minimize such interference. Intellectual skills are also dependent upon a great deal of specific transfer. Over time specific details tend to be lost in re-organization. Overlearning and emphasizing the importance of the specifics should increase retention. However, because of the above described characteristics retention of infrequently used intellectual skills is poor.

TRANSFER

Transfer of intellectual skills may be specific or broad, depending upon the uniqueness of the skill. Intellectual skills such as reading or summing have wide transferability. Other intellectual skills have narrow transfer and may even be quite esoteric, such as being able to figure out what day of the week November 1, 1805 was.

EVALUATION

Evaluation of intellectual skills should conform closely to the level of the intellectual skill hierarchy and the scope of transfer addressed in instruction. Extreme care should be taken to avoid the pitfalls of testing verbal information when the instructional objective was an intellectual skill or of testing for far transfer when only specific transfer experiences were provided in instruction.

SUMMARY

In summary, intellectual skills are those capabilities which mediate symbolic interactions with the environment. Task analysis of intellectual skills involves identifying the prerequisite intellectual skills directly impacting on the to-be-learned skill. Such a learning hierarchy specifies the conditions necessary in order for instruction on a new skill to be successful.

Curriculum development has been positively affected by the research and theory building on learning hierarchies, although all researchers do not operate within the same paradigm. Current research emphasis is on validating the hierarchical nature of specific learning hierarchies and on establishing the unique character of intellectual skills distinguished from other kinds of learning outcomes.

REFERENCES

Beeson, G.W. Influence of Knowledge context on the learning of intellectual skills. American Educational Research Journal, Fall 1981, 18, (3), 363-379.

Brown, J.S. and Burton, R.R. Diagnostic models for precedural bugs in basic mathematical skills. Cognitive Science, 1978, 2, 155-192.

Eisenberg, T. & Walhesser, H. Learning hierarchies -- numerical considerations. Journal for Research in Mathematics Education, 1971, 2, 244-256.

Gagne, R.M. & Briggs, L.F. Principles of Instructional Design, 2nd Edition. New York: Holt, Rinehart, and Winston, 1979.

Gagne, R.M. Learning hierarchies. Educational Psychologist, 1968, 6, 1-9.

Gagne, R.M. Domains of learning. Interchange, 1972, 3, 1-8.

Gagne, R.M. Learning and instructional sequence, in Kerlinger, F.M. (Ed.) Review of Research in Education. Itasca: Peacock, 1973.

Gagne, R.M. Mayor, J.R., Garstens, H.L. & Paradise, N.E. Factors in acquiring knowledge of a mathematical task. Psychological Monographs, 1962, 76 (7, whole No. 526).

Markle, S. They teach concepts, don't they? Educational Researcher, 1975, June, 3-9.

Merrill, M.D. Necessary psychological conditions for defining instructional outcomes. Educational Technology, 1971, August, 34-39.

Merrill, P.F. New directions in procedural learning. Paper presented at the meeting of the American Educational Research Association, New York, 1982.

Acquisition of verbal information is discussed in this chapter within the framework of rote versus meaningful information. Associate and Neo-Behavioristic approaches leading to mnemonic techniques is contrasted with categorical and advance organizer theories which emphasize modification of cognitive networks. Problems connected with the empirical testing of theories are explored.

1. In what ways does the learning of rote verbal information differ from the learning of meaningful verbal information?

2. How do advance organizers enhance retrieval?

3. What constitutes a good test of a theoretical explanation?

CHAPTER TEN

VERBAL INFORMATION

INTRODUCTION

The domain of verbal information includes all the facts, principles, rules, and generalizations that are the subject matter of any curriculum (Gagne, 1972). Verbal information constitutes a major portion of school learning. In terms of learning outcomes, verbal information is stored knowledge. The use or application (intellectual skills) of this body of knowledge is not pertinent to the study of learning verbal information. What is pertinent is the availability of the knowledge to the learner at some later date. The memory of verbal information has been the subject of psychological research since Ebbinghaus (1885).

THEORETICAL POSITIONS

BEHAVIORISTS

Associative Viewpoint. The Associative viewpoint dominated early research on memory of verbal information. Subjects learned serial lists of words or nonsense syllables, or they learned paired-associate lists.

Repetition of simultaneous pairings was assumed to create a bond or association which would be activated at a later date when one item of the pair or list became a stimulus. Reinforcement theory attempted to explain the acquisition of verbal information by postulating success or knowledge of results or vicarious reinforcement. The associative and/or reinforcement theory was a generally accepted theoretical view and the emphasis on research was on delineating the parameters of verbal information learning and retention: how many items could be remembered, which item positions were best and worst for retention (first, middle, or last in serial lists), what characteristics of the to-be-remembered items were most salient (rated meaningfulness), and so on. The use of nonsense syllables and/or unrelated words was heralded as methodologically rigorous procedure which permitted the study of learning, uncontaminated by prior associations or bonds. Such an approach was theoretically consistent for behaviorists and associationists.

Neo-Behavioristic Viewpoint. Science, however, properly pursued, is a self-correcting discipline. As data accrue, theoretical postulates which fail to parsimoniously interpret or predict behavior must be amended or abandoned. A neo-behavioristic theoretical approach grew as several strands of data evolved. Miller (1956) reported his research on the limits of short-term memory. Seven plus or minus two bits of information could be held in short-term memory. This was important, but even more important was the data suggesting that by "chunking" information human subjects could overcome the 7 ± 2 limitation in short-term memory. Chunking, however, implied some conceptual linkage not easily explained by traditional Behaviorist or Associationist theory. Another strand of research noted that subjects in recalling lists of words tended to "cluster" words semantically linked. Yet another strand observed that subjects used various devices to help themselves remember and recall meaningful lists or pairs of words or syllables. They created meaningful links between the to-be-remembered items; they mediated. Still subscribing to a success of knowledge of results reinforcement theory explanation of verbal learning, neo-Behaviorists increasingly explore the acquisition and retention of meaningful verbal information. A different set of research questions is posed by the neo-Behaviorists to delineate the parameters of verbal information learning and retention: what mediational devices are used, is verbal or imaginal _mediation_ more effective, what semantic categories are most salient, how are hierarchically ordered lists of words organized for retention, is retrieval a distinctly different process from storage, how do cues interact with storage, with retrieval, and so on. Interesting research with interesting results continues.

Mnemonic Devices. _Bellezza_ (1981) offers a framework for thinking about and studying the class of mediational techniques commonly called _mnemonic devices_. Neo-behaviorists have studied the devices of categorization, rehearsal, recording of stimuli, subjective organization, language and imagery mediation. Not as well studied are the method of loci, pegwords, digit-consonant encoding and other similar devices.

Bellezza makes a distinction between rote learning, meaningful learning and learning through _cognitive cuing structures_. _Rote learning_ is under the control of associative principles of learning and rehearsal is the appropriate strategy. _Meaningful learning_ is under the control of cognitive principles of learning and activating a schema that can accept new information is the appropriate strategy. _Cognitive cuing structures_ appear to be an _intermediate memory strategy_ for verbal information, providing a meaningful framework for verbal information not easily related to a prior schema. Therefore, mnemonic devices are cognitive strategies that can be learned and later used to learn non-meaningful verbal information.

Organizing Mnemonic Devices. Mnemonic devices may be of the organizational or encoding type. _Encoding devices_ transform the to-be-learned information into a different form so it will fit into a prior schema. _Organizing Devices_ build associations between to-be-learned verbal information and easily retrieved, earlier learned verbal information.

Organizing devices which create retrieval cues that are extrinsic to the new material are called _peg type_ devices. The classic strategy of associating words with parts of a room or other structure (_method of loci_) is a peg type mnemonic device. The same place can be used over and over for remembering new words. Research indicates that there is little proactive interference (Bellezza, 1981). However, remembering the words from an earlier use might be difficult (retroactive interference). Another peg type device is imaging a concrete object and then associating the to-be-remembered word with the conjured image. This strategy often inolves first learning a strategy for remembering the pegs. The "one is a bun" strategy is an example of a device to remember the images to which the new information is to be associated. As with the method of loci, the same peg-word strategy can be used over and over. However, not all peg-type strategies have multiple uses. Some are specific to the to-be-remembered material. Examples are first letter strategies. Creating the word "homes" from the first letter of each Great Lake is an illustration cited by Bellezza (1981). Another is remembering the nine planets in order from the sun by use of the sentence "Men very easily make jugs serve useful nocturnal purposes." With all of these peg type devices, the cue must be remembered first and then the associated information is retrieved.

A second organizational device builds the to-be-remembered information into the mnemonic device, an intrinsic cuing structure. These are termed chain type devices. Linking two to-be-remembered things, incorporating new information into a story and using rhymes are all intrinsic, chain type devices. If the new material is concrete, linking by visual image is very effective. Imaging a toad sitting on the head of a pin will facilitate the later retrieval of the association "toad-pin." If a serial list of semantically unrelated items must be remembered, overlapping a series of images can be effective. For example, if the next pair of words to be remembered after "toad" and "pin" is "rabbit" and "snow," image the toad on a pin, the pin stuck in the rabbit that is running up a snow bank. The story technique is similar in that new information is embedded in an ongoing scenario that is self-cuing. Rhymes are intrinsic sound cues, illustrated by the "30 days hath September" popular strategy.

Successful organizational mnemonic devices have characteristics of constructibility, discriminability, and associability (Bellezza, 1981). That is, they must be easily and reliably called to mind, not easily confused with other cues, and easy to connect to new material.

Encoding Mnemonic Devices. Encoding mnemonic devices require associability and invertibility. Since encoding devices transform the new information into old forms, the cuing structures must be easily converted back to the new information. Therefore a conversion strategy is required as part of the encoding strategy. Transforming words to numbers or numbers to words is a case in point. Remembering numbers by transforming them to words requires a prelearned conversion strategy. Each digit, 0 to 9, must be associated with a consonant sound that can be reliably used to create a word by inserting vowels. For instance, prelearning that "2" is "L" and "5" is "N", I can later remember my locker is #52 by encoding "new locker." Another time I can remember that Sean said 25 books were needed by encoding "loony."

Other encoding strategies include semantic, phonetic and imagery transformations. Concrete words are often encoded as images. Abstract words do not lend themselves to imagery but can be remembered by semantic or phonetic transformations. In semantic transformations the abstract word is changed into a concrete word that has similar or associated meaning. "Anger" might be encoded as "red." Phonetic transformations convert abstract words to concrete words that sound similar. "Anger" might be encoded as "anvil." A related strategy is used in foreign language learning. The foreign vocabulary word is transformed into a concrete word that can be imaged; its meaning in the native language is associated with the image. This is called the key-word technique.

Organizational and Encoding mnemonic devices are mediational strategies that make retrieval of nonmeaningful verbal information more probable. They represent a set of cognitive strategies that can be learned and later utilized to learn other things. Learner generated mnemonic devices appear to be more facilitative than instructor generated devices. However, when learners cannot or do not generate their own strategies, instructionally provided cognitive cuing structures are effective. In terms of metacognition, it would seem that knowing one has the ability to generate and/or use mnemonic devices to facilitate the learning of nonmeaningful verbal information would be the precursor for consistently engaging in such a cognitive strategy.

Verbal Information

From a cognitive point of view, both traditional associative and neo-behavioristic theory have inherent weaknesses. In the interest of rigorous methodology, Associative research has relied on nonsense syllables and words out of context. The outcome has been mountains of data about rote learning of meaningless items. The neo-Behaviorists utilize meaningful items and explore use of context as aids to acquisition and retention, but also seem to be studying rote learning. Another potential weakness of this last approach is that the research has been almost exclusively on the acquisition and retention of already known verbal items. The thousands of studies in this strand of research seem only to be asking: How do humans remember a unique presentation of already familiar verbal items? This, of course, is of interest. You have seen and read all of the words in this chapter before. What is new and what must be remembered is a new arrangement of those words -- a unique presentation.

COGNITIVE THEORY

The cognitive psychologist, however, is not as interested in the mechanistic process potentially involved in the storage and retrieval of lists of words, as in the cognitive structure that underlies and supports acquisition and retention. Developmental research has shown that the acquisition of new words is largely dependent upon underlying cognitive structure (Grippin, 1977). The role of cognitive structure in the learning of meaningful verbal information receives major emphasis by cognitive psychologists.

Categorical Theory. Jerome Bruner (1966) theorizes that humans interact with their environment in terms of the categorical structures they mentally possess. A category is defined as a concept and a precept which operates as a rule for classifying things as being equal. Incoming information is organized and stored in terms of pre-existing categories, or forces the modification of categories. Totally new input is not processed at all. There must be a prior category which directs the selection or perception of environmental stimulation. As categorization skills and the number of categories possessed increase, coding systems develop which allow cross-referencing of related categories. Such coding systems are seen by Bruner to be essential to memory and transfer. To remember a specific item of verbal information, it is sufficient to recall the system to which it belongs and the stored criterial attributes of the appropriate categories permit the recreation of the item.

Meaningful Verbal Learning. Working from a similar cognitive theoretical viewpoint, David Ausubel has developed a theory of meaningful verbal learning. According to Ausubel (1977) meaningful learning occurs whenever new information is related to prior cognitive structure. The prerequisites for such learning are (1) that the learner be disposed to relate new information to prior structure rather than disposed to engage in rote -- verbatim memorization and (2) that the new information is relatable to prior knowledge on a "nonarbitrary and nonverbatim basis" (p. 163). By "nonarbitrary" Ausubel appears to mean that the relationships between new and old information must have a conceptual, rather than associative, basis. By "nonverbatim," he appears to mean that the relationship be categorical; that is that the meaningfulness is not restricted to the narrow confines of specific words, but is generalizable to other terms with similar meanings in a categorical network.

A theory of meaningful verbal learning is an attempt to explain the human capacity to acquire and retain very large amounts of verbal information in spite of the research-revealed limits on information-processing space. Ausubel (1977) proposes that learners overcome the human limitations on processing information by utilizing existing cognitive structure as scaffolding to subsume new learning. By attaching new learning to old, the learner is no longer dependent on his limited ability to retain discrete items in memory. Since concepts, rather than verbatim "recordings," are related, more information processing space is available. Many words are relatable to an underlying concept which is subsumed; therefore, stored. The Associationist research on serial learning and paired-associate learning does not illumine meaningful verbal learning. It addresses only rote learning and clearly demonstrates the limited value of such learning. Few pieces of information can be processed at a time, acquisition requires many trials, interference is strong and retention is poor.

Advance Organizers. Ausubel (1977) points out that

although much school learning turns out to be rote learning, good _expository teaching_ can produce meaningful learning and poor discovery teaching can produce rote learning. Since expository teaching is more efficient in time and cost, Ausubel endorses expository teaching leading to reception learning as the most appropriate model for classroom instruction. To avoid rote learning of verbal information, instruction must prepare the learner in such a way that relevant prior cognitive structure is available to subsume the new learning. The use of _advance organizers_ is theorized to accomplish the readiness of cognitive structures for further differentiation.

An _advance organizer_ (1) is introduced before the lesson, (2) is designed to cue relevant prior knowledge, (3) is presented at a higher level of abstraction, generality and inclusiveness than the planned lesson, and (4) makes _explicit_ the connection between the organizer, the prior knowledge and the lesson to follow. "_In short, the principle function of the organizer is to bridge the gap between what the learner already knows and what he needs to know before he can successfully learn the task at hand_" (Ausubel, 1977, p. 168).

Do Advance Organizers Facilitate Learning? Since the success of advance organizers to enhance meaningful verbal learning is crucial to Ausubel's theory of meaningful verbal learning, the utility of advance organizers has been the object of much empirical research. The jury is still out. About as many studies report insignificant effects as report significant effects (Barnes and Clawson, 1975). Critics point to the lack of clear operational definitions for "subsumer" and "advance organizer" (Barnes and Clawson, 1975, Strihe and Posner, 1976). Proponents cite prior definitions in the literature, repeat and expand the definitions, and decry the use of research studies which do not adhere to the operational definitions for evidence against the efficacy of advance organizers (Ausubel, 1977; Lawton and Wanska, 1977).

Problems of Advance Organizers. The problems involved in testing hypotheses derived from Ausubel's theory include _individual differences among learners_, _operationalization of the advance organizer_, and _instrumentation of dependent variables_. Ausubel's early studies indicated that low verbal ability learners benefited from advance organizers more than other learners (cited in Ausubel, 1977). The inference follows that high verbal ability learners provide their own advance organizers and therefore do not demonstrate facilitation from experimentally provided organizers. Graber, Means, and Johnsten (1972) use this inference to explain their insignificant results in an experiment testing effects of advance organizers on college student achievement in a science lesson. They suggest that equivalent numbers of subjects in both control and experimental groups possessed appropriate prior knowledge and the ability to provide their own organizers. While such a rationale is plausible, theory is not advanced by such studies. Hypotheses cannot be disproved if negative results can be explained away. A rigorous experiment which tests the theory must, then, include an assessment of prior relevant knowledge and subject ability to generate self-organizers.

The second problem _operationalization of the advance organizer_, plagues many experimental studies. While Ausubel feels that advance organizers or subsumers have been clearly and adequately defined (Ausubel, 1977), a cursory glance at the research literature reveals a wide variety of interpretations. For whatever reason (unclear operational definitions by Ausubel or failure to study Ausubel's theory on the part of researchers), different experimental studies call quite different treatments "advance organizers." Hartley and Davies (1976) distinguish advance organizers from pretests, overviews, behavioral objectives, and other _pre-instructional strategies_ that supposedly tune the learner to receive instruction. They write: "pretests _alert_, behavioral objectives _inform_, overviews _prepare_, and advance organizers _clarify_" (p. 246). Hartley and Davies do not include in their review the voluminous literature on adjunct questions and other preinstructional strategies. Legitimate questions can be asked: Is there more than a surface difference between advance organizers and these other pre-instructional strategies? Do advance organizers create a different learning experience from behavioral objectives or adjunct questions? Is the learning more or less meaningful? Are such distinctions important in building a comprehensive theory of meaningful verbal learning or are they just variations on a theme?

Verbal Information

Besides the problem of defining exactly what constitutes an advance organizer, research in the area suffers from poorly conceived and constructed *dependent variables*. A typical study presents an advance organizer designed to enhance meaningful retention of verbal information, presents a lesson to be meaningfully subsumed, and then tests the learning by a dependent measure that appears to tap mostly *rote* learning; for example, see Rickards and McCormick (1977). In such a study, it really doesn't matter whether the experimental group scores significantly higher. Meaningful learning is not being assessed. The theory defines meaningful learning as "nonarbitrary" and "nonverbatim." Studies using verbatim recall or recognition of presented material neither disprove nor support the theory. A cognitive position, that meaningful verbal learning is dependent upon a conceptual relation to prior conceptual/categorical knowledge, is being inappropriately tested by methodology more consistent with an associative position. Appropriate dependent measures which assess retention on a conceptual, not verbatim, level are needed to test the theory.

Better Research and Clearer Answers. More recent research has attempted to disentangle the pros and cons of advance organizers. Luiten, Ames and Ackerson (1980) use a different *statistical methodology* than Barnes and Clawson (1975) to determine how many studies have demonstrated facilitating effects of advance organizers. Barnes and Clawson used a voting technique, counting the number of studies reporting significance versus the number reporting nonsignificance. Luiten, *et al*. (1980) looked at the number of studies that showed an increase in mean performance for advance organizer groups over control groups, disregarding tests of significance. Using this technique, they demonstrated that subjects receiving an advance organizer were, on the average, better off than subjects that did not receive advance organizers. In addition, they found that the effect of advance organizers increases over time, was beneficial for all grade levels studied, for all subject matter studied, for all ability levels, and was more effective in aural than in textual form.

Mayer (1979) criticizes earlier reviews of literature on the question of effectiveness of advance organizers for being atheoretical. Making the point that assumptions about learning can only be tested successfully within a theoretical framework, he presents such a framework.

Testing the Efficacy of Advance Organizers. Four theoretical viewpoints which provide a test ground for advance organizers are described by Mayer (1979, p. 373). Reception Theory states that retention of verbal information is a function of how much information is received into working memory. Beyond such learner variables as motivation, the amount of information going into long-term memory from working memory is a direct outcome of the amount of information offered as input and how quickly that information is offered. Under such a theory, advance organizers should have no effect on retention since they offer no specific information.

Addition theory, according to Mayer, hypothesizes that advance organizers should have an effect if they precede learning and activate or provide an anchoring item in LTM. Retention is a function of the additive nature of receiving information into WM and having prerequisite knowledge in LTM to serve as anchors. Under this theory new information is added to LTM in the form it is received into WM. Advance organizers do not change the perception of the information; neither does previously stored information. A new page is just added to the old file in LTM.

The assumption of Retrieval Theory is that advance organizers do not affect learning at all; rather, they affect retrieval. What is learned would not be influenced at all by the advance organizer. However, the organizer provides a cuing mechanism which increases the likelihood of retrieval.

Assimilation Encoding Theory hypothesizes that advance organizers will not affect learning under all conditions, but when they do, the learning outcome is something different from the information input. According to this theory, new information is integrated (assimilated) with old information and what gets stored in long-term memory is this new integration. When advance organizers are effective, they activate prerequisites in LTM which are brought into WM where they interact with the received new information from short-term memory. Advance organizers will not be effective if they are redundant to instructional materials, if they do not activate appropriate prerequisites in long-term memory or if the learner already has a cognitive strategy of activating prerequisite organizers.

Relationship between Data and Theory. Since each theory predicts a different outcome on tests of retention as a function of advance organizers, scientific tests of the theories are possible. Reception theory predicts no effects of advance organizers. Retention tests should reveal the same acquisition of new information for experimental and control groups. Addition theory predicts positive effects of advance organizers with new information but not more or qualitatively different learning outcomes. Effects of advance organizer would be revealed in differences between recognition and recall tests or in speed of retrieval. Assimilation Encoding Theory predicts qualitatively different learning outcomes from information input when advance organizers are effective.

Mayer (1979) put these theories to the test in a series of verbal information learning studies. He reports that Assimilation Encoding Theory best fits the data. When advance organizer groups demonstrate better retention than control groups, their performance reveals a reorganization of information on a conceptual basis that promotes far transfer, but loses specific detail. In cases where advance organizers did not facilitate far transfer, the above listed excepting conditions prevailed. Either the instructional materials themselves acted as advance organizers, or the learners were high ability performers who appeared to develop their own advance organizer, or the mismatch between learner prerequisite and new information was too great to be bridged.

Advance Organizers: An effective Instructional Methodology. Instruction for meaningful verbal learning probably should include advance organizers. Research to date indicates that carefully constructed advance organizers will probably enhance the learning of most students and will probably not interfere with the learning of the others.

Mayer (1979, p. 382) offers a checklist for producing effective advance organizers:

1. Does the organizer allow one to generate all

or some of the logical relationships in the to-be-learned material?

2. Does the organizer provide a means of relating unfamiliar material to familiar, existing knowledge?

3. Is the organizer learnable, i.e. is it easy for the particular learner to acquire and use it?

4. Would the learner fail to normally use an organizing assimilative set for this material, e.g. due to stress or inexperience?

Mayer's research on advance organizers reinforces the cognitive view that meaningful verbal learning is dependent upon the structural properties (schemata) of the learner. Unless some prior schema can be activated to assimilate the new information, meaningful learning cannot occur. The success of mnemonic devices (cognitive cuing structures) is also explained in terms of prior structures. Associating nonmeaningful verbal information with previously learned information ("52" is my "new locker") ties it into a schema that can be accessed in multiple ways, increasing the probability of retrieval.

Gagne's contention that the learning outcome of verbal information is dependent upon "its presentation within an organized, meaningful context" (1972, p. 3) receives support, then, from both neo-Behaviorists and cognitive theory. However, a "meaningful context" and what is learned are defined quite differently by each. Gagne (1977) makes a distinction between rote verbal learning and meaningful verbal learning. He explains the former as basic associative learning and the latter as a distinct domain of learning. However, many questions remain unanswered. Is a network of associative links equivalent to a stored categorical structure with subsuming properties? Or are Associationists and Cognitivists talking about two different processes of learning leading to two different learning outcomes?

CURRENT THEORETICAL DIFFERENCES

In an excellent review of the literature, Ellen Gagne (1978) comes to the conclusion that the theoretical lines are blurring between associationist/behavioristic explanations of verbal learning and cognitive explanations. Both theoretical viewpoints embrace a cognitive structure model in which prior knowledge and experience mediate new knowledge acquisition. Disagreement continues on whether that mental network follows the rules of association or the rules of schemata. Association rules require a serial linkage between specific cognitive units previously connected by contiguity or reinforcement. Schema theory posits a much more integrated network where the cognitive unit is "a 'plot' which contains variables" (Andre, 1979, p. 305). Rather than specific information linked to other specific information, schema theory hypothesizes that the "plot" contains a record of the constant features of a schema, the different variables related to the schema, and the ways in which those variables might differ from one experience to another.

The mental structure for a swimming pool as conceptualized in the Behaviorist tradition would consist of a network of specific information about specific swimming pools experienced in the past. When this network was activated, the excitation would flow through linkages between nodes of specific information. More frequently associated or reinforced nodes would be more likely to be activated because the links would be stronger. If rectangular pools were experienced more often than circular pools, initial activation of the swimming pool network would retrieve rectangular pool. If rectangular pool did not match the input data, further search of the network would be initiated, perhaps finding a prior weak link between round and rectangular pools. In the cognitive tradition the mental structure (schema) of swimming pool would be a mental blueprint of the constant features of a pool, e.g. water and container and swimmers; and any other variables previously abstracted from pool experiences with the potential values they could take, e.g. above ground, below ground, inside, outside, kiddie pool, Olympic pool. Once activated, the swimming pool schema completes its match-mismatch process on incoming data on the basis of the general schema, not on the basis of any specific feature. Both rectangular and circular pool input would immediately be accepted as a match.

Andre (1979) hypothesizes that both theories are right. Learners have and use both associative networks and schemata. The procedure (executive-management strategy) activated by the learner will depend upon the task demands. In terms of verbal learning, nonmeaningful information may be handled by the associative network, meaningful by a schema.

Empirical tests of these theoretical questions are complex and difficult. The answers are being gradually evolved by researchers such as Mayer (1979), Andre (1979), and Ellen Gagne (1978).

SUMMARY

In the meantime, practitioners taking an eclectic viewpoint, should help learners create meaningful mediational links for to-be-remembered verbal information, should provide a variety of pre-instructional organizers designed to bridge the gap between what is already known and what is to be learned, and should require sufficient rehearsal of nonmeaningful verbal information.

MEMORY

As discussed throughout the chapter, retention of verbal information is dependent upon many different factors: the nature of the to-be-learned verbal information, the cognitive strategies and intellectual skills of the learner, the instructional context. In general, for most learners retention of *rotely learned verbal information* is poor. Whether this is an effect of underdeveloped associative links or lack of prerequisite supporting structure or both is unclear. What is clear is that overlearning is essential for good retention.

Meaningful verbal information, on the other hand, results in excellent retention. However, what is retained tends *not* to be identical to the presented information. The input is transformed into more general dimensions and integrated with previously held information. Since meaningful verbal information is learned in one trial, it is essential that important specific details be made very salient or they will be lost in the transformation.

TRANSFER

Transfer of learned verbal information is also a function of whether the learning is rote or meaningful. Rote verbal information has only specific transfer potential. Identical elements must be present in the transfer situation in order to trigger retrieval of the stored rote verbal information. However, over-learned rote verbal information can be triggered in a later meaningful verbal information context and become part of a conceptual network with more general transfer potential.

Meaningful verbal information has the potential for all forms of transfer. Since the information is stored semantically, any similar information can trigger retrieval, leading to transfer in all such similar instances. Retrieval of meaningful verbal learning may not be facilitative, however, if necessary specific details have been subsumed in such a way as to be lost or if re-organization has distorted or made indiscriminable the aspects relevant to the transfer situation.

Good pedagogical procedure calls for incorporating transfer experiences into the instructional sequence so that part of the original learning experience, whether rote or meaningful, is learning when and where transfer might be appropriate.

EVALUATION

Nonmeaningful verbal information learning is evaluated easily by recognition or recall. Evaluation instruments should reflect the specific information taught. Transfer questions would not be appropriate. Depending upon the task demands, providing structural cues during evaluation may be appropriate. Cuing during evaluation makes sense if future instances in which the verbal information will be needed can be expected to contain the cues. In such cases recognition would be a more sensitive measure of learning. Since rote learning of verbal information is probably only justified in terms of efficiency of retrieval, e.g. times tables, speeded evaluation tests may be appropriate.

Evaluating the learning of meaningful verbal information may also take the form of recognition or recall. Whether transfer questions are appropriate or not depends upon your theoretical orientation. If you believe that cognitive structure is an associative network, transfer must be specifically taught or the connections (linkages) cannot be fairly assumed to exist. However, if you believe that cognitive structure consists of schemata that assimilate new information and are modified by that input, transfer questions provide a vehicle whereby the structure of the schema may be evaluated. Transfer questions could be very useful in diagnostic evaluation in either case.

When evaluation is used in the narrow sense of giving students tests to see if they learned the verbal information offered in instruction (summative evaluation), transfer questions for which no instruction has been provided are probably unfair. In such a case the learner is being evaluated on her cognitive strategies and intellectual skills, as well as the verbal information which has been taught.

REFERENCES

Andre, T. Does answering higher-level questions while reading facilitate productive learning? Review of Educational Research, 1979, 49, (2), 280-318.

Ausubel, D. The facilitation of meaningful verbal learning in the classroom, Educational Psychologist, 1977, 12, 162-178.

Barnes, B.R. and Clawson, E.D. Do advance organizers facilitate learning? Recommendations for further research based on an analysis of 32 studies. Review of Educational Research, Fall, 1978, 45, 637-659.

Bellezza, F.S. Mnemonic devices: Classification, characteristics and criteria. Review of Educational Research, 1981, 51, (27), 247-275.

Bruner, J.S. Toward a Theory of Instruction. Cambridge: Harvard University Press, 1966.

Ebbinghaus, H. Memory. New York: Teachers College Press, Columbia University, 1913.

Gagne, E.D. Long-term retention of information following learning from prose. Review of Educational Research, Fall, 1978, 48, (4), 629-665.

Gagne, R. Domains of learning. Interchange, 1972, 3, 1-8.

Gagne, R. The Conditions of Learning, 3rd Edition. New York: Holt, Rinehart & Winston, 1977.

Graber, R.A., Means, R.S. and Johnsten, T.D. The effect of subsuming concepts on student achievement on unfamiliar science learning material. Journal of Research in Science Teaching, 1972, 9, 277-279.

Grippin, P. Classification Skills and Cuing Conditions in Free Recall of Familiar and New Words Among 3rd and 4th Grade Children. Albany, New York: College of Saint Rose, 1977. (ERIC Document Reproduction Service No. ED 137 758.)

REFERENCES CONTINUED

Hartley, J. and Davies, I.K. Preinstructional strategies: The role of pretests, behavioral objectives, overviews and advance organizers. _Review of Educational Research_, Spring, 1976, _46_, 239-265.

Lawton, J.T. and Wanska, S.K. Advance organizers as a teaching strategy: A reply to Barnes and Clawson. _Review of Educational Research_, Winter, 1977, _47_, 233-244.

Luiten, J., Ames, W., and Ackerson, G. A meta-analysis of the effects of advance organizers on learning and retention. _American Educational Research Journal_, 1980, _17_, (2), 211-218.

Mayer, R. Can advance organizers influence meaningful learning? _Review of Educational Research_, 1979, _49_ (2), 371-383.

Miller, G.A. The magical number seven, plus or minus two: Some limits on our capacity for processing information. _Psychological Review_, 1965, _63_, 81-97.

Rickards, J.P. and McCormick, C.P. Whole versus part presentations of advance organizers in text. _Journal of Educational Research_, 1977, _70_, 147-149.

Strihe, K.A. and Posner, G.J. Epistomological perspectives on conceptions of curriculum organization and learning. In Shalam, Lee S. (Ed.). _Review of Research in Education_, Vol. 4. Itasca, Illinois: Peacock, 1976.

In this final chapter, an attempt is made to demonstrate how the principles presented in this book can be applied to specific learning problems. To accomplish this three different student projects are edited to follow the suggested outline for analysis of an instructional unit. Peggy Byrnes discusses the problems encountered by a blind piano student; Rochelle Robinson writes about the motor problems of a small boy; while Judy Pinsonnault considers a unit of a college statistics course.

1. What specific problem can I identify in an instructional situation with which I am familiar?

2. What questions should I use to analyze this setting?

3. What information and principles can I bring to bear on this problem?

CHAPTER ELEVEN

INTEGRATION

This text has offered a model for analyzing instructional units that is grounded in theories of learning. The model utilizes the Gagne domains of learning outcomes, a global contrast between behavioristic and cognitive explanations of learning, and applications of selected particular theories of learning to specific learning outcomes. In addition, the model emphasizes the importance of assessing the characteristics of the learner and the learning setting.

Analysis. A thorough analysis of an instructional unit involves (1) clearly specifying the desired learning outcomes, (2) categorizing those outcomes by characteristics that permit application of appropriate theory (this text has used categorization by Gagne's domains), (3) describing the learner and learning setting in such a way that the limits of learning are clearly understood, (4) selecting theoretical frameworks that are appropriate for the outcomes desired, that can generate multiple instructional interventions, and that allow empirical verification of results, (5) developing instructional interventions which reflect 1 through 4 above and which address the essential requirements for initial learning, retention and transfer, and, finally, (6) creating evaluation processes that are clearly related to the desired learning outcomes and that assess both the achievement of the learner and the success of the instructional intervention.

Such a detailed analysis is a complex and time consuming project. The practitioner could not and should not be expected to embark upon this level of analysis for <u>all</u> instructional units. A detailed analysis is appropriately utilized for those units of instruction that past experience indicates are particularly difficult to learn or for new units of instruction for which established prior instructional interventions are unknown.

However, although a thorough analysis would not ordinarily be done for all instructional planning, this general procedure and approach should be followed for all instructional planning. Instructors should have clear thoughts about what the learning outcomes are, who the learner is and from what theoretical framework they are operating. Each planning session should include a quick self-check to assure that instruction is not merely a mindless repetition of tradition. The self-check list should include such questions as: Do I know what my objectives for the learner are? Do I know what learning outcome domains they represent? Do I know my learners? Do I have a learning theory framework for my instructional interventions? Have I remembered retention and transfer? Is my evaluation relevant? With practice, these questions are posed and answered within the time constraints of the busiest practitioner. The payoff for both instructor and student lies in a systematic approach to instruction that can be evaluated precisely enough for modification to make a difference. Teaching is a subtle mix of science and art. The best artists know the science of their craft and use that knowledge to become better artists. Your authors hope you will use theories of learning in that way.

EXAMPLES

Edited analyses carried out by three former students follow. Peggy Byrnes (1979) analyzed beginning piano instruction for a blind, adult learner. Rochelle

Robinson (1978) analyzed an intervention strategy for a pre-school child with ambulation problems. Judy Pinsonnault (1979) developed an instructional unit for an adult class in statistics.

Each of the reports has been edited to conform to the six steps listed above and to protect the privacy of individual learners. Aside from these minor editing processes, the papers are presented as verbatim records of final student projects in the course for which this text was written.*

PROJECT ONE: Peggy Byrnes

1. Clearly specify the desired learning outcomes.
   The teacher must have a clear idea of what terminal performances are desired after instruction and specify these as precisely as possible using both observable, active verbs and delineated statements of content.

Long-Term

1. Acquire basic understanding of and facility at the keyboard.
2. Eventually, to make the transfer from a rote-aural approach to learning music to one which relied at least in part on music reading.
3. To use the keyboard in a functional way for accompanying singing as well as in teaching.

Short-Term (in sequential order)

1. Identify left from right at the keyboard.
2. Equate left with low and right with high.
3. Find groups of 2 raised keys with left hand, then with right hand over entire keyboard.
4. Find groups of 3 raised keys with l. h., then r. h. over entire keyboard.
5. Note to left of 2 raised keys is C. Find all D keys with l. h., then r. h. After C, E and D have been found, play tunes with C,D,E, e.g. Hot Cross Buns. Play on all C, D, E's.
6. Expand to 3 raised keys. Find F, B, G, and A. Find Hot Cross Buns on B, A, G, then on A, G, F.

---

*Student papers are used with the written permission of the authors.

Expand across keyboard. (Use both hands)

7. Find basic 5-finger patterning in key of C (C, D, E, F, G). Do finger-play with r. h. then l. h. to equate 1, 2, 3, 4, 5 in r. h. with thumb to pinky (and the reverse in the left hand).
8. Transfer 5-finger pattern to G, A, B, C, D.
9. Identify whole and half steps (half step being 2 keys next to one another with no other key between). Feel the keyboard. Repeat process for whole steps (one key between two keys). Again, feel.
10. Go back to finding single notes and concentrate on finding whole and half steps from a given note. (Explain raised keys function and that there are only two places on the keyboard where there is not a raised key between 2 keys (E-F; B-C).

2. Categorize those outcomes by characteristics that permit application of appropriate theory.

The final outcome can be broken down into categories or types of learning processes that are similar across content areas. The studies reported here use the Gagne model of motor skills, attitudes, cognitive strategies, verbal information and intellectual skills. For any instructional unit, one or more of these domains of Gagne's model may be used.

Facility at the piano is primarily a motor skill. Music reading and the use of the keyboard in a functional way are clearly intellectual skills.

In addition, since verbal information will facilitate communication between the teacher and student in the learning of the other skills verbal information is included to a lesser degree. Further, for this learner, there is a clear attitude component and a necessary development of new cognitive strategies.

3. Describe the learner and learning setting in such a way that the limits of learning are clearly understood.

A theoretical framework based on the outcomes and domains may need to be significantly altered when matched to the characteristics of the learners or the situation in which the learning must occur. For example, instructional strategies which work well in a small group may fail in a large group, or techniques which may be derived from theory and demonstrate good success with some learning styles or ages may need to be modified with those who have different learning sytles, ages or handicapping conditions.

Subject is a twenty-year old woman who is congenitally blind. She has entered the music education program to become a certified music teacher and a performer in her skilled area of voice. The subject, upon entrance into the program, could not read braille music and, therefore, relied for her musical development totally on a rote-aural approach. She was also not independent in her movement, being unable to cross the campus alone or go from one room to another without help. In fact, she walked securely only when aided by another. (All of this in spite of the fact that she had help for two months prior to entering from the Association for the Blind to acquire mobility on the campus.) The subject is of average intelligence, is one of triplets, both others being normal, and comes from a middle class background.

When subject was introduced initially to the idea of learning to play the piano, she reacted negatively. Not being able to read braille music, and being able to play the guitar well in a folk-style, she could not see any need for herself to play the piano. (It ultimately took four years to overcome this attitude. This would agree with the theory of dissonance which states that a person cannot simultaneously possess two attitudes which are logically inconsistent. Also, the subject did leave Saint Rose for one year to learn to read braille music at a special school in New York City and to improve her independent mobility.)

The subject's initial acquisition of skills at the keyboard was very slow. It took several weeks to accomplish a basic left, right feeling and to begin to find given notes and three-note patterns on the keyboard by ear. Looking back at the slowness of the learning, and given that her problem was not an aural one, it would seem that the subject had not overlearned those basic underlying motor abilities acquired during childhood and adolescence which Fleishman hypothesizes become part of a person's basic skills. Thus, the rate of learning and final level of achievement on a specific task (in this case, playing the piano) is limited by these previously acquired basic abilities. Also, as this pattern is evolving, contributing non-motor skills, such as the intellectual skill of following directions, decrease in importance and the need for speed, or for speed of aim movement, the concentration on the movement itself rather than on the accuracy becomes most important.

4. <u>Select theoretical frameworks that are appropriate for the outcomes desired, that can generate multiple instructional interventions, and that allow empirical verification of results</u>.

Beginning with an appropriate theory allows the teacher to develop several alternate routes to the desired outcome. Further, with a theoretical base the teacher can account for the success or failure of a given technique so that transfer of successful strategies to new appropriate situations takes place and systematic (rather than shotgun) modification of less successful strategies occurs.

5. <u>Develop instructional interventions which reflect outcomes, domains, learners and theoretical underpinnings and which include initial learning, retention and transfer</u>.

In designing the instructional interventions, themselves, the instructor must be clear about what is to be learned and by whom and must select an appropriate theory. Further, the teacher must not only reflect on the initial learning but also consider how the student remembers the material for later use through transfer.

Because the process of acquiring a motor skill is significantly different for an adult than a child, it was necessary to try to combine successful routines (after trial and error practice) to bring about increased anticipatory patterning and thus make the routine not only rapid and smooth (Bruner's modularization) but hopefully produce a sub-routine which would lead on to the next routine.

The ability to acquire any speed in finding keys to begin patterning would depend on how well the keyboard itself is known. If this has not become a subroutine the entire process will be slowed down and little expansion will be able to take place. In other words, a fast response on the first routine will help make it a sub-routine. (Unfortunately, this did not occur with the subject because I moved too quickly through the beginning steps.)

Conventional theory states that speed will depend on the amount of practice and how strongly the student is motivated. Logan's micromolar theory would support this. It assumes that a child learns a task at a particular speed and that speed will depend on the speed at which he practiced and how strongly the conditions differentially reward the speed. (In this case, the reward was praise and the knowledge that the next step would be begun when this step was mastered. In the future, now possessing this knowledge, I would assign a practice partner to the subject and use the tape recorder for motivation. Also, I would incorporate more actual manual help making her hand an extension of mine to begin to build a spatial pattern as well as to help facilitate speed.)

The following diagram indicates the assumption that learning is optimum at the speed at which training is given.

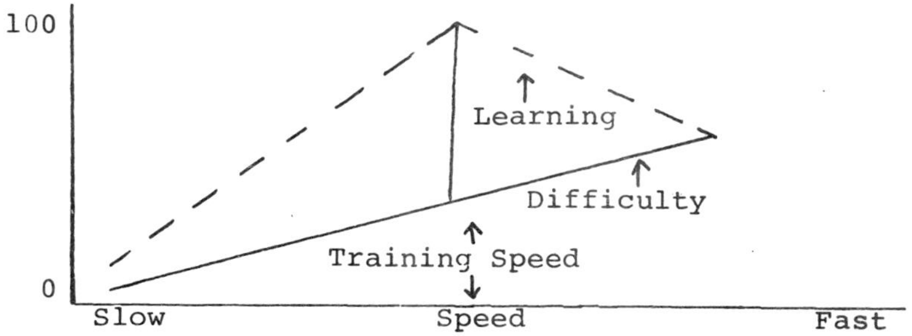

The distinction between learning and performance is critical. It is generally recognized that performance depends on various motivational factors in addition to learning. (In this case, low motivation played a role in producing a slow response.) In a micromolar theory, "learning refers to how well the response is known at any particular speed." Hence, response may be slow at first because of low motivation, and then remain slow even after motivation is raised because the slow progress the subject made in attempting to play the piano over a four-year period.

Bandura's social learning theory, which relies on vicarious reinforcement, states that when an observer identifies with a model, that observer will imitate the behavior of the model and be reinforced vicariously through that identification. It does not seem possible that this theory would be of much use to improve motor development and coordination in a blind student. It is not possible to hear how a person moves, though the result of that movement can be heard, but it is possible to feel that movement with them, so this seemingly reinforcing motivation builder could only be realistically applied in this case by extending the use of the model. Also, with the behaviorists the reinforcement may be internal feedback, informational feedback or affective feedback.

Bolles and the cognitive theorists state that when acquiring a motor skill, what is learned is an expectancy that anticipates a response. What has to be learned and reinforced are the cues which predict certain consequences. This stored information about the environment becomes a prediction for future behaviors.

Since the subject did not have an expectancy level regarding her motor skills, it seems reasonable that this theory would apply in that the difficulty of training a new response has to compete with a previously learned strong expectancy, namely not possessing basic motor skills. The speed and flexibility of skill performances, such as playing the piano, reflect an internal system that can anticipate cues and respond with little processing of external criteria -- the anticipation of cues, then, is essential. (There was much emphasis in the instruction to interpret cues given and to do them as automatically as possible. For example, objectives 9 and 11 relied heavily on this process.) The information processing of such a skill suggests that the behaviorist interpretation may not be as compatible here as the cognitivist theory.

Therefore, the amount of information that can be processed, the level at which it is processed, and the amount of practice are the limiting factors in skill acquisition. When cues are known and anticipated, and pre-set responses are available, those cues can be processed and responded to with a minimum of conscious attention (again, providing that the motivation and the developmental motor abilities are present).

There is a great deal of verbal information inherent in learning the keyboard: describing the keyboard itself in the subject's terms, defining up and down, defining a steady beat, 5-finger pattern, whole and half steps, keys and where sharps and flats occur. As soon as the subject is required to find high and low, up and down, to keep a steady beat, play a 5-finger pattern in a given key, or simply to find given notes, the area of intellectual skill enters in. This is not to minimize their importance for they both play upon the area of motor skill development in terms of actually playing the piano.

Certainly, the subject did employ a cognitive strategy in her unique approach to the keyboard.

Conclusion. There would be a much more effective learning situation to teach such a complicated skill as playing the piano to a blind person under the conditions such as were stated if several factors were given attention from the very beginning.

Before any attempt was made at the keyboard itself I would do some large motor movement activities especially using the arms to force the subject to contract those movements into more refined ones needed at the keyboard. (The finger dexterity itself was never a problem which is the opposite of what is usually encountered, especially with children.)

The need for greater motivation on a daily basis (rather than on a weekly one) might be overcome with the use of a practice partner (who might share the lesson and serve as a model) and a tape of each lesson to reinforce the practice.

An attempt to increase the speed of the earliest learnings (namely, finding actual keys) with as much speed as possible, and then transferring that to single notes, to 2 or 3 note groupings, etc. would be significant.

It would seem important to make an attempt to do even more relating of new learning to old, hoping to increase the information processing space (e.g., since guitar was known, relating V^7, I chords to guitar chords). Also, the use of as many advance organizers as possible to impart as much information before the lesson about what is to be learned, making it as relevant as possible to what went before in an attempt to bridge the gap between what the learner already knows and what he needs to know to successfully learn the task at hand.

It would be important to remove as much interference (Hunt) between similar learnings (since the visual aspect of learning is not present to supplant this with much tactile and aural reinforcement) as possible. An example of where this might occur would be key signatures. It would be necessary to group them according to 5-finger feeling at the keyboard with their initial presentation, e.g., D major and A major would have the same touch since their patterning of white and black keys is the same. This would be essential as an advance organizer as well as attempting anticipate interference.

Finally, had a more definite goal in terms of accomplishment been stated to the subject upon her entrance to the program for her first year of piano, her attitude might have been different from the beginning.

6. Create evaluation processes that are clearly related to the desired learning outcomes and that assess both the achievement of the learner and the success of the instructional intervention.

Most teachers consider at some point in their planning how they will assess student success in learning the desired outcomes. Fewer, however, plan specifically for assessing their instructional techniques with any regularity. Such evaluation is essential if continued appropriate modification and effectiveness of the instructional strategies is to take place.

(Although evaluation of the major objective "basic facility at the keyboard" is apparent here, we have suggested in this text that a more complete delineation of the formative evaluations and evaluation of the program would be more helpful to the instructional planner.)

When finally faced with the ultimatum that unless

a given level of achievement at the keyboard was met, the subject could not student teach or graduate, her progress this year has been amazing compared to her previous years.

In spite of all my failure at teaching the keyboard to this subject, she is playing simple Bach pieces and can take a melody she knows well and add an appropriate chordal accompaniment.

BIBLIOGRAPHY

Bolles, R.C. Reinforcement, expectancy, and learning. Psychological Review, 1972, (5), 394-409.

Fleishman, E. Individual differences and motor learning. In R.M. Gagne (Ed.) Learning and Individual Difference. Columbus, Ohio: Charles E. Merrill, 1967.

Grippin, P. and Peters, S. Theories of Learning: An Expansion of Gagne's Domains. Albany, New York: The College of Saint Rose, 1979.

Logan, F.A. Micromolar behavior theory and performance speed in education. Harvard Educational Review. 1963, 33 (2), 157-283.

Integration

PROJECT TWO: Rochelle Robinson.

1. Clearly specify learning outcomes and

2. Categorize learning outcomes

After several informal tests such as walking a straight and curved line, standing on one foot, hopping, jumping and throwing and catching an oversized ball (L'Heureux, 1978), it was determined that the desired learning outcome would be the motor skill balance or "gross body equilibrium" (Fleishman, 1967). Fleishman described "gross body equilibrium" as the "ability of an individual to maintain his balance despite forces pulling him off balance, where he has to depend on non-visual (e.g., vestibular and kinesthetic) cues."

Balance has also been described as the state of stability produced by the equal distribution of weight on each side of a vertical axis (Barsch, 1967). Static balance and dynamic balance were the two components of balance addressed by Barsch. Static balance referred to the even distribution of weight at a rest-stance while dynamic balance referred to the "postural orientation of the body when the organism is performing a specified motor activity which involves relatively large motions of all or parts of the body which act to disturb the gross orientation of the organism."

3. Describe the learner and the learning setting.

The learner is a 5.7 years old Kindergarten student. There is one sibling, an older sister, 7.5 years old. He is a bright active child who has not displayed any school learning problems either in Nursery School or Kindergarten. Since he began walking at 11 months, he has fallen on the average of twice daily either when walking or standing still. Medical examinations have excluded any vision problems, orthopedic problems or abnormalities, epilepsy or atopic seizures, middle ear damage or fluid. He has excellent eye-hand coordination and fine motor control. Kindergarten physical education screening, taken when he was 4.7, indicated that he was functioning at a level normal for a 5-year old.

The present instructional setting is the learner's home which has provided him with the usual gross motor activities, including swimming, ice skating and cross-country skiing, and apparatus such as tricycles, swings, jungle-gyms, etc. There has been no formalized instruction in gross motor control either in the school -- or home-learning situation.

4. Select appropriate theoretical frameworks.

...the behaviorist position of Albert Bandura (1969), social learning theory. In this theory, Bandura contended that when an observer identified with a model, that observer will imitate the model and be reinforced vicariously through that identification. Because the observer was not an overt learner, the action would be symbolically stored in the memory to be retrieved later. This theory inferred that the accuracy of the actual performance will then be a function of the stored representation but it will also be a function of the availability of the prerequisite skills necessary to the performance of the action (Grippin, 1978). Bruner (1972) has termed this "observational learning" and imitation. Bruner has described the prerequisites for observational learning as the ability to differentiate or abstract on oneself from a task, that is, to be able to view one's own performance in terms of others' performance. The second prerequisite for observational learning was the construction of an action pattern by appropriate sequencing of a set of constituent sub-routines to match the model's performance. Imitation, according to Bruner, allowed the individual to incorporate what has been observed into behavior that was not mere mimicry but directed intelligently to an end. This would depend on the individual's ability to match to the model a construction of behavior while being able to distinguish and relate what was analogous in the individual's behavior and that of another member of the species. These actions have a self-rewarding character which would be comparable to Bandura's affective reinforcement.

Bruner (1973) has provided a cognitive approach to motor skill acquisition. In Bruner's theory, early skill was dependent upon the initial arousal of an intention, specifying a goal and minimal directions concerning means. The initial arousal of an intention involved the "internal discharge in the nervous system whereby an act about to occur is not produced in the effectors by the usual motor volley but is also signaled to related sensory and coordination systems by a corollary discharge" or by internal feedback preceding action. Initial arousal was followed by a "loosely ordered sequence of constituent acts" which would later, if the contingencies for reinforcement were met, occur in appropriate serial order to achieve the goal toward which the intention seems to be leading. As the constituent acts were arranged into a successful combination, aspects were refined for better performance. As these routines became smooth and rapid (or modularized) the routine became a subroutine in a more complex action.

Barsch (1967) in his theory of movigenics has applied the concepts of cognitive theorists to an instructional curriculum. Bruner (1973) has postulated a learning theory for motor skill acquisition while Barsch (1968) has described a theory of instruction to correspond with it. Barsch (1967) has defined the three stages of motor learning as (1) learning the proprioceptive mechanics of the action (Bruner's loosely ordered sequence of events); (2) fixing the mechanics through practice (Bruner's trial and error organization of constituent acts and refinement into a rapid smooth order) and (3) assigning the act to the cognitive file to be retrieved as necessary to variable demands (Bruner's modularization of a subroutine into a more complex routine).

Both Bruner (1973) and Barsch (1967) have stressed the need for an intelligently directed sequence of events toward a goal. Bruner and Barsch have stated that as serial structured acts were modularized or became automatic, more information processing space was available to the learner.

5. <u>Develop instruction based on theory</u>.

Using Bruner and Barsch's approach to motor skill acquisition one would initiate an intention for the learner, observe a disorganized sequence of events which would continue until the performance was successful. After repeated trial and error combinations or practice, the learner would be better able to refine his/her constituent acts until these acts became smooth and rapid, modularized or automatic. The learner would then be able to pursue other areas of exploration. The implications of these two theories for the learner would be that he has not modularized the subroutine balance into the more complex routines walking and standing. This would also suggest that he has had to concentrate on the mechanics of shifting his weight from side to side. His falling would be considered an indication of his inability to consistently concentrate on either static or dynamic balance mechanisms.

Barsch (1968) has recommended the use of the Harmon walking rail to assist the learner in "coming to balance." Using Barsch's activities and evaluation techniques, the learner should show improvement in initial informal testing situations as well as a decrease in his falling.

This instruction will be presented to the learner as a playtime activity. Bruner (1973, 1972) has stated that one of the functions of play was that it allowed the learner to try different combinations of behavior that under functional pressure would never be tried. Play also provided a means of minimizing the consequences of one's actions.

In keeping with Barsch's (1968) recommendations the Harmon walking rail will be utilized. Barsch recommended the Harmon walking rail over the traditional walking board because he felt that by repeated traversing of the walking board the learner received only practice in traversing the board. The Harmon walking rail consists of two four foot sections that are fastened together as an eight foot long surface. The treads are slanted outward and downward about 15 degrees. A visual target will be placed about 18 feet in front of the starting end of the rail.

The instruction will consist of as many training sessions as the learner needs to be able to perform the task of traversing the rail in a variety of settings and contexts. The learner will be expected to walk slowly, rapidly, forward and backward to establish that he has learned the task.

The learner will be able to explore the apparatus and get accustomed to the "feel" of the rail. The instructor will verbally guide the learner to discourage the walker's lowering and twisting of his head. The learner will be instructed to fixate on the visual target placed in front of him.

Integration

The walker will be instructed to walk forward and backward on the rail. The learner will not turn around at each end of the board to maintain a forward walk. The instructor will continue to give the learner verbal cues as he traverses the rail.

It is suspected that the learner's head stance and shoulder alignment will need improvement. The instructor will initiate the following activities to improve alignment. If after picture analysis, it is shown that other areas need improvement the instructor will initiate techniques suggested to improve those.

To improve head stance, a bean bag will be placed on the learner's head as he walks. Other suggested "headware" would include a cup, book, etc.

To improve shoulder alignment, a yardstick will be held in the learner's extended arms in a horizontal line at the level of his shoulders, sighting over the edge of the stick toward the target.

6. <u>Evaluation</u>.

Evaluation Games: The following activities will be photographed with a polaroid camera to allow for a detailed analysis of: the way the learner visually steers his walk, head position, shoulder alignment and the placement of feet for the directional aspect of walk. Barsch has stated that these activities should be executed without loss of balance or alignment. Fleishman suggested that this ability is best measured by tests conducted with eyes closed.

Giant steps, baby steps, scissor steps (crossing feet in front of one another), scissor steps backwards, side steps to the left and to the right, limping with one leg and then the other, walking a curb with one foot on the elevation and repeating the evaluation games with his eyes open/closed. Pictures will be taken under both conditions and analyzed according to the initial criterion. After the learner has gotten the "feel" of the rail, pictures will again be taken and analyzed for the various aspects of alignment such as: Carriage of the head and sustained sightings of the visual target, horizontal line of the shoulders, pelvic line and placement of the feet on the treads to establish the best possible method of bringing the walker's body to alignment.

If a comparison of the evaluation games -- eyes open -- demonstrate an improvement in head stance and shoulder alignment and the learner demonstrates a decrease in falling, it will indicate that he has modularized the subroutine balance into the routines walking and standing. If a comparison of the evaluation games -- eyes open/eyes closed -- demonstrate an improvement in head stance and shoulder alignment and the learner demonstrates a decrease in falling, it will be a better indication that he has modularized the subroutine balance into the routines walking and standing.

If a comparison of the evaluation games under both conditions indicates an improvement in postural orientation but the learner continues to fall, it will indicate that the learner has only received practice in walking the rail or that the proper remedial balance activities have not been provided.

If a comparison of the evaluation games under either condition do not show an improvement in postural orientation but the learner ceases to fall, it will indicate that the Harmon rail activities improved balance but not head stance and shoulder alignment.

If a comparison of the evaluation games under either or both conditions do not indicate a change in posture and the learner continues to fall, it will indicate (1) that the learner has not received sufficient practice; (2) that the activities were inappropriate and/or (3) there is a physiological reason for the learner's inability to "come to balance."

REFERENCES

Bandura, A. Principles of behavior modification. New York: Holt, Rinehart & Winston, 1969.

Barsch, R.H. Achieving perceptual motor efficiency. Seattle, Wash.: Special Child Publications, Inc., 1967.

Barsch, R.H. Enriching perception and cognition. Seattle, Wash.: Special Child Publications, Inc., 1968.

Bruner, J.S. Organization of early skill action. Child Development, 1973, 44, 1-11.

Bruner, J.S. Nature and uses of immaturity. American Psychologist, August 1972, 27, (8) 687-708.

Bruner, J.S. Toward a theory of instruction. Cambridge Mass.: The Belknap Press of Harvard University Press, 1966.

Bruner, J.S. The course of cognitive growth. American Psychologist, January 1964, 19, (1), 1-15.

Dunham, P. Jr. Effect of practice order on the efficiency of bilateral skill acquisition. Research Quarterly, May 1977, 48, (2), 284-287.

Fleishman, E. Individual differences and motor skill learning. In R.M. Gagne (Ed.). Learning and individual differences. Columbus, Ohio: Charles E. Merrill, 1967.

Gagne, R. Domains of learning, Interchange, 1972, 3, (1), 1-8.

Grippin, P. Motor learning and performance, unpublished manuscript. CSR, 1978.

Halverson, L.E., Robertson, M.A., and Harper, C.J. Current research in motor development. Journal of Research and Development in Education, Spring 1973, 6, 56-70.

Halverson, L.E. A real look at the young child. Journal of Health, Physical Education & Recreation,

REFERENCES CONTINUED

May 1971, 42, (5), 31-33.

Henderson, S.E. Role of feedback in the development and maintenance of complex skill. Journal of Experimental Psychology, May 1977, 3, (2), 224-233.

Kleinman, M. The effects of practice distribution on the acquisition of three discrete motor skills. Research Quarterly, December 1976, 47, (4), 672-677.

L'Heureux, R. Best of tests, unpublished manuscript, CSR, 1978.

Wrisberg, C.A. & Herbert, W.G. Fatigue effects on the timing of performance of well-trained S's. Research Quarterly, December 1976, 47, (4), 839-844.

PROJECT THREE: Judy Pinsonnault

1. Clearly specify learning outcomes

The topic of the unit concerns the types of measurement scales used in the social sciences -- nominal, ordinal, interval, and ratio (Stevens, in Mueller, Schuessler, & Costner, 1970, pp. 14-16).

The goals of instruction are that, as a result of the unit, the student will possess a knowledge and understanding of the four types of measurement scales and the rules and principles governing their use, as well as the ability to apply these rules and principles to the solution of practical probelms in the social sciences.

In general, as a result of instruction, the student will evidence an understanding of the various types of measurements scales, as well as the ability to use this understanding in novel practical situations. A further goal here is that the student be convinced of the importance of measurement in the social sciences and be comfortable with numerical manipulations.

2. Categorize learning outcomes

A set of more detailed instructional goals is provided in Figure 1. These goals are stated in terms of instructional objectives and have been divided into groups reflecting Gagne's domains of learning as they apply in this situation (Grippin & Peters, 1979).

It would seem that an important domain to consider initially in analyzing this unit in terms of Gagne's domains is that of attitudes. Here there are two particularly important attitudes that might color a student's approach to the instructional unit.

First there is the attitude that the social sciences are as valid scientific pursuits as the "pure" sciences. Many people are of the opinion that the social and behavioral sciences are "common sense" and that predictions can be made as accurately on this basis as they can on a theoretical one. It would seem important that a student of the social sciences see the contributions to be made here as being extremely valuable and important ones. They should appreciate the value of theory and its uses. As it applies to this instructional unit on measurement, this would mean that a student should be aware of the importance of numerical representation of data in the social sciences if we are to arrive at a means of making predictions. The student, then, must evidence an appreciation for the need to develop new types of scales other than physical ones to measure behavioral traits.

A second attitudinal concern is one that is encountered in many students -- a fear of anything that appears to involve mathematics -- the idea that "statistics" and "sadistics" have some similarity other than an acoustical one (Gay, 1976, p. 214). Very often a student will presume ahead of time that a topic involving any kind of numerical manipulation will be too difficult for her/him. It will be an important instructional outcome, then, for students to feel at ease and confident about approaching problems involving numerical concepts.

The domain of verbal information is also important in this instructional unit. This domain involves the stored knowledge -- facts, principles, rules, and generalizations -- that apply to the topic at hand (Grippin & Peters, 1979, p. 41). In this unit on types of measurement scales, several new terms, concepts, and rules will be introduced. This will involve a good deal of verbal information learning. A content analysis is provided in Figure 2 that outlines the basic concepts of concern in this unit and the relationships among them.

This verbal information will need to be readily brought to mind if the learner is to supply definitions and descriptions of the various types of scales. It also is what is involved when a learner is asked to state a rule or principle or provide an example of a concept. An ability to label the types of scales will be needed in making later use of them. It is also important that the student associate key aspects of a stimulus situation with the correct scale type to aid in evocation of the appropriate rules or principles for application. For example, when a situation involves "ranking," the term "ordinal scale" should come to mind. In terms of Ausubel's distinctions (Grippin & Peters, 1979, p. 44), this will involve both rote and meaningful verbal learning to some extent. No doubt some rote learning of totally novel terms will occur, for instance in learning the following s-r associations:

True Zero -- Ratio Scale

Equal Scale Units -- Interval Scale

Rank Order -- Ordinal Scale

Qualitative Categorization -- Nominal Scale

A good deal of the remaining verbal information, however, will probably be best acquired in a meaningful context. As the content analysis and charts indicate, the four types of scale are related in a hierarchical fashion. Learning the necessary verbal information in an organized manner should facilitate later recall of the terms, definitions, etc. as well as be helpful in application behaviors. This idea will be discussed further in the instructional strategies section of this paper.

While the domain of verbal information involves the ability to recall and supply the pertinent facts, terms, and definitions, this will not result in the student meeting all of the instructional goals. The domain of intellectual skills involves the ability to <u>apply</u> the information.

A task analysis chart (Figure 3) outlines the things that a student should be able to <u>do</u> as a result of this instructional unit. In this domain, transfer of learning is vertical, with lower level skills contributing to the successful learning of higher level ones. This will be of importance in designing an instructional strategy. In this domain, we are concerned with observing evidence that the learner is able to apply the rules and not that s/he merely be able to <u>state</u> them, as we were in the domain of verbal information (Grippin & Peters, 1979, pp. 73-77). Here, we will be looking at performance rather than strictly possession of verbal information. A learner may frequently be able to <u>use</u> a rule when s/he cannot state it. The task hierarchy in Figure 4 breaks down performance in terms of Gagne's model (Grippin & Peters, 1979, pp. 78-79). The tasks in the chart are broken down as far as the level of the discriminations required in forming definitions of the four types of scales. It should be kept in mind of course, that a further breakdown could be accomplished with each of the concepts at the lower levels, e.g. variables, degree, category, magnitude, etc.

INSTRUCTIONAL GOALS

As a result of this unit concerning the types of measurement scales used in the social sciences, the student will evidence competency in the following areas:

ATTITUDES

Value the contribution of the social sciences to human knowledge.
Support the viewpoint that measurement is as important in the social sciences as it is in the physical sciences.
Display confidence in solving problems that involve numerical concepts and manipulation.

VERBAL INFORMATION

Provide definition of terms:
- Describe the characteristics and uses of each scale.
- Describe the limitations of each scale.
- Give examples of each type of scale.

Provide an explanation of the relationships among the four types of scales.
State the criteria for using one type of scale rather than another.
State the principles and rules used when selecting the appropriate type of scale.

INTELLECTUAL SKILLS

Identify novel examples of each scale type.
Convert from one scale type to another.
Predict the consequences of using one type of scale over another.
Apply rules for each scale type in a novel practical situation:
- Discriminate important criteria of situation.
- Select appropriate type of scale.

Integration

Explain rationale for selection.
Predict outcome. Consider limitations.
Develop appropriate measurement tool.

Figure 1 Instructional Goals.

VERBAL INFORMATION

CONTENT ANALYSIS

Measurement

The assignment of numerals to objects or events according to rules.

Classification

Grouping objects or events according to a common characteristic, attribute, or quality.

Nominal Scale

Qualitative Classification
Crudest type of scale. Not very precise.
Classifies data into mutually exclusive categories.
Indicates numerically how many persons, events, etc. are in each category.

Examples: Experimental - Control Groups
Pass-Fail Choices A,B,C,D, or E
Marital Status Introversion - Extroversion Sex

This type of scale is used in the social sciences frequently in tests from which more sophisticated measures are compounded.

Ordinal Scale

Classification by rank
Ranks items in terms of the degree to which they possess a particular characteristic, in order of least to most, high to low, etc.
This type of scale reveals any given item's relative standing as compared to others in the same classification category.
More precise than a nominal scale. Conveys more information.
Ordinal data can be reduced to nominal data.
Limitation: The scale gives information about relative standing, but doesn't tell how much so.

e.g. the difference between ranks 1 and 2 may be much larger than that between ranks 3 and 4.
Examples: Attitude and Opinion Scales

Strongly Agree - Agree - Disagree - Strongly Disagree
Class Rank
Percentile

Interval Scale

Classification by magnitude of the difference between one value and another, according to their position on a scale that possesses units of equal intervals.
This type of scale allows for computation of the scale distance between values. This allows for addition and subtraction of scale values. Not only can we determine that a particular item is larger than another, but we can tell how much larger.
Such differences can only be compared qualitatively, however.
This type of scale does not allow for multiplication or division, e.g., any IQ score of 120 is 60 points more than one of 60, but we cannot say that the first person is twice as intelligent. This is due to the fact that there is no fixed zero point, no point of origin.

Interval scales convey more information than ordinal and nominal scales, and thus can be reduced to these less complex forms.

Interval scales are employed frequently in the social science.
Example: IQ Scores
Temperature
Standardized Scores

Ratio Scales

Possess a fixed origin, a true zero point.
This quality allows for quantitative comparison of values on the scale, e.g., a 10-year old child is twice as old as a 5-year old.
Ratio scales are the most precise type of scale and are the kind most frequently used in the physical sciences.
They are not as often found in the social sciences, due to the indirect nature of the measurement required by social data.

Integration

> Ratio scales convey more information than the other three types and can be reduced to a less complex type when necessary.

(Gay, 1976, pp. 221-223; Lefrancois, 1975, pp. 272-273; Morgan & King, 1971, pp. 289-292; Mueller et al., 1970, pp. 14-16)

Figure 2 Content Analysis

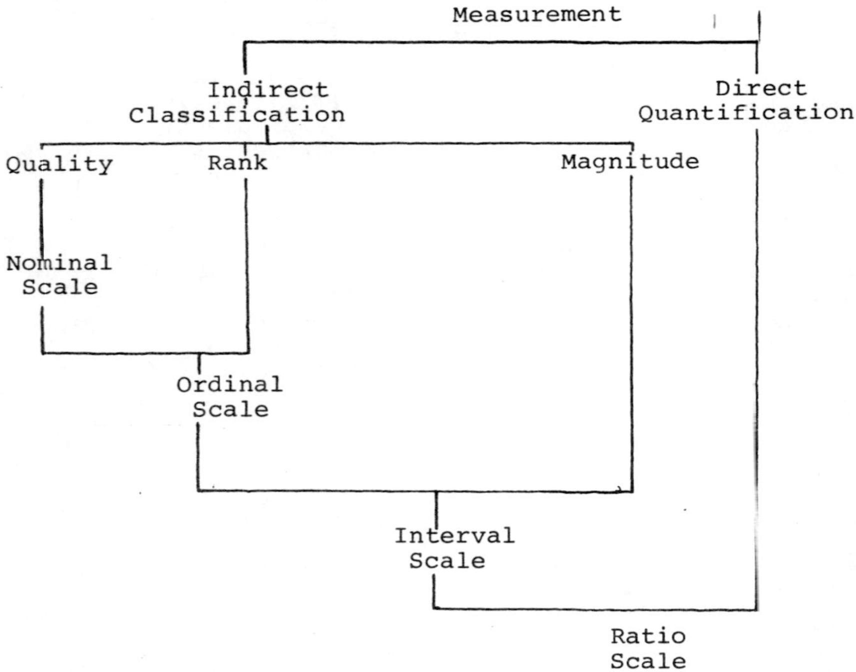

Preliminary concepts required: Scale, category, unit of measure, addition, subtraction, etc.

Figure 3 Task Analysis Chart

Integration

Select and make use of the type of measurement scale that is appropriate in a given situation

Analyze the situation as containing the potential to be numerically symbolized but that the variables can be at best indirectly measured and only qualitatively compared.

Analyze the situation as containing a variable that can be directly measured and quantified.

Figure 4a Analysis of Task Hierarchy for Use of Measurement Scales. (Intellectual Skills)

Integration

Analyze the situation as containing the potential to be numerically symbolized but that the variables can be at best indirectly measured and only qualitatively compared.

Identify the situation as involving qualitative comparison of variables according to their possession of a given quality. Aware that values of the variable cannot be numerically compared.

Identify the situation as calling for the classification of data into categories

Apply the rules for use of nominal scales.

Recognize the presence of properties and criteria which define a nominal scale.

Recognize the presence of mutually exclusive classification categories.

Recognize the possibility that membership in these categories can be represented numerically.

Identify the situation as calling for the ordering of data in terms of degree with categories.

Apply the rules for use of ordinal scales.

Recognize the presence of properties and criteria which define an ordinal scale.

Recognize that values of the items can be ranked in terms of degree.

Recognize that the variables have value relative to each other.

Figure 4b Analysis of Task Hierarchy for Use of Measurement Scales. (Intellectual Skills)

Analyze the situation as containing a variable that can be directly measured and quantified.

Identify the situation as requiring a scale that will represent the difference in magnitude between values of the variable. Aware that the potential for numerical comparison is present.

Apply the rules for use of interval scales.

Recognize the presence of properties and criteria which define an interval scale.

Recognize that the scale may have units of equal intervals.

Recognize that variables may differ in the magnitude of their numerical value, and may be added and subtracted.

Apply the rules for use of ratio scales.

Recognize the presence of properties and criteria which define a ratio scale.

Recognize the presence of a value of absolute zero.

Recognize that values may be expressed as ratios, and may be divided and multiplied.

Figure 4c Analysis of Task Hierarchy for Use of Measurement Scales. (Intellectual Skills)

3. Describe the learner and learning setting.

This unit of instruction is one that will be contained in an introductory research methods course in the social sciences. The learners involved will be adult-aged undergraduate students of normal intelligence majoring in some area of the social sciences.

4. Select appropriate theoretical framework and

5. Develop instruction based on that theory.

Several researchers have noted that attitudes include three components: affective, cognitive, and behavioral (Grippin & Peters, 1979, p. 122). All of these need to be considered in outlining an instructional strategy. A strategy often used in the past in an attempt to overcome negative or fearful attitudes held by students regarding content involving numerical exercises was to repeatedly tell the students that the material was "not as difficult as you think" or that "The formulas are long and look complicated but are really very simple" and comments of a similar nature. Such urgings probably failed to break the associations that a student had developed between math and the negative feelings associated with failure to succeed. According to conditioning theory (Grippin & Peters, 1979, pp. 123-235), the relationship involved here would be as follows: Math = Lack of Success. A strategy to combat this learned association would be to provide success at problems involving numerical manipulation early in the instructional unit and continue to provide repeated opportunities for the experience of success. This would result in the formation of an incompatible response -- Math = Success, and the earlier response would be extinguished. The student would no longer have an expectancy that s/he won't be successful with problems of this nature.

A cognitive dissonance theory such as Festinger's (Grippin & Peters, 1979, pp. 126-127) would be useful here. This theory holds that the cognitive and affective components of an attitude must be consistent in order for it to remain stable and affect behavior. In this case, the student attitude would be, "I don't like problems involving math because I can't do them. I always get them wrong." This attitude will not remain stable if a student finds that s/he does not always get them wrong, that s/he can do them. In order to reduce the dissonance that this discrepancy might create, a change in attitude toward liking problems involving math, or at least feeling neutral about them would result. This will be accomplished by providing students with repeated occasions to experience success at problems involving numerical exercises.

A similar strategy will be used regarding the attitude that the social sciences are "common sense" and do not require the rigorous numerical measurement techniques that the physical sciences do. The students will be presented with problems in the social sciences that cannot be solved by common sense but call for the use of numerical approaches. Real-life examples of which they cannot deny the import will be presented and it will be illustrated how the social sciences, through theoretical models and numerical approaches, was able to solve these problems. The student will have to modify his/her attitude that the social sciences are merely common sense, having been presented with discrepant information.

Prior strategies used in teaching a unit of this nature involved verbal presentation in lecture and textbook form. In some cases, the textbook would present exercise questions designed to assess students' mastery of information. While such an approach usually succeeds in supplying students with examples and definitions of the concepts involved, it seldom provides opportunity for students to generate examples and rules on their own. Based on Gagne's distinctions (Grippin & Peters, 1979, pp. 9-20), such a method would mainly be dealing with verbal information and not devoting much attention to the intellectual skills involved. A method that involves more application of the rules and concepts rather than mere articulation of them should prove more useful.

Based on this, I will attempt to outline an instructional strategy that involves discovery learning of the rules and concepts involved in the use of measurement scales. By using this method, the learner should arrive at an intuitive knowledge of the rules and concepts and will then be provided with the necessary verbal labels for them.

This approach is basically a cognitive one,

involving an active and constructive involvement on the part of the learner. Wittrock (1978) explains that activities in instruction should be designed to facilitate this active construction by the learner, rather than provide them with the rules and definitions in totally verbal information form. Such an approach requires that the learners use their information processing strategies to organize and understand the information. This is somewhat complicated by the fact that intellectual skills and verbal information are learned in different ways. However, intellectual skills are bound by the content on which they are operating -- and this will usually be verbal information. This creates a need for verbal labels when using rules, concepts, discriminations, etc.

Gagne (1973) tells us that intellectual skills are learned as a result of positive transfer from other subordinate intellectual skills. He observes that the prerequisite skills provide an internal component whose presence is crucial in the interaction of the entire stimulus situation. A discovery approach would involve general movement from the lower to the upper levels of the task hierarchy outlined in Figure 4. This does not mean that the task hierarchy provides an instructional sequence. But it does provide a description of the prerequisite skills that need to be called into service at various levels of tasks.

The strategy used here will involve a preliminary discussion of the concept of measurement and its uses. This will function as an advance organizer for the introduction of later concepts (Ausubel, 1977). The students will be asked to give examples of measurements. These will then be compared and contrasted in such a way that the learners arrive at the "Direct" -- "Indirect" distinction. Here, given a meaningful context, the terms "classification" and "quantification" will be introduced. (Refer to content analysis.)

Next, two scales will be presented for discussion -- e.g. an attitude scale and an IQ score scale. The students will be asked in a discussion to discriminate the differences between these two. Questions designed to facilitate and guide this discussion will include the following: Which measure is more direct? Which is more limited? Which score can be more directly compared to other scores? When the students have arrived at the identifying criteria for each, the terms "ordinal" and "interval" will be supplied for the classificaion they have developed. The definitions will then be further articulated, further examples provided, and the students will be asked to generate other examples. A similar approach will be followed presenting a nominal with an ordinal scale and a ratio with an interval scale. At this point the students have made the necessary discriminations that define the concepts and have discovered the criteria for the rules used in each specific case. They have proceeded through Gagne's hierarchy from the level of discriminations -- concepts -- rules for each individual scale type. Next, they will be presented with a lesson involving the relationships among the scales conducted in a similar manner. Hopefully the skills already learned will transfer and the learned rules combined to form new higher order rules and relationships.

Regarding the domain of verbal information, it should be noted here that at each point where a concept is generated, the new verbal label is introduced. Thus the verbal information is being learned in a meaningful context, as Ausubel, Bruner and other cognitive theorists would suggest (Grippin & Peters, 1979, pp. 43-49). For example, the students have discussed the difference between a pass-fail grade and a percentile rank and have delineated the criteria that make the scales two different types. With this context, they need a label for each type and the terms "nominal" and "ordinal" are introduced. As mentioned previously, this may also involve some association learning (Ebbinghaus, in Grippin and Peters, 1979, pp. 57-58). Through voluntary contiguous pairing the term "qualitative categories" might come to evoke the term "nominal" hereafter. But the supplying of these new labels in the meaningful context is what is crucial here. In this respect, the strategy meets Ausubel's criteria for meaningful verbal learning (Ausubel, 1977). The learner has intentionally engaged in the memorization due to a need for a verbal label to describe the rule or concept s/he has generated. The new information has been related to a prior conceptual network through use of the preliminary discussion of measurement, quantification, and classification as advance organizers.

This strategy involves discovery learning of intellectual skills, from discriminations to problem-solving skills. This creates a need for verbal information to summarize the data at various points. For example, a student doesn't want to repeatedly say "the type of scale that ranks data in order of degree of possession of a given attribute." The learner has arrived at the concept, and then is provided the verbal label "ordinal scale" and likewise for each of the other four scale types. This allows for chunking (Grippin & Peters, 1979, pp. 42-42) of the definition into one word. That word represents and evokes the definition. This allows for more efficient use of the student's information processing space. The four verbal labels can be compared and contrasted in the information processing space more easily than four sentence-long definitions. Similarly, this discovery approach should lead to the student having a feel for when a nominal scale is used and s/he could probably correctly identify a novel example of one. The student possesses the rule -- and at this point the instructor helps articulate that rule. In this approach, the discovery and attainment of an intellectual skill creates a need for verbal information so that the students may articulate the concepts and rules that they have generated. Thus the verbal information will almost always be supplied in a meaningful context, as Ausubel would advise (Ausubel, 1977). A good deal of research has suggested that when new verbal information is learned in a meaningful context, memory of the information is facilitated (Grippin & Peters, 1979, pp. 46-48).

The past instructional strategies mentioned earlier -- lecture and textbook format -- have proceeded in a different direction from this one. They have presented the learner with verbal information -- definitions of the concepts, examples of the discriminations, statements of the rules -- and from here they have hoped that the intellectual skills would follow deductively and be strengthened by a use-disuse kind of mechanism such as that proposed by Thorndike (Grippin & Peters, 1979, p. 58). Wittrock (1978, p. 10) advises that in a discovery approach, the rules are discovered through gaining an <u>understanding</u> of the rule and the ability to <u>apply</u> it and relate it to other rules. This strategy attempts to facilitate this process by using a discussion technique and providing concrete examples from which the learners abstract the rule. As Wittrock advises, this involves encouraging the learner's use of information processing strategies in the induction of the rules (Wittrock, 1978).

To aid in memory, a diagram such as that shown in Figure 3 might facilitate recall. It would be of assistance in illustrating the relationships among the concepts. In the approach outlined here, the chart would be provided <u>after</u> the learners had themselves generated the discriminations, concepts, rules, and relationships among them. It should help them to more efficiently organize the material.

To aid the students in seeing the relationships among the concepts that define the discriminations among the rules needed for problem-solving activities (Gagne, in Grippin & Peters, 1979, pp. 78-79), an exercise similar to the following would be provided:

> How can we distinguish among a group of people varying in age?
>
> Divide into young -- old
>
> Rank from youngest -- oldest
>
> Assign ages

This would aid students in seeing that the various types of scales provide various levels of information about a set of data. Diagrams might also aid in memory by providing imagery that might aid in recalling relationships among the various concepts (Grippin & Peters, 1979, pp. 61-62; Wittrock, 1978, pp. 9-10).

Another illustrative discussion might involve presenting the students with a novel situation such as the following:

> An inventory that measures the degree to which children stereotype occupations. Each child receives a numerical flexibility score from 1 - 25, with 25 being the most flexible, i.e. the least amount of stereotyping used by the child. What type of scale is this?

The teacher would facilitate this discussion by designing questions to direct it. For example: Does the scale involve direct measurement? Can values be multiplied and divided? Can we say that one child is more or less flexible than another, given their score?

Exercises and questions like these would provide

practice in using the intellectual skills. Opportunity for practice of intellectual skills has been found to be helpful in promoting retention and transfer (Grippin & Peters, 1979, class notes). Instruction would involve maximum use of this principle -- providing sample exercises and short ungraded quizzes, scored in class should increase mastery of the skills and the verbal information in addition to providing the experience of success needed to cultivate positive attitudes. This strategy is also based on the principle that immediate knowledge of results facilitates memory by acting as a reinforcer in the learning situation (Grippin & Peters, 1979, p. 26).

It is hoped that this strategy will result in successful learning of the rules involved in the use of measurement scales. A focus on intellectual skills should make more efficient use of storage space than attempting to store many discrete pieces of verbal information (Grippin & Peters, 1979, p. 75). Storing a rule facilitates response to a class of things with a class of responses. To the extent that we need words to talk about these things and responses, the verbal information should be well-learned and recalled in the meaningful context of the rules themselves.

6. Evaluation

A table of specifications using a behavior-content matrix, and outlining how these goals might be weighted in an assessment of the instructional unit is provided on page 250 (Gage & Berliner, 1975, pp. 793-796).

SUMMARY

In this final chapter the authors have demonstrated the value of analyzing an instructional unit. When a teacher clearly states and categorizes the learning outcomes and describes the learner, she has a good basis on which to make decisions about what theory (theories) may apply; what instructional strategies flow from those theories and what evaluation processes may be appropriate. The teacher, then has a clear idea of what she should "Do Monday morning."

Throughout the text, the authors have tried to describe and use learning outcomes so that they would become almost automatic categories for the reader's thoughts about any learning process and content. At the same time, we have attempted to suggest the theories that make the best predictions about each of the various domains. Our hope is that you, the reader, can now answer our initial question: "Learning Theory and Learning Outcomes: Is There a Connection?" with a resounding "YES," and that further you can use that connection to solve the learning problems in your instructional setting.

Integration

Behavioral Competencies	Types of Measurement Scales	Ratio	Interval	Ordinal	Nominal	Total
Attitudes	Display confident approach to problems involving measurement and numerical manipulation. Support belief that measurement and quantification are important aspects of the social sciences.					10%
Verbal Information	Define terms and concepts State criteria for scale selection State rules and principles of scale selection Explain relationships among the four types of scales.					30%
Intellectual Skills	Convert from one scale type to another. Predict consequences of using one type of scale over another. Apply rules for scale use in a novel situation. Identify novel examples of each scale type.					60%
Totals		25%	25%	25%	25%	100%

Figure 5 Table of Specifications for Evaluation

REFERENCES

Books

Gage, N.L., & Berliner, D.C. *Educational psychology.* Chicago: Rand McNally College Publishing Company, 1975.

Gay, L.R. *Educational research: Competencies for analysis and application.* Columbus, Ohio: Charles E. Merrill Publishing Co., 1976.

Grippin, P., & Peters, S. *Theories of learning: An expansion of Gagne's domains.* Unpublished textbook. Albany, New York: The College of Saint Rose, 1979.

Lefrancois, G.R. *Psychology for teaching.* Belmont, California: Wadsworth Publishing Company, Inc., 1975.

Morgan, C.T., & King, R.A. *Introduction to psychology.* Fourth edition. New York: McGraw-Hill Book Co., 1971.

Mueller, J.G., Schuessler, K.F., & Costner, H.L. *Statistical reasoning in sociology.* Boston: Houghton-Mifflin Company, 1970.

Periodicals

Ausubel, D. The facilitation of meaningful verbal learning in the classroom. *Educational Psychologist*, 1977, *12*, 162-178.

Gagne, R. Learning and instructional sequence. In Kerlinger (Ed.), *Review of Research in Education.* Itasca, Illinois: Peacock Publishers, 1973, 21-25.

Wittrock, M.C. The cognitive movement in instruction. Abstract of article appearing in *Educational Psychologist*, 1978, *13*.

INDEX

Index

Index

Index